THINGS I SHOULD HAVE TOLD MY DAUGHTER

This Large Print Book carries the
Seal of Approval of N.A.V.H.

THINGS I SHOULD HAVE TOLD MY DAUGHTER

LIES, LESSONS, & LOVE AFFAIRS

PEARL CLEAGE

THORNDIKE PRESS

A part of Gale, Cengage Learning

GALE
CENGAGE Learning·

Farmington Hills, Mich • San Francisco • New York • Waterville, Maine
Meriden, Conn • Mason, Ohio • Chicago

GALE
CENGAGE Learning®

LIBRARY OF CONGRESS CATALOGING-IN-PUBLICATION DATA

Cleage, Pearl.
    Things I should have told my daughter : lies, lessons & love affairs / by
Pearl Cleage. — Large print edition.
        pages ; cm. — (Thorndike Press large print African-American)
    ISBN 978-1-4104-6965-6 (hardcover) — ISBN 1-4104-6965-4 (hardcover)
    1. Cleage, Pearl. 2. Women authors, American—Biography. 3.
Self-realization in women. 4. Motherhood—United States—Biography. 5.
Large type books. I. Title.
PS3553.L389Z46 2014b
813'.54—dc23
[B]   2014008402

Published in 2014 by arrangement with Atria Books, a division of Simon & Schuster, Inc.

Printed in Mexico
1 2 3 4 5 6 7 18 17 16 15 14

I've been heading in this direction
for years. I light a candle.
I light a joint. I turn down
the music and begin to write.
— PEARL CLEAGE, 11/30/80

THE QUESTION

I told my daughter over lunch at our favorite hamburger joint that upon my death, which, as far as I knew, was not imminent, I wanted to leave the diaries and journals I've been keeping since I was eleven years old to my granddaughter, Chloe, who was three at the time. My daughter didn't even pause to consider the idea.

"Absolutely not," she said calmly, reaching for the ketchup. "She doesn't need to know all that."

"All *what*?" I said, surprised by her reaction.

"All *that,*" she said, raising her eyebrows as if I knew perfectly well what all *that* was, so she wasn't required to provide any specifics.

"You've never even read my journals!"

I knew this to be true since she had politely declined my offer to provide her with unlimited access to them when I thought she might be curious somewhere around her fifteenth birthday. I didn't want her to have to sneak and read them the way I did when I discovered a volume of my own mother's diary, carefully concealed in the back of her closet. That discovery made me understand for the first time that my mother had a rich interior life, not to mention a sex life, that didn't include me at all. Far from being hurt by this, it deepened my affection and respect for my mother, who had now been revealed to me as a mysterious, passionate, creative woman engaged in a valiant struggle to balance love and freedom.

My daughter didn't see it that way. She saw the journals as uncensored, unedited slices of my life, meant for my eyes only. Any attempt to include others in such an intimate experience, after the fact and through no fault of their own, struck my child as self-indulgent, insensitive and unnecessary.

"Aren't you even curious?" I said.

"Curious about what?" my daughter said.

"About my life," I said. "About what happened."

"Mom," she said gently but firmly, "I know what happened. I was there, remember?"

After that it seemed wiser to move on to

more neutral topics, but I couldn't get her reaction out of my mind. If part of any sane woman's life is figuring out how to spot the lies, remember the lessons and engage passionately in the love affairs, aren't my journals among the most primary of primary sources? And even though my daughter is telling me they are probably nothing more than a toxic brew of rage, whining, scandalous behavior and unreliable memories, I am not convinced.

After all, she only has one half of the equation to consider. Yes, she was there, but my daughter was not privy to the relentless soul searching, merciless self-observation and rigorous self-analysis that allowed me to survive my early womanhood and emerge with my health and sanity still relatively intact. Those crucial conversations only took place in the pages of my journals, where clarity came slowly, over years, and the resulting behavioral changes occurred gradually enough that my daughter could not be expected to draw a straight line from one state to the other. She only saw the Sturm und Drang of my mad flight toward financial independence, sexual liberation, creative fulfillment and free womanhood, not necessarily in that order. Looking back, I wonder if it's possible that the things I *didn't* tell her are as necessary as the things I did.

"Do us all a favor," she says gently, dropping me off at home later. "Burn them up and be done with it."

I am shocked by her suggestion. If I was going to burn them, I could have done that every year as part of my usual New Year's rituals: *give thanks for what has just finished and what is about to begin; make your resolutions; drink champagne with the beloved; burn your journals.* No way. There is a reason why I saved them all these years, carting them from my baby girl bedroom, to my college dorm, to a series of apartments and finally home. There is a reason they have survived and even if I'm not exactly sure what that reason is, I probably ought to think about it a little longer before doing anything as irrevocable as burning. I decide there is only one way to figure out who's right. I'll read them all and then decide.

I am surprised to realize how many there are. Stacked in cardboard boxes; stashed in my great grandmother's Alabama steamer trunk; spilling over the sides of an overflowing and badly tattered basket, demanding organization and attention. They have mutely rebuked me many times as another year passes and I add a few new volumes to their number without going back to be sure that 1967 isn't crowding 1996 and that those pages I took out from December of 1982 were correctly replaced and not stuck in April of 1984 by mistake. Clearly, the first challenge is narrowing my search for mystery and meaning to a manageable number of notebooks. I need an organizing principle, but based on what? *Dates? Times? Places? Decades?*

The idea of a couple of decades appeals to me. Twenty years is not enough time to be overwhelming, but it is more than enough to be a representative sample. As best I can recall, the two decades between 1970 and 1990 were pretty action-packed as far as those lies, lessons and love affairs I was talking about earlier. I know for a fact that I left college, moved to Atlanta, got married, finished college, got a job, had a baby, quit a job, wrote a book, helped elect a mayor, quit another job, got divorced, lived by my wits, became an artist, had a play produced, had my heart broken, mended it, found my honor, found my smile, realized I was a lot stronger than I had thought I was. A lot wilder, too, but all that came much farther up the road. This particular twenty-year journey begins in Atlanta on January 9, 1970 . . .

THE JOURNALS: 1970–79

JANUARY 9, 1970

It seems fitting somehow that the first entry into this journal should deal with the increasing repression and retaliation that is coming down in this country — white to black. Donald Stone is going to jail today with two other brothers. They had a demonstration in front of the Atlanta Draft Board a couple of years ago, did twenty-three dollars' worth of damage to the door frame, and now he, Stone, has to serve three years. Leah and Stanley Wise gave a party for him last night. It was crowded and it was tense at first because everybody knew what was going on, but nobody was talking about it. His wife, Flora, was smiling and talking to people but when she stood by herself, her face looked stretched. Stone was drinking. He danced once with Lonetta and laughed. Stanley brushed past him and didn't even look around. Like he was there, but gone, too — already gone.

When he spoke, Stone said: "I had alternatives. I had alternatives open to me. I could have done other things. But going to jail is in keeping with my political reality and I figure black people are going to have to deal with jail and so I am going to serve." His wife was not around when I heard him speaking. I guess she didn't want to hear him talking like that. She didn't cry, though. She was just kind of tight. I smiled at her and she smiled, but she doesn't really know me and who wants to talk to somebody they don't know at a moment like that? So, I didn't approach her. A lot of SNCC people were there. Some of us went swimming at the park before we went over to Leah's and then on the way back, we sang songs. Mostly Charles, Stanley and Porter sang. Me and Michael didn't know all the songs. Freedom songs. Movement songs. SNCC songs. The one I like best is "One More Time." Bernice Reagon sings it, too. My mind is opening now. I want to write things! I feel more into what is happening. Whatever is going to come down in this country is not about looking sharp. It is not about abstaining from things or really getting into a deep thing about "the people." Whatever comes down and how we deal with it is only important at all in terms of how we learn to deal honestly with each other. Those people tonight were trying to deal not only with the abstractions of a political reality, but with the very real feelings they have for somebody they love; with how to show him what they feel for him, even though they aren't going where he's going — yet. At twelve noon we are going to watch him turn himself in at the post office downtown. Liberation is a constant struggle. And this is a new year.

JANUARY 12, 1970
I think that a black poet can do one of two things for his people:

1. Reflect the beauty of their black life; whole, broken and mending.
2. Lead them in a righteous direction by showing them the path and what lies ahead in liberation and victory.

If you call yourself a black poet and you ain't doin' that, you ain't bein' truthful and you ain't bein' fair and in general, you ain't doin' nothin' for yr people/yr self/the struggle/the nation/the community. In short, you ain't doin' shit.
So there.

Last night we saw *The Battle of Algiers,* and afterward, we were talking and wondering if it was going to get like that here. Then this morning, they say on the news that two SNCC people were blown to bits outside of the town in Maryland where Rap Brown is on trial as of yesterday. They were Che, from here, and Ralph Featherstone, who I think was working out of D.C. now. Porter looks like he is going to cry. I know Stanley is about to cry. Everybody around here is trying to deal with it and what it means. The press is already saying some shit about how they were carrying explosives to make trouble in the town and that they blew themselves up. That is obviously a goddamn lie. Would they ignite a bomb on themselves? Would they carry nitroglycerin? What do they think we are? Folks here are going to have a memorial service. Stanley is trying to get it together. I feel helpless and sick. What can we do? What should we do? We are so unready to retaliate to anything. We talk so damn much and ain't five guns among the whole damn group. What are we going to do? People keep talking about being ready "when the shit comes down." It is already coming down! Every day. All the time. God. I feel horrible and that is an ego trip to even be worrying about how I feel. Che's real name was William Payne. They can't find his parents to notify them and they are already saying his name on TV. No consideration for human things. Why are you surprised? I can't write any more now. It doesn't seem like it is worth shit anyway.

MARCH 11, 1970
(Presented at Sister's Chapel, Spelman College, Atlanta, Georgia)

THIS STATEMENT HAS BEEN PREPARED BY PERSONS FROM DRUM AND SPEAR BOOKSTORE WHERE RALPH WAS MANAGER, AND THE AFRO-AMERICAN RESOURCE CENTER

Ralph Featherstone and William Payne were killed by a bomb placed in the car they were driving. These murders took place on a highway leading out of Bel Air, Maryland. We understand the reason for Ralph and William being in Bel Air was specifically to arrange for the entry of H. Rap Brown into that city. Rap was due to stand trial in Bel Air for alleged charges of arson and inciting to riot. We know from past experience the danger of assassination of black leaders is ever present. Ralph and William were very concerned and took upon themselves the heavy responsibility of arranging a safe entry into the city of Bel Air, Maryland, for Rap.

Borrowing a car on the evening of March 9, Ralph and William drove to Bel Air to survey the situation. At 11:50 p.m. that evening while on the highway leaving Bel Air the car exploded into a thousand pieces killing Ralph and William instantly. William's body was mutilated beyond recognition. We believe that that bomb was intended for H. Rap Brown.

It is significant to note that the car that was driven and destroyed had been used over the past five years throughout the black belt of the South. The car was well known to State and Federal authorities. Ralph and William's presence in Bel Air was almost certainly known. A bomb was planted at some point during the night under the right seat of the car.

Ralph Featherstone, manager of the Drum and Spear Bookstore before coming to Washington, D.C., had worked in some of the most dangerous areas in the South: Neshoba County in Mississippi where the three murders took place in 1964; Lowndes and Wilcox counties in Alabama and the city of McComb in Southwest Mississippi. During this period of intense political activity a close and lasting friendship developed between him and H. Rap Brown. In his work in the South, Ralph has seen many black people killed. A number of those killed were personal friends of his. It is important to remember that H. Rap Brown is still missing. We do not know whether he is dead or alive.

MARCH 12, 1970

This morning, a note from the revolutionary front: Three establishment buildings were bombed successfully in New York last night. The Mobil Oil Building, the General Telephone Building and IBM. They said that a letter sent to the papers claimed that a group called the Militant Revolutionary Nine did it. Black or white? Who knows? It is a blow against the shit that is going down and that is a positive move. The memorial service for Featherstone and Che was really sad. None of the people who spoke blew their cool and cried. The tone of the things they said was that we should not be sitting around crying but that we should be uniting and working together. Stanley said it should be very clear that this is not like the Mississippi killings where three nuts come up and do something. He said it was an organized government thing and should be called that. He was swollen in the eyes and looked like the effort to talk without breaking down was intense. Porter said "death is no stranger to me," and he looked sad, too. They said at the meeting last night at Porter's house, Stanley cried for a long time and then got himself together. Lynn Brown thinks that Rap was in the car and is dead. They have not heard from him at all and everybody thinks he is either captured or killed. The car was not going to the courthouse so how could they be going to bomb it anyway? The news and all are acting like it had nothing to do with the trial. The ugly judge said it was not related. Yesterday morning, somebody bombed the goddamn courthouse anyway. They arrested a white woman behind it. Also in New York the apartment of some SDS folks blew up. They said they were "playing with explosives." Weathermen. It sounds like part of the same shit to me. The Chicago trial, and now SDS, and now Featherstone, and now New York. This country must look pretty damn awful to the outside world. I am trying not to be hysterical. Times are getting worse. How do you get to the point where you are like the people in *The Battle of Algiers,* and can face all the shit and not break down? I am not there yet and I know it. We are both afraid. For us, for friends, for families, for what is happening here. I wonder what it's going to be like in five years. Maybe I should have a kid now while we are still out of the camps.

To: Staff
From: Wife and Family of Ralph
   Featherstone
Date: March 12, 1970
Re: Funeral

The body of Brother Featherstone will lie in state at the Stewart Funeral Home, 4001 Benning Road, N.E., Washington, D.C. The body will lie in state 6 p.m. Thursday and Friday.

Memorial Services will be held Saturday at 1:00 p.m. at the Stewart Funeral Home Chapel prior to cremation.

Donations may be sent to:

Center for Black Education
1431 Fairmont St.
Washington, D.C.

MARCH 12, 1970
It seems that I have been operating on the edge of hysteria since this first began. I am overreacting to everything. I feel like I can-

not respond exuberantly to any emotional thing or I will slip off and become hysterical. This afternoon, we went out to eat lunch and coming back, I started laughing and then I started crying and it was awful because I couldn't stop it. I don't know what's happening. Dorie just contacted a very old woman who knew Featherstone to tell her about the memorial service and Dorie was saying, "Yes, ma'am," and, "No, ma'am," and it sounded so nice. She wouldn't have ever said it to anybody here, so it was really nice and funny to hear her talking like that to an old lady. I teased her about it a little and she just grinned and said "that is my training." The other day we were looking through some materials and we found an old SNCC agenda for some important meeting or another. It was all about bad things happening and what they were going to do about it, but at the bottom, somebody had written an order for lunch: "chicken and potatoes and some sweet potato pie," it said. It was written in pencil and it was just weird to see it and realize that the folks doing all that dangerous Movement work in places like Neshoba and Philadelphia, Mississippi, were still having to eat and sleep and order lunch and go to the bathroom.

Working here, I am surrounded by the Movement. In the materials we are collecting and in the voices of the people who work here. Most of them are longtime activists and organizers. I listen to the stories they tell and I am in awe of their determination and their courage. They all know Daddy and respect him. I actually think he is part of the reason why I got this job. We're charged with gathering archival materials documenting freedom struggles all over the country. They would love to have Daddy's papers here. I think it's great that Mrs. King started this huge project so soon after Dr. King died. I wonder if they knew what a radical Vincent Harding was when they asked him to run it!

She has been very nice to me the couple of times I've met her. She looks *exactly* like her pictures. I wanted to tell her I think the name of the place is unwieldy: The Martin Luther King, Jr., Library and Documentation Project. But then somebody told me they had thought about making it even longer: The Martin Luther King, Jr., Library and Documentation Project and Center for Non-Violent Social Change, so I figured I would let well enough alone.

I wonder: where is Rap?

MARCH 27, 1970

My cousin Deedee is going to Algeria. Why? Because somebody in a dream came to her and said "Go to Algeria!" So she got up, looked in the dictionary to make sure where it was and then started getting ready to go. She is selling her furniture and giving her things away and getting ready to go. Sonny is gone and Barbara is going to Japan in a VW bus, so I guess it makes sense that Deedee is splitting to Algiers. Kris, on the other foot, is growing the kid and becoming fed up with the women's role in the revolution — cleaning up; doing dishes; and feeding the man. What a revolution. Stokely said the place of the woman in the revolution should be prone. Then the Panther guy said, "On the other hand, any woman walking behind her man should be getting ready to put her foot up his ass."

Are those my only choices?

JUNE 17, 1970

We saw a movie last night called *Women in Love*. It was weird as hell. Some parts were really good, but some parts were dragged out and heavy-handed. There was one part where this man gave an explanation of how to eat a fig. A fig! The way he said it was so vile and nasty, but really funny. Lots of really thinly veiled double meanings and stuff. Really well done.

Kenneth Gibson was elected the first black mayor of Newark yesterday. He was supported by LeRoi Jones and the folks at Spirit House. The Newark Negroes are pretty glad, but the Mafia is pissed off. I hope that is not going to be a big hassle with all that mess! That is my political note for the day.

But, back to the movie. It had all these really corny scenes of romantic love. I object to that in movies because I think that it messes people up in real relationships. They always want to make a pretty picture, never reality. It always has to be like the movies. But other parts of the movie included really raunchy love scenes and they were just as awkward and messy as real life can be, but the realness was overshadowed in certain sections by the romantic thing. I mean, running nude through the grass and all that! A real drag. Not believable.

Kris is having her baby in about another four days. I hope she is all right and the kid is all right and that she will come for a visit in August!

DECEMBER 16, 1970
Well, today a man stopped me on the street

to say something smart but before he could get it out, I said, "How are you doin' today?" And he kind of regrouped and said, "I trust in the good lord. They done killed King, so I'm on my own, I guess." Wow. That is too depressing to deal with. I wonder if he felt anything about ol' King for real. It kind of set him back when I greeted him before he could hit on me. Although he did remember to ask me for my phone number before I walked away, he did it in a haphazard, half-assed kind of way. Just to keep his hand in . . .

JANUARY 14, 1971
Last night at Vincent Harding's house was strange. Mrs. DuBois and the adoring folks at her feet. I don't quite know why. She is very intelligent, but the attitude of waiting for wisdom from the fountainhead is foreign to me in terms of Mrs. DuBois. But later, after she had exhausted herself, Howard Moore began to talk about Sister Angela Davis. He is a beautiful brother and a great lawyer who is defending Angela in California in connection with George Jackson's brother killing a judge, trying to free his brother. She is innocent and Howard said he thinks she can win. I hope he's right. I almost started crying when he was talking

about the horrible conditions in the jail where she is being held. Later, he leaned over to Mrs. DuBois when there weren't many people around and said: "Mrs. DuBois, do you think you could give me a word of encouragement for Angela?" Wow. It was just like all the shit that is going down rushed into that room and was right there. The whole thing was real — Angela in prison, roaches in the soup, black, communist, woman, mice tails in the food, jail conditions, political prisoners and the whole shit. Everything was present in the room with us. At the end of the party, Stanley Wise told Mrs. DuBois, with typical Wise enthusiasm, "My wife and I are coming to Africa and we will stop by Egypt and see you." Like it was on Beckwith Street! Crazy black folk! I have to call Jane about organizing a rally for Angela at Spelman. We can do it, I'm sure. We have to do something about raising funds and keeping public interest alive. We can't just fade away and let them kill her!

JANUARY 15, 1971
Well, it has come to Spiro Agnew on television telling us that if the State determines that a mother is unfit, the State will place the child of the welfare mother in an or-

phanage. Also, if a welfare mother has too many children, the State will sterilize her. Also, if someone on Medicare takes "too long to die," the State will be empowered to "put them out of their misery." Isn't that horrible? He is the polluted wave of the future. I have only one comment on him: I WANT OUT!!

FEBRUARY 9, 1971
New York City

On the road with Karen for the Southern Education Program recruitment tour. We're recruiting black grad students to teach at black southern colleges for two years after they finish grad school. We present it kind of like a Peace Corps thing, which is weird, but I think a lot of people see the South as a foreign country anyway, so. . . . Our slogan is "Teach A Brother!" Karen gives the spiel, answers questions, I hand out information on SEP, then the sponsor takes us out to dinner. It's fun. Glad I don't have to do the speech!

FEBRUARY 11, 1971
Princeton, N.J.

Karen made me give the speech! She didn't even tell me until right before the program started. I tried to freak out, but she wasn't having it, so I had to get up and do it. Once I got started, it was pretty cool. I believe in what we're doing, so I talked about how important it was and how much they would get out of it. People seemed pretty responsive and came up after to thank us for coming and take our brochures.

When we got ready to walk across campus for dinner, the whole group of us were together, but I started talking to this guy from Trenton. He said his name was Zaron Burnett and he was a conscientious objector leaving the next day for two years of alternative service in a state mental hospital! There was snow and ice on the ground and while we were walking, he offered me his arm. It was nice. Old-fashioned and kind of courtly. We ended up sitting together and kept talking all through dinner. I really liked him. It almost felt like we were picking up a conversation in progress. He walked with us back to our car and it was really cold and very clear. Dark sky and lots of stars. I wished him luck, but he didn't seem worried about going. Like it was another adventure and he was ready for it. It seemed like a movie scene. Little snowflakes swirling around us. A brief moment before returning to the struggle. I felt like I should kiss him, but Karen was standing right there, so I didn't.

Home tomorrow!

JULY 22, 1971

This morning on Hunter Street, I passed a black woman at the bus stop. She was simply dressed in a green-and-white checked shirtwaist dress. It was a little too big and little bit too long, but not really sloppy. It had a little fabric-covered belt to match, too. But on top of her head was a huge, platinum blond wig. It was curled and flipped and teased and in general fixed to look as hideous as possible. It wasn't even pulled down very far. It was just sitting there like it was a bird who had decided to light there and visit with her for a while. She had a very serious expression and she was looking down the street intently for the bus. The wig was looking, too, but I don't think it was looking for the bus. It looked like it had had a hard night and would welcome an Alka Seltzer.

AUGUST 4, 1971

Seems like Sharon and I always talk about old times. Like when we see each other we go right back to Freshman Week at Howard when they marched us to the chapel in black dresses to take an oath by candlelight that made us officially Howard women. And how you had to come in for curfew at eight o'clock when it was still light outside and you could look right out the dorm window and watch the switching sophomores swoop on the brother you hoped would wink at you. I remember all the politics in D.C., traditional and non-traditional. I remember the counter-inaugural me and Kris went to that ended up a muddy mess no matter how much hay they threw down to soak up the puddles of rain. I remember two white boys offering us "a quarter for a dance and a cigarette for a screw." I remember two shadowy brothers who offered grass guaranteed to "open up your head." I remember old Phil Ochs singing anti-war songs while we sat on some bales of hay, smelling the reefer in the air so thick you could float up above the crowd on your own if you breathed long enough and deep enough. And what did President Johnson think about it? No cops came. They had bribed the God of Rain so why did they need cops? Ain't nobody gonna riot when the mud is up to your knees!

Old times. New times will have to come later. Peace!

Friday the thirteenth. Does that mean bad luck? Does a black cat mean bad luck? Seems to me we have to sluff off these white-oriented symbols of bad luck along with all the stuff about how scary black is. I refuse to be intimidated.

Saw *McCabe and Mrs. Miller.* Beautiful pictures and some really spirited cussing. However, in totality, the movie somehow just missed being really hip. I dug it, though. He thought it was superficial. Maybe it was, but we all like to indulge in a superficial thing or two every now and then. After the movie, we passed by the Snooty Hooty Boutique and even though it was closed, you could see inside through the glass and in among the long dresses and suede coats were scattered six or seven real boys. They looked to be about sixteen or seventeen. They were all fragile and floaty and delicately posed like little pieces of white taffy candy. They were smiling like they had a secret we wanted to know and wearing their hair in long curls around their shoulders. One waved at someone who went by, but none of them waved at us. They looked like their eyes would glow in the dark. Like cats or mice or snakes.

I have been madly in love with this man for years. He came to Detroit once to talk to my father about some anti-war activities when I was in high school and then I met him again when I got here. He was in SNCC with Karen and sometimes he drops by our office to say hello. Today he comes in wearing a pale blue flowered shirt, blue belt, baggy gray pants and tiny little black pointed toe shoes. His eyes are always the same; curious and peaceful. He has planted a garden and he is talking about it to Karen. "I wish I had listened to the old folks," he says. "They say you must plant okra and curse it when you put it in the ground or it won't come up. They say if you plant at a full moon, you will get tall plants, but they will be bare. If you plant on the waning moon, you will get short plants, but they will be full and good bearing." He says the ones he planted rebelled against the rows and the renegade plants are now growing successfully all over the yard. He says a friend of his who works for the railroad brought him some cotton seeds and he will plant them by his front steps so he can say: "When I was in Georgia, I had cotton growing right outside my door." I don't think he knows how nice it is to see him. I remember seeing him one day at the library. He called me "Jewel Child." That did not, of course, help the case of unrequited love.

SEPTEMBER 14, 1971
Because Library School will take up two whole years of my life, I have decided to keep a journal of events/feelings/reactions to it as long as I can stick it out. Judging from today, that might not be too long, but I will start with a reaction to yesterday so it will not be forgotten.

First, they gave us a tour of the library, starting with the Margaret Mitchell Room. Somehow, that didn't quite put a right taste in my mouth, since her most famous character is the well-known slave-owning Scarlett O'Hara, but I didn't let it faze me and kept right on. We proceeded to all the dusty recesses of the library and ended up in the children's section, standing in our uncertain little group, facing a fireplace lined with a series of tiles from 1903, which tell one of the Uncle Remus stories. And there at the top, wearing his beautiful, angelic smile, was the old uncle himself, telling his stories to a little white child with a blond pageboy. That, of course, did nothing to brighten my mood or my general outlook on the whole adventure. But, onward and back upstairs to meet Mr. Rochelle.

First of all, as soon as he opened his mouth, my prejudices immediately took over: a white man with a southern accent. Two strikes. He talked on and on in a strikingly boring monotone. He said that there had been some question about whether he could function as head of the library system in a city that was now over 50 percent black; whether he could "think black enough." Of course, he dismissed the question as not really relevant in most instances and said he was sure he could deal with it effectively. Very bored. Very patronizing. I was totally turned off. Then a young brother talked to us about bookmobiles. He was all right, but not an exciting speaker and after Mr. Rochelle, we needed pepping up. Finally, he said something about how he had been told by a warden of a prison in Atlanta not to bring "those controversial kinds of books" into the prison for the prisoners to read. That was interesting, especially in view of the whole Attica thing and George Jackson and the general level of awareness of the brothers in the prisons and the repression that is coming down on them. But the young brother did not dwell on it. Then, we were introduced to Miss Smith, a young sister from Cleveland who spoke enthusiastically about how great a chance this was for creative folks and how much she dug her work. Finally, some enthusiasm! I was much heartened.

We had lunch at Emile's, around the corner from the library. Nothing of note, except nice little hot loaves of bread on little wooden bread boards at your table. They have good fish, too. Then we're off on a tour of the inner-city branch libraries. I was surprised to see all the storefront libraries. They really reminded me of Kris and Jim and the Black Conscience Library they had in Detroit where they used to have free showings of *The Battle of Algiers.* Some of the libraries were interesting looking, but most of them did not look too alive. But it was an interesting overall tour and I was enthusiastic about it by the time it was over. Visions of working in one of those places became more real and I felt somewhat relieved, although I was still dreading courses with titles like "Libraries and Librarianship." The night class in political science is still too new to judge. It should be interesting, I hope. But on to today . . .

At the end of the day, they told us that our entire group, including myself, of course, will be taking a remedial language arts seminar! That idea is too awful to even put on paper. Can you imagine being told that as a graduate student, you will be expected to make outlines, do topic sentences, diagram and give speeches and do all the insanely time wasting and elementary things you should have been doing all along? I was incensed. I was indignant. I will drop out of the entire program rather than take that course. I will not do it. I think it is totally absurd and insulting. Miss Bynam said that the reason was that so many people come into Atlanta University graduate programs and can't write and read and effectively communicate. That may be true, but I, fortunately, am not one of that number. So why, why, why? I really cannot deal with it further at this time. I hope to be able to report something more positive tomorrow.

The real problem is that I don't really want to be a librarian. I love books. I love reading and this program is a multi-year fellowship that will allow me to quit my other job and have more writing time, but can I survive a whole class on the Dewey Decimal System??

SEPTEMBER 23, 1971
An old man with a long cigar and a straw hat cocked to the side walked me from Cyn-

thia's house back to work. He talked the whole time and took my elbow crossing the street and only toward the end of our stroll did he begin to get a little off the point, but I was saved by having reached my destination. Working for twenty-five years as an inspector at Sears. Very proud of that. Inspects steering wheels. Very proud of that, too. "Well," he says, "you certainly are a beautiful kid. Look like you never been loved." It seems that is my great charm, according to other folks' assessments also. My pure, sweet, untouched innocent look. Ha!

SEPTEMBER 24, 1971

Karen and I come out of the office at noon and see a man lying on the floor just outside our door. He is lying on his side and can't be seen breathing, but has the smell of wine strong around him. Bill Mahoney is with us and he asks Karen if she knows who he is. She said, "Yep," and headed for the alcoholic rehabilitation center. Mahoney stands over the man for a while and then leans down and gently shakes his shoulder. "Are you all right?" he says. The man slowly opens his eyes and says, "Yeah, yeah," and turns back over to go to sleep again. Mahoney says, "Are you sick?" The man says, "Help me, help me," and extends his hand, then pulls it back. Mahoney, with the beautiful, bland expression that is his alone, squats down by the man and says, "How do you feel?" The man says, "Why can't my people get together? Why can't they just get together?" Mahoney says, "We're going to get together. Don't worry about it. We are going to get together." The man says, "Even after black power, we still can't get together." Mahoney says, "Yes, but after Attica, I think things will be a little different." The man lapses into groans and tosses his head back and forth. Mahoney helps him sit up and the man holds Mahoney's hand very tight. Mahoney asks him his name and where he lives. The man says it, but Mahoney can't quite understand and asks him again and the man repeats it, a little indignantly like he's annoyed to have to repeat himself. Then Karen comes with a man from downstairs at the rehab center and the man says roughly, "You better leave that dope alone. It will kill you." Mahoney takes one side and the rehab man takes the other and they hoist the drunk guy, who says, "O-o-o-o-o! Dope! Did you hear what he said?" And he looks at Mahoney and shakes his head like "This is just what I was talking about," even though, of course, it wasn't. They head off down the hall and I remember what I know of Mahoney's history. Freedom rides with baseball bats and firebombs waiting at the end of the line. Parchman Prison with holes in the ground for political prisoners. How did he manage to come through all of that still able to reassure a drunk man that everything is going to be all right?

All this, and it's only noon.

OCTOBER 1, 1971

Damn if the new month doesn't start with a bang. It's hotter than it should be outside and I creep into the Morris Brown College snack bar to get a hot dog and prepare to head back to work. I take out my book, but a short, chubby, intense-eyed young man joins me with a brisk, "Are you busy?" "No," I say. What else can you say? He pulls up a chair and tells me he heard me question the presence of television cameras at the rally the other day and how hip he thought that was. "Thank you," I say. "I just don't like to see strange white folks taking our pictures." He smiles in a mysterious way. "I am a member," he says, "of section one." I nod. What the hell is section one? I wonder. No need to wonder long. He tells me. "Section one," he says, "is a military organization that was started by my brother and is kind of a backup to the Black Panthers. It is a secret group that cannot be arrested by the FBI," he says with a madman's glow of satisfaction. "Yes." I nod again. Why is he telling me, I wonder? For all he knows, I could be an FBI agent who asks hip questions at rallies to throw folks off. I almost suggest this to him, but the mad glow in his little eyes makes me take another bite of hot dog instead. He says softly, "We have been planning to do something big for nine years and in 1973, we will be ready to blow the lid off and really do our thing." I am remaining cool and taking slow sips of Coke. "Is that so?" I say, trying to sound supportive and noncommittal at the same time. He nods. "Yes." He also tells me how they believe in an eye for an eye and if the police beat up someone, section one takes a policeman and beats him up and ain't that revolutionary? I listen a while longer and then excuse myself, gently folding the remaining half of my dog and my chips up in a napkin for disposal. I'm still hungry, but I figure it's time to go. It is a trip what people say sometimes. Section one? "No one knows," he says in parting, "how many members we have." "Good," I say. "Very good."

OCTOBER 4, 1971

I need some time to myself by myself! There must be time for thought and music and peace and solitude! Also: No one can keep a creative house and work every day from nine to five. Can't be done, folks. Ain't no way.

OCTOBER 6, 1971

Miss Victoria Delease. I don't know how to spell her last name, but it sounds like "de-leez." A big woman with red coat/hat/dress ensemble. Nice gravelly voice and nice easy smile and relaxed manner. Rev. Jackson: small and quick, wiping his face under his glasses. "Are you a good public speaker?" he said to me. "I don't know," I said, surprised to be asked. "I haven't done much public speaking." "Well," he said, "come to South Carolina and we'll put you to speaking." She is running for Congress. She is from Ridgeville, she says, in Dorchester County. The South always designates things in terms of counties and my mind fills up with lynch mobs and Klan hoods and night riders. But she smiles like it holds no terror for people with sense. "Yes," she tells Karen, "it will take a hard fight, but I don't think it's hard enough to make me quit." Rev. Jackson doesn't talk. He drove six hours to get here this morning. She says, "It would have taken longer but he drove eighty the entire way." She is trying to get a day care proposal funded and they are messing over her. She is not taking it though. Karen is to help them get it together. I hope they do. Her name sounds like fleur-de-lis on the wallpaper. Victoria Delease. I wish I knew how to spell it! She is really big. When she walks toward you, you can see her getting bigger and bigger like in a cartoon or something. Victoria Delease. Anyhow, when I saw her, I wasn't scared anymore. Just that quick. White folks are a bitch. Scared to go someplace in my own country because the white folks might get me. Isn't that a bitch? I never thought of it like that. No wonder folks are so easily intimidated. And I never saw anybody get shot or anything. Take heart! This week Atlanta, next week Dorchester County, next week, Jackson, Mississippi! Ha!

OCTOBER 6, 1971
Slow afternoon. It is hard to say how these folks who just left have affected me. They really made me feel so optimistic and hopeful and really good. Rev. Jackson and Mrs. Delease. They are back up there in Dorchester County just doing their thing. Over there

45

in the woods, just doin' it. The Dorchester Community Educational Project. Right on! The first year of integrated education in that area, all the black kids failed a standardized test!!!! You don't hear about shit like that on the news. All of the black kids failed! Now that is a real weapon. If you can control everything and even make folks think they ain't shit, it is a bitch. It really, really is. But they are tutoring and doing a whole community center thing. I dig the South for days. I really do. There is something different about southern people. They are warm and nice and they speak to you and stuff. It is amazing. I do dig me some southern folks. I wish the whole country could have black folks like down here, not crazy Californians and other crazies. People can say everybody down here is backward and country. I know better.

OCTOBER 7, 1971
Early in the day. Not much happening yet. Paschal's Restaurant is quiet and smells like early morning coffee and sleepy people. Yesterday Julian was in here, smiling wanly and shaking hands with people who know his name. He looked slightly bored and even a little put upon, but why come in Paschal's if you don't want folks to pat your back and

squeeze your hand? Not if you're Julian Bond! The Julian Bond!

"Think white," Mayor Massell told us yesterday. "We must stop the flow of white folks from Atlanta to the suburbs. That would be a tragedy," he says. He is all het up because the mayor of Dallas said he didn't want Dallas to be another Atlanta. Isn't that a bitch? Think white, folks! Think white! Only thing is, we've been doing that for years and the white folks are still running. So . . . fuck 'em.

Fania Davis says that in Angela's little cell there is not enough light and so Angela is losing her eyesight. When she comes to the visitors' area, the sun makes her squint and she can't see so good anymore. Huey Newton is in China with Elaine Brown. The people applauded him at a public meeting of some sort and he smiled and applauded them back. That was nice, I thought. I don't think Eldridge Cleaver would have had the sense to do that. I wonder how it is for him now in Algeria. Probably a big, fly-ridden bore, knowing him. So strange. There must be a lesson in there someplace.

OCTOBER 8, 1971
I think that the thing is to take your life into your own hands. I think that is the only way

that you get anything together. I look back nostalgically because I'm forgetting the boredom and the lack of direction. Only the good times stand out. It ain't gonna do. I am proceeding to give some work to Carlton Molette and will continue to give some work to A.B. so that I can get my writing shit together and do it. I want to write, so why not write? I know I am as good as Nikki Giovanni and Johari Amini and probably a lot more of them, but who will know if I am busy doing dishes and shit like that? Best grab your own life and run with it. And that is just what the kid intends to do.

So there.

OCTOBER 12, 1971
The day before the trip to Wallace country. I am not scared yet. I went to Madison, Georgia, so I guess I can make it to Birmingham, Alabama. Just read *The Feminine Mystique.* The "problem with no name" is really a trip. The women's lib anthology that I'm reading really makes me see how universal the problems of "women" are. This may be a sweeping generalization, meaning middle-class women in America, but you know what I mean. I mean, the frustration of finding yourself saddled with a lot of chores and stuff that are a drag and

it is weird when you find what is expected of you. Last night: dishes to be done, but he has reading to do, so he just leaves them for me. It is not like he feels he has to do them. It is never his job to do them; he is just helping me when he does them. That is a basic and very important difference. It means that the housework is my work to do. He never comes home an hour early from Emory to start dinner. Of course, most husbands don't even do anything at all, but that is not my problem, is it? But housework is not even the totality of the problem because the lady in one of the chapters had a maid. The problem it seems to me is the total submergence of your personality into the life of your man. It would be unthinkable for me to say, "If I get a Master's degree at Atlanta University, I'd like to pursue a Ph.D. at Howard." Would the entire family move? I doubt it very seriously. I really do. But I, for no reason other than he said it, would move wherever: Dartmouth, California, Yale, Harvard, etc. etc. etc. It is strange. I would like to live in New York for a little while in order to just be there and exploit whatever possibilities are there in terms of writing. However, it will not happen unless he is in the mood to move. I understand all of this a little more now, but still not enough. I am reading more and understanding more. It is interesting, but it is weird. This feminist anthology is really well put together and interesting. Makes you feel good to read it. All that stuff about how conditioning of girls starts so fast was really frightening. I wonder if I will do that to my daughter. I am going to consciously try not to. That would be a drag. It is bad to get them into that cutesy thing. I think it is bad anyway.

So, on to Alabama and maybe I will broach this subject with Karen about "the problem that has no name." It is funny how embarrassed you are to admit that sexism even exists. Men have done almost as good a job as white folks.

OCTOBER 22, 1971
This is a misty Friday and I am remembering days when my bangs would swell up and become afro-fied and I would be embarrassed lest someone see my nappy hair. Days of wine and roses. Gone now. Seems one of our friends has flipped out again or so goes the story that is making the rounds. His problem seems to stem from people's reactions to how light he is. A lot of people don't realize he's black and I guess it makes him feel bad. I need to have an old-fashioned talk with him so I can advise him

to tell the folks who mess with him about being light to go fuck themselves. Karen said a woman in The Lovin' Spoonful coffee house once talked about him like a dog and asked him how he liked "coming up here to party with us." And he would not tell her he was black. I would have said: "Bitch, kiss my black *us* ass." But I know that kind of shit is hard to do. It really is. I remember the time they told me to get out of a March in D.C. They said: "Get out. We ain't lettin' the beast march with us." They thought I was white and they refused to believe me when I said I wasn't. But what can you do? They wouldn't let Kris and Jilo into the Topographical Research Center in Chicago because they didn't have PROOF of being black. Isn't that a bitch? Weird folks in weird places. I feel for our friend. A.B. says he wrote a math book for six-year-olds based on the metaphysical concepts of the sixteenth and seventeenth centuries. Okay, but my mind fixes on stories of a Mississippi prison guard telling him, "If you want to eat, you gotta act like a monkey." I can see his eyes gleaming up from that hole in the ground and not wanting to act a fool, but hungry, so hungry . . .

DECEMBER 1, 1971

I am going to write a little note to Robert Hayden. I think his poems are wonderful. I really dig his poem "Runagate, Runagate," and I think I will tell him just that. I would like to send a note to Langston Hughes, but I waited too late . . .

DECEMBER 2, 1971

Yesterday in NewArk (that's the way we're supposed to spell Newark since they elected a black mayor) they passed a regulation on the school board to make it mandatory that all classrooms in the city have a liberation flag in the room displayed the same size and quality as the good old stars and stripes. Isn't that amazing? That is something for little kids to grow up seeing that! It will change their whole outlook right from the beginning. Rather than saying the American pledge of allegiance, they should say some kind of pledge to the liberation flag. I wonder what they would say? "I pledge my life to the liberation struggle of my people and dedicate myself to that struggle until victory is won and we live in peace." Something like that, I guess.

Pictures of Nassar's funeral: all those people crying in the streets. I wonder how it will be when Mao dies or Fidel.

Peace in our time and a chicken in every pot.

DECEMBER 2, 1971
The Palestinian guerillas killed the prime minister of Jordan at a meeting. They shot him down dead. They showed them on television after their capture. They were in no way down and out or cowed or anything like that. They were giving victory signs and carrying on. They also said they had intended to kill him for a long time and would only increase their opposition to Israel and "the lackeys of the West." And they showed one man and said: "This one is reputed to have had the blood of the man to drink as he slid down on the floor and lay dying in the hotel lobby. This man drank his blood." And the story was corroborated by witnesses. "He really did it," they said, nodding. The thing is the blood drinker looked just like a regular person. He gave the victory sign and then the thumbs-up sign. He was smiling, too. That is enough to make you stop and think. About everything.

DECEMBER 7, 1971
A moment of peace to record some thoughts for my twenty-third birthday. Isn't that weird? I still feel seventeen . . . eighteen at

the most. It is nice though. This has been a very good birthday so far and it is only ten-thirty. Michael got up early this morning and fixed breakfast for me! Eggs and bacon and hot coffee cake and orange juice and coffee. And he wouldn't let me help or do the dishes or anything. It was very nice and I feel properly spoiled. Carolyn Lewis called from New York to wish me happy birthday. I felt good to know she is okay. Nice that she still keeps in touch. We've known each other since seventh grade!

I am very happy today. I have no complaints. Peace and power!

DECEMBER 15, 1971

Things here are getting to be a drag. All the crazy folks see our office as a haven or something. It is really sad, but also scary. A brother came by yesterday and asked Pat if she would "aknead" with him after work. What does that even mean? It's a made-up word, but what does he think it means? We don't know, but it was really frightening. He had come in here the Friday I was out with his pants sitting wide open and no drawers on. Dick floating in the wind. I think he digs Pat. That is a drag, too. How is she supposed to deal with these insane, insane, insane niggas? She brought a gun to work today, so I guess that is her answer to that question.

DECEMBER 20, 1971

This occurs to me as if it were my own original thought and brand new to the world. White folks don't have to do anything to you specifically. After they do it to a couple of other people that you know about, you are so incapacitated by fear that you ain't no use to the struggle anyhow. For example, I was terrified of going to Alabama. I have never been there so I don't know how it is, right? Gut reaction: terror. I am in fear and trembling for days before we go, hoping Karen won't say anything out of the way to the white folks so we won't get killed. Not talked at, but killed. A death fear. That kind of fear just for a non-offensive first visit to Birmingham. How did those Movement folks ever get up enough courage to start marching and demonstrating? I don't know what I could/would have done. Being in Detroit is different from being in Mississippi/Alabama/Georgia! It is so depressing. If you know one person who got lynched, you are immediately fearful that next time it might be you. And these Movement folks I know all knew folks who got killed; murdered. It's horrible. It is a psychological thing mostly, I think. Oppression is built on a series of assumptions, and if they begin to crumble, the system is in grave danger. The assumptions have got to be just as strong with the oppressed as with the oppression mongers. The oppressed must feel inferior and then he will act inferior. Amazing. I just thought about this in terms of me going to Alabama and it all became very clear. Damn these racist white folks! They are a bitch!!!!!!!!

JANUARY 6, 1972

It is strange the way black folks deal with each other in public sometimes. In front of the white folks. Sometimes even when we know each other real well, black folks get into a whole funny bag. Acting real weird and ill at ease. Like their whole being is screaming, "Don't let me do nothin' niggerish in front of these white folks and don't let this person with me who I think I love do nothin' foolish either." What a weight to carry around! It's like the Léon Damas story about the black man on the bus who felt bad because the only other black man on the same bus was ugly and sweaty and dirty and ill-kempt. It is hard to express it. So sad.

Other strange things, too. . . . The women

in Northern Ireland put their kids out in the street as a diversion so that the British green beret types could not come and find the guerilla IRA folks. That is an amazing thing to me. Can you be ready to sacrifice your children to the idea of the revolution? It is a real thought. Can you put Jilo out? Or baby Kofi? Knowing that the British will just as soon blow their little heads off as not? It is a real thing. The women there are really involved in their struggle in such a passionate way. They shaved a girl's head and tarred and feathered her because she was going to marry a British soldier. They have half their men in British detention and she is going to marry a British soldier? They say it ain't gonna happen. It is a trip to think about it all.

Today on the street, this couple was walking down the block, real cool, and all of a sudden a car tried to run them over. They recognized who it was and fled, running, cool forgotten, down the street. The car gave chase and the dude ran into a grocery store and the girl hid behind a cop. They argued for a while and then the girl went off by herself, the dude in the car went off by himself and after a long time, the dude in the grocery store crept out, ran up the street, hopped into his green Cadillac and split, going real fast. Wonder what the deal was on that? Power to the people!

JANUARY 7, 1972
It's like coming into a combat zone every morning. I am more frightened every day. I hate working/living like this. I am going to have to move, quit or do something because this shit must end! I don't know if I am acting edgy or just feeling edgy. I can't even get up in the morning anymore without being depressed. I won't work in a situation like this. I absolutely refuse. Today, first thing I see when I get out of the car is Marvin the drunk coming out of Councilman Q.V. Williamson's office and going into our building. I ask Michael to come in with me and we open the back door and who is standing there but Marvin! Goddamn! What a way to start the day. Michael has to go to class, so I went and got a man from Q.V.'s office to walk all the way up to the office with me. They're supposed to be managing the building so I didn't feel bad asking him to do it. I intend to ask him every morning. It ain't supposed to be about the shit you see in this building! I don't know what to do, but this shit must end and soon! I ain't gonna deal with it much longer. And I have to go to the dentist today! How much is

one body expected to bear? I hope I get seven thousand dollars to go to graduate school at Atlanta University and don't have to work, period. I will never work in this kind of situation again if I can help it, but as Paul Newman tells Joanne Woodward in *The Long Hot Summer,* "Never say never."

Help! This is Friday but I feel no relief at all.

JANUARY 16, 1972

It is so cold in this office that my fingers are about to fall off!

Jules and Jim was on television yesterday. That is such a sad movie. Beautiful, but so sad. In the war, they are on different sides and Jules is afraid he will kill Jim. "I am glad to go to the Russian front," he says. "Here I am afraid I will kill him." And Jim says to his girlfriend, "Sometimes I am afraid I will kill Jules." "They were good friends," Jim says in his book. "Everyone called them Don Quixote and Sancho Panza." And Jeanne Moreau sings that pretty little song that I can't get out of my head afterward. Jim says, "She was quiet after her triumph of jumping into the canal." And we see her carrying her pajamas in that little package like she's going to the post office. I really dig it. And at the end,

Oskar Werner walking with that little catch step after the other two are cremated and we see the bones getting ground up. How final can you get? "Catherine wanted her ashes thrown to the wind," Jim wrote, "but that was against the rules."

One observation: It is hard to cook and watch a movie with subtitles!

JANUARY 23, 1972

A journal is a very weird thing. I remember when Kris found part of my journal and read it, I felt really bad, but of course didn't say anything to her about it. How can somebody read a journal that you have really put shit into that you don't intend for other folks to read? When A.B. asked me what was in the folder and I said, "My journal," I felt like I had been exposed in some kind of weird sex crime or something; like I had discovered my fly was open.

Deedee writes from L.A.: "Each day I breathe fire and flames."

JANUARY 24, 1972

I had a strange dream last night. I must have been reacting to the Fred Hampton documentary, which was depressing as hell. The Panthers talked so bad and sold so many wolf tickets and when the police came, they

60

didn't even have a damn lookout. Couldn't even wake up before they get killed. Revolutionaries . . . but Fred Hampton himself said some really hip things. He said when he was in jail, "There was nothing around me so I put my ear to the ground, and when I put my ear to the ground, I heard the voice of the people." That is so sad I can't stand it. But anyhow, I dreamed that we were in Chicago and in this long protest march and I was not really sure I wanted to be in it. A lot of black folks were standing around the edges of the crowd and not looking too pleased, but I couldn't get out of it. So we ended up in this warehouse district and this girl was saying, "Yeah, this is a cool way to go," but we were heading right into a field that would box us in and I said, "No, I ain't goin' this way. When the police come, we can't even get out." And I started going back out and other folks did, too, and the girl was pissed. She had straightened hair and may have been white, but I can't remember. Anyhow, then we all were in a gym-like place singing "Lift Every Voice and Sing," and the police came in and started standing around, so I got scared and sat down at the edge and tried to look off like I wasn't in the whole thing, but it was obvious that they knew everybody there was in it. So finally folks started getting scared and running out and I said, "That's a good idea," so I ran out, too, and in the lobby, all the folks who had run out were lined up and the police were all over them saying, "All right, all of you are going to get shot." And they lined us up and I had to line up and I was looking for a place to sneak out to. Absurdly, I thought maybe I could say I came out to go to the bathroom, but then I woke up before they shot us. The movie scared me, obviously. It's hard to see people selling all those wolf tickets, but no action.

JANUARY 25, 1972
Note on *Ms.:* It has some fairly decent articles, but they are all/all/all, down to the last woman, middle class and overwhelmingly white. A few examples: an evening where a housewife has her moment of truth. There are three couples there in the story. The husbands are all lawyers. The wives are a teacher, a doctor and a writer. How middle class can you get? And they are all white. The woman who is a writer also tells feminist fables, has published a novel and gives lectures on modern poetry. Gloria Steinem is the epitome of the women *Ms.* is talking to. The women working on the magazine all try to identify with non-white

women and say that among women "there are no barriers," but the only black woman in the whole issue is a black welfare mother who is in the fucking back of the magazine. She is obviously being used as a token. Her piece is not a lead article, but her picture is in the table of contents so you will think they are into a black/third world thing. It is not addressed to women. It is addressed to white women, and not even all of them. I don't know why I feel so pissed about it. I guess I hoped for more. I must be a more radical feminist than I thought, plucked eyebrows and all. I am letting them grow back. Fuck this fake shit! I don't care if Nefertiti did do it!

JANUARY 26, 1972
We have to go look at another building today so we can move the SEP office. I hope that it offers some relief to the siege conditions that exist where we are now. Every morning, Michael and I come up here ready for combat. It is a real drag. What is the function of having to be scared every morning coming to work? I feel like this will end like the movies. They will look in the dead girl's journals and see all these references to how scary it is and how she wants out and then one day her poor mutilated body is

found raped and stabbed to death.

Last night, I had a dream that was like a remake of *Straw Dogs,* except it wasn't people trying to get in, it was mice and rats and squirrels. I mean big squirrels, like human size. It was a trip. A bad trip.

JANUARY 28, 1972

Various images in my mind. Today, Kofi X came by again. He is a great artist, but he is in bad shape. Yesterday, he was talking real fast and very hyper. Today, he is literally slurring his words and blinking real slow. I guess he is still taking dope. That is horrible enough, but the really bad thing is, I came back from the barber shop and I was on my way to the bathroom, and when I turned down the hall, there he was, standing outside the doctor's office, slumped against the wall. He looked just like that other man with the little hat and closed eyes who is always out there waiting. When he looked up and saw it was me, he kind of smiled and tried to get it together. He said he was going back to California pretty soon, but at the moment, he was obviously looking for that doctor. There is nothing else down here but the bathroom and Hazel's Hairtique and I know that wasn't what he wanted. I feel so sad and screaming inside to see that. The goddamn dope help center is at one end of the hall and the weird doctor is giving out fixes at the other end. Lord. It is so horrible. Kofi's face was all drooped down like dough. If I knew how to keen, I would.

JANUARY 29, 1972

This morning we go hear a talk by the little man who used to be Langston Hughes's personal secretary. His name was Raoul Abdul and he was a mixture of Indian and black. His father was from India and he talked about how when Langston Hughes would wake up at one in the afternoon, he would be a real bad-tempered person and would scream out, "Raoul! Where is the tea? Bring the croissants!" Like a real movie star thing. But he said that was okay. "That was just the way he was." Then he said Langston would get up and put on a Japanese kimono and complain and always had to have a heater (winter and summer) by his feet. He said Langston would play Alex Bradford and Clara Ward and rouse himself with gospel music. Raoul confessed that he didn't like gospel music then and didn't ever like it until he figured out there is a connection between gospel music and flamenco! Get to that! Langston wanted everybody to love him, Raoul says. And I

65

did love him/do love him and hope he rests in peace.

As I walked by our favorite militant book store later, the owner was playing "Suite: Judy Blue Eyes," by Crosby, Stills, Nash and Young. That is a nice contradiction and shows he is a man after my own heart.

FEBRUARY 21, 1972
I am invited to visit the senior poet. His room seems bare and filled to bursting at the same time. Old newspapers and printed junk everywhere. A chair filled with makeup, roses and other supposedly feminine para- phernalia. He greets me at the door with the odor of someone who has been drinking for a long, long time. Are all artists this way? (Hell, no!) He has the smell of drinking and vomiting on yourself, of drinking so much that you sweat Scotch. Strange. He makes himself so ugly. He is too pot-bellied for the shirt he has pulled across his stomach. The shirt is brown with brown print. All in all, it is a strange monotone appearance, but he wants to use four of my poems in the magazine! "Aunt Abbie," "For Diana Danc- ing," "Untitled," and "Deaconess." Right on!

FEBRUARY 22, 1972

Dreamed about Angela Davis last night. I was sitting with her and we were talking and I asked her if she wanted a bangle. And she said, yes, and I took one of mine and gave it to her and she slipped it on her arm and smiled and we went to some stores and looked around, but we didn't buy anything. It was a very real dream. When I woke up this morning, I really felt like I had been with her. Strange to deal with that. She was thin and looked tired but she did smile some. She liked the bangle, I think.

MARCH 3, 1972

Lately, I have been obsessed with having a baby. Wonder why. I have not mentioned this to Michael since it is still an abstract thing, I think. I mean, I don't want to mess up and not get a Master's and probably begin a Ph.D. before I get pregnant so I could write my dissertation over the diapers and stuff. I think I will write on the Marquis de Sade . . .

Mark sent me a Shirley Chisholm for President button!

I wonder what our kid would look like . . .

MARCH 9, 1972

I was reading *Slaughterhouse Five* and Vonnegut says that he knew a man who said that after the war, he was going to get a hired gunman to kill all of his enemies. He was at war when he said this, killing people every day, but he couldn't kill his own enemies. He could only kill folks who hadn't ever done anything to him in the first god-damn place. That is weird as hell.

The bad mood broke yesterday. I am really glad. Don't know what the fuck the bad mood was about, but I am so glad it is over.

APRIL 23, 1973

This is one of those days when I am glad to have a job in television. Three of us went down to get the story for our show, *Ebony Beat Journal.* Me, the producer/writer. Ngaio Killingsworth, our cinematographer. And Ashia Nanji, our associate producer. The station (WXIA-TV) thinks of us as their way to fulfill a community responsive-ness commitment to the FCC. We think of ourselves as journalists. Filming the picket line outside of Rich's Department Store downtown gave me a strange feeling. I remembered all the picket lines I was on in Detroit. Like the time we were boycotting my high school because of overcrowding and Robert Higgins, who went to our church, but didn't go to our school, was walking with us instead of going to class at his own school because he said he was a socialist and his first allegiance was to where the struggle of the people was. That was the day I spent in a sound car with Mr. Boston, driving around the west side, urging people to come out and support the Northwestern High School picket line and everybody had one ear on the radio because President Kennedy was sending his ships to Cuba and so were the Russians and we were all thinking we should have gotten those fallout shelters like they told us to in the first place. Nobody came down to the school to join us and a lot of kids, my friends included, were going on in to class like we weren't even there. Then I started thinking about the picket line in front of the A&P store, walking with Oscar Hand, who was the choir director at our church, and when the policeman tried to break up the demonstration, he told the policeman that we didn't have to move and I got this sickish, green feeling in my throat because I knew the policeman wanted to hit Oscar and Oscar wouldn't run and I would be there, helpless, all by myself . . .

But Rich's today was different energy. There was a lot of tension and determination; anger and pure Negro defiance. It was beautiful. Ngaio was putting the silent camera in everybody's face and walking in the street to get the shot and Aisha said to one of the leaders, "You're a Leo? Fantastic!" Insane. It felt a little like Detroit that morning just before the riot started. There was that same free-floating tension and looseness in the crowd. Like they're thinking, why don't we just . . . do ANYTHING? Whatever we want! Nobody can stop us from doing it! Beautiful. Made me feel like old times and I almost started crying. The brothers and sisters were not scared at all. Beautiful!

MAY 7, 1973
Have just seen *Two English Girls,* directed by François Truffaut, the same one who directed *Jules and Jim,* and *The Wild Child.* It was very, very good. The women were very well done. They did not have happy-ever-after endings to their lives, but they seemed to live very intensely, which is better than the ho-hum. One girl, Anne, was more fulfilled, I think. She had lovers and was very liberated. At one point after she decides to give up her virginity and take Claude as a lover, they part company. They are staying on a Swiss lake and she climbs into a rowboat and rows away by herself.

He does the same. Beautiful. At another point, she has two regular lovers. The subtitle says: "The two lovers suffered greatly. Ann thrived on it." *It* being the multiple relationships; not the suffering. It was a very, very good movie.

I feel a weird desire to be alone for a while. I am tired to death of catering to, playing games for, the folks at work and in a different sense, here at home. Just the mere presence of someone else is irritating to me just now. Don't know why. I suspect because of all the bullshit, famously boring games I am forced to play at work to placate everybody. Today, I am not going to get involved. I'm going to be quiet and serene. I wonder if that will last past 9:30 or 10:00 o'clock. Probably not.

I feel that I have a weird stillness inside me that keeps being interrupted by everything from the necessity of eating to the worry about gaining weight when you do eat. What a bore! I have to get back to my writing; to my solitude. But the phone, the people, people, godawful people are around all the fucking time!

Maybe I, the consummate social being, will eventually turn out to be a hermit. I begin to feel that tendency begin to rise in me. I also feel like letting my hair grow and wearing long skirts and no makeup. I wonder if that is a fad. Also, no more birth control pills. Ever! Let the chips or sperm fall where they may!

"Ann thrived on it." At the end of the movie, Claude, Ann's lover, looks in the mirror and he is about forty-five years old and he sort of looks startled at his reflection and says to himself with a little push up to his glasses, "What is wrong with me today? I look so old." I am going to take Kris and go see the movie again.

JUNE 2, 1973

A friend from the past, still crazy as hell, but nice. He and another jive brother are talking about how "a black man needs three or four women to fulfill his needs." God! Such arrogance. He is nice, though, my friend. Doesn't take it all too seriously. "Your problem," he says with a rueful smile, "is that you are number one, too intelligent." What man would ever say that to another man? They know not what they say or from whence their incorrectness comes! We gave a little party for him last night and a lot of folks came. Carolyn Gerald, Tobe and Goldie Johnson, Karen and A. B. Spellman, Paul Carter Harrison, Donna, his lady friend, Luther Weems, Beni Ivey, Gaye

Cobb, O. T. Hammonds, Dr. Napper, Vern Odom, Pamela Lake, Deirdre McDonald, Ojeda Penn, Clint Deveaux, Doris Dozier, Sharon and Tom Jones. A weird little group, but nice. Shirley Franklin was there, too. I like parties, but they cost too much to give!

JUNE 3, 1973

So many things are going through my head. Emily Evans is dead. She was killed in a car accident. Her husband was in it, too, but he was in a coma for a while and then he woke up and lived, but Emily died. Deirdre told me at the party last night and I can't stop thinking about it. It is so unreal. How does it feel to be dead like that? Do you know at a certain point that you are dying? Do you try to fight it? Do you feel scared? Do you feel frustrated? In a car accident, you probably are gone too fast for you to feel anything. Emily. I remember so many scattered things. Like her in that concert with Diana Ramos, singing that song and dancing with that orange dress on and carrying her tights and her shoes in a rope bag like a real dancer. And wearing those white tights and black leotard and white shoes with pink ribbons. And dancing and worrying if her butt was too big to be a real dancer. And going to New York to study with Arthur Mitchell and going on exchange to Dartmouth where she met her husband and not knowing that started the chain of events in time and space that would mean she would die. She would die. She would die. Deirdre said she thinks it was because of snow. They couldn't see the road. I wonder if they lay there in the snow and nobody knew they were gone for some time. Did they almost freeze? Did she die right away? Did he know she was dead? Did he do the driving? How does he feel now? She was twenty-two or -three. Younger than me and she died. I remember talking to her in class about Ken Lee and what a good actor he was and about black men and women and how hard and confusing the whole love thing is. And this brother she married made her really happy and she said he was different. She was teaching dance at Dartmouth while he finished school. I can't stop thinking about it. How long has she been dead? I can't deal with it.

JUNE 4, 1973
Today, into our little dungeon office, sauntered none other than Kip Kano, the Kenyan runner from the Munich Olympics. I guess they figured since we produce the black public affairs shows, we might want to interview him. He was just a medium

height, slender, slender, slender man with a close haircut and a gap in the bottom row of his big, square white teeth. What luck for Aisha! She was decked out in African garb, as she often is, and she rapped to Kano about things in general in perfect Swahili. She gets big points from me for doing this since she seemed to do it really well. It was weird to see him in the studios of Channel 11. I can't describe the essence of the weirdness, though. Somehow, it was rather uncomfortable because I didn't know what to talk to him about. I can never treat folks from Africa as easily as I do folks from here. I always feel pushy like it is not cool to let on that you want to talk to them about their country. I can't describe it, but I never feel relaxed talking to Africans.

(There is a sucker fish on the bottom of the tank in our office, and he is eating away. He is humping along the bottom of the tank, just sucking up the slime after the other fish eat and puke and crap all over the bottom of it. That fish is one weird dude.)

JUNE 6, 1973
I asked Murdell if she knew about Emily and she said she knew and that Emily was six months pregnant and was conscious when the accident happened. She was

pinned in the car and they couldn't get her out and she was awake. Awake and bleeding to death. She could have been saved, but they couldn't get through the rush hour traffic to get her out from under the car and she lay there and died. That is really depressing. That is probably the last I will say about Emily because I can't deal with it. Not at all.

SEPTEMBER 30, 1973
It is almost a month now since Poppy died. I think I am ready to try to deal with it, but I'm not sure. Kris and I kept dreaming about him when we got back from the funeral in Detroit. She had a dream that he and Aunt Daisy were back and they said they would be around. "You didn't think I'd stay gone, did you?" he said to Kris. I dreamed that he was back and he said, "Don't touch me!" but I hugged him because I was so glad to see him and he died again. It was at the funeral home, too. Weird. Kris also had a dream where he was riding in a car where there was no driver. Like a rocking chair rocking with nobody in it means death is rocking the chair. Anyhow, they all got in the car and drove away with him. It is all weird. I do not remember grandfather dying. I was too little. But

Poppy is another feeling. It's like not really being able to believe he's gone. Nanny didn't even know he was dead until the night of the funeral. I went downstairs and Mommy and Nanny were sitting at the kitchen table. Nanny had ice cream in a bowl, but she was crying. And she said, "I knew somebody was dead and I thought it might be him." But she's senile and couldn't really get a handle on the thought. Barbara brought the ribbon and two flowers off the family wreath and put it on Nanny's dresser since she couldn't go to the service. The ribbon said: "From his loving family to a wonderful husband and father." Well, when Mommy went downstairs, Nanny had torn it all to pieces and thrown the ribbon and the flowers in the corner of her room. She knew then, but she couldn't stand it. Mommy and Henry had seen the light going on and off in the bathroom and went downstairs to see if everybody was all right. Nanny had gotten up and gotten dressed and was walking/walking/walking through the house to see where Poppy was. And she kept turning on the bathroom light to see if he was in there. She knew he was dead, but how could she fathom it? They had been married for fifty years! There is no separateness after all that time.

At the cemetery, Mommy was crying after the last prayer and she said: "I can't leave him here. How can I leave him here?"

OCTOBER 17, 1973

I am still too exhausted to make much sense. Want to just get some impressions down. Thank god, the election is over! We won! Maynard Jackson has been elected the first African American mayor of Atlanta. Incredible! People everywhere last night. The returns coming in and Buddy Jordan screaming and Shirley got hit in her car by a truck, but she didn't get hurt and came on down to the hotel. Maynard comes out of the inner sanctum of the suite when victory is obvious and kisses his family; shakes some hands; and a kiss for me. He has soft, fat little cheeks like a little fat baby. Nice. And the speech downstairs in the ballroom, and me and Shirley Franklin upstairs, listening to the reports and eating black olives. And the total insanity afterward with people trying to get in the suite and get to the new mayor and me sitting on the floor, working with the press, trying to reason with a hysterical brother from the black audio network and him saying, "Let me speak to a man!" Good grief! Male chauvinism and the awful depressed feeling that sneaks over you when it rears its ugly head. Strange how you seem to feel the city will change overnight. So many women were trying hard to hit on Maynard's brother, Paul, and the cops with small guns under their arms, but also trying to hit on the women and Jay Cooper winking at me around the corner. Finally the tired, tired ride home and the amazing feeling carrying over to this morning and both of us admitting we liked the excitement and wondered how we will ever adjust to normal living and wanting a job at city hall and feeling guilty about that and loving the telegram from Mommy saying congratulations. I already know that working in this campaign has changed my life. The question will be how? The wonderfulness of winning!!

DECEMBER 13, 1973

I had a dream last night. In the dream we went to the movies and there was a scene with Maynard in it and all the black folks in the movie cheered. And then these teenage white boys got up and peed on all the black people in the place. Alderman Marvin Arrington was there and he got up and said that he had information to the effect that they were going to sing the Nazi national anthem at 7:30 and we better split. So we did and when we got outside, they had slit Maynard's tires and he had to ride with us, but he and Michael went somewhere else and me and Deirdre went to the car and we saw some people lifting up a little dead black child and putting the body into a white car next to us. Then the police came over to us and put a gun in the door and told us to get out because they knew we were the killers. We were scared and got out and Deirdre wouldn't talk to them and they kept rubbing her arm and putting the gun against our cheeks and trying to touch her breasts, but she wouldn't talk to them. It was such a weird dream. Very realistic, too. Maynard said: "They were big boys because in the dark I could see they were very well developed." Weird, weird, weird . . .

DECEMBER 14, 1973
It has gotten so that now I cannot even look at television without getting angry at what the shows are doing to women's self-conceptions. That is an awkward sentence. What I mean is, it is difficult to giggle at the comedy sketches when all they are doing is perpetuating myths about women. Flip Wilson is the prime offender of the week. Last night on his show he had a skit about a woman who accused someone of

rape. Funny topic, right? Anyhow, the woman turns out to be a real sex freak and only uses the rape charge to meet men and get turned on by re-enacting the crime for the officers (both men also). She finally decides she digs one of the policemen and they go off for a tête-à-tête. A real drag. Especially since there is so much controversy connected with rape anyhow. It must be awful to have been raped and then see some shit like that. A few weeks ago there was a movie called *Rape.* It was a drag, too. It started off trying to be progressive. The woman was raped and put through a lot of really horrific shit by the police in terms of questions, and the hospital trip and all that. And then the movie totally copped out! Turns out the guy she identifies in the lineup and that a lot of other rape victims identify is innocent, but that he is the identical twin of the real rapist. How many times has that ever happened? I would bet not even once. That is the whole subtle, sexist crap that implies that a woman who accuses a man of rape will probably make the wrong identification and send some poor innocent guy to jail. Besides, since she isn't really hurt (especially if she wasn't a virgin at the time of the rape . . .) why not just let the whole thing slide? That is horrible. I think that to be raped must be just about the most frightening, painful, degrading thing that could happen. It hurts. It is a really personal assault on your body. I mean someone doesn't just hit you or beat you up, they enter your body, without your permission of course! Anyhow, I didn't dig that movie and I definitely didn't dig the rape sketch on Flip Wilson's show. It is so important to be conscious even when it makes you realize how much negative stuff you have enjoyed all your life until you realized it was all anti you.

To: Mayor Jackson
From: Pearl Cleage Lomax, Press
    Secretary/Director of
    Communications
Date: January 18, 1974
Re: Startling Revelation

My doctor informed me yesterday that I am approximately two months pregnant. I felt that you should be apprised of this situation and in order to facilitate matters, I propose the following:

1. I will continue to work throughout my pregnancy until it is time for me to go into the hospital. I am in

perfect health and do not anticipate having to curtail performance of my duties in any way.

2. We should move to hire an assistant communications officer who could be taught to perform the duties of the job. (This is necessary in any case due to the heavy work load of this office.) This person should be hired as soon as possible to give her or him time to adjust to things here. I would suggest the beginning of March as a good time.

3. I will request two months of maternity leave after the baby is born. I will have fully trained my assistant by this time and the transition should be a smooth one. She or he will perform in my position during the two months that I am out of the office.

4. At the end of two months, I will return to work. During my leave, I will be available for writing assignments and other duties that can be performed at my home.

I hope these suggestions are agreeable to you. I would like to discuss the matter with you at your convenience. I felt that a brief memo outlining the situation and my proposed handling of it would facilitate our later follow-up conversation.

Pearl

JANUARY 23, 1974

Now that I know that I am pregnant, I remember all those resolutions to keep this dynamic diary of thoughts, feelings, etc. The fallacy of that is that it assumes that your thoughts, feelings, etc. will suddenly begin to revolve around the fact that you're pregnant. ("Carrying life in your belly," as A.B. so poetically put it!) However, I do not find that I am constantly thinking about the baby. I do think more about what I eat and all, but since I am no bigger and not sick, I do not feel pregnant. It is nice. I feel positive about the whole thing, but not at all consumed. That may come later, according to the findings in *Ms.* magazine, which make pregnancy seem like one step from hell. I don't believe that to be the truth.

I am eating better and drinking milk and taking vitamins and stuff. Weird trip for me, the junk food queen. But, I assume this diary will begin to get more babyfied as time goes on and the appearance thing changes. Bought my first maternity dresses today.

They are nice, too. Not tacky at all. Looks like I might survive. Karen and Kris say they are glad I am pregnant so now they can see what a stylish pregnant woman will look like. Ha!

JANUARY 28, 1974

What a rotten day! I don't know what I did to give myself this much indigestion for two days, but I imagine it was flying to Washington with the mayor yesterday morning; the jangled nerves that come with flying; the not eating until 10:30 that night; and then eating that goddamn acidic grapefruit. I've had horrendous indigestion ever since. Mostly at night, but off and on during the day, too. A real drag. I will have to be more careful now that the kid will be taking his toll on the old body, too. Indigestion is a bitch.

This last-minute news conference thing is a real drag. The mayor is going to have to get that together. I can't deal with things the way they are now. It's just one long ball of stress. I feel really weird about this job. I feel like I am now part of the establishment. That is a drag. When Donald Stone and them presented a petition for action on the Police Department to the mayor today, I felt good. It is good to have some black folks making demands on Maynard. Black folks need to be heard! Otherwise, his mind will be buried under the mass of information from the Chamber of Commerce types who are always on the case.

Anyhow, the weather is horrible. I am ready to wear my new maternity clothes, but I ain't got the stomach for it. My joke for the day . . .

MARCH 13, 1974
I have let so many days go by. Tsk, tsk. What an awful mother already! I am getting bigger, but still feel fine. I am fearful of gaining a lot of weight, but have not been putting on so much that I am running to diet books. I am trying to hold down the junk food consumption. I remember about two weeks ago, I had this strange feeling. I realized I was indeed pregnant. I mean, I felt like I was really carrying around a lil' person in there who was growing and developing and I had no control over any of it. It was weird. Not a hostile feeling, but weird.

It is also weird for people to respond the way they do. Gloria Gayles says to me: "Are you excited?" I went into my standard response about how I was pleased and looking forward to it, etc. "Yes," she said with obvious concern, "but are you excited?" I didn't really know what to say. I am not really "excited." Excited suggests an all-consuming elation that I do not have time to have! The thought of the baby doesn't enter my mind for hours at a time. It is a pleasant undercurrent, but "excited"? That especially seems to be offensive to me. It means a whole altering of your style and your life and your specificity to make you into a big glowing maternal being. I think that is negative to you and the kid. How can he or she possibly survive the strain of having to be EVERYTHING in the mother's life? I am not getting down what I mean, but it is hard to figure it out. I mean, it is good to be having a baby, but it is not the be all/end all of my life. There!

Daddy says to be sure to put something on my stomach so I won't get stretch marks. I will do that! I am not necessarily worried at this point, but I will try to be careful.

I am already thinking that the two-month leave won't work. I want to see the kid grow for a while. I ought to be there to help it grow and get humanoid before we throw it into a nursemaid's arms. But there is time to figure it all out.

APRIL 6, 1974
First of all, let's say this . . . there is

absolutely nothing glamorous about being pregnant. There are a lot of nice things about it. There is the moment when the doctor first tells you that you are expecting and you feel like you want to laugh and cry and holler all at the same time. There is the relief and happiness you feel when your mate responds with the joy you had hoped he would feel. There is the brief time you carry around your secret without telling anybody in case "something happens." There is the fantastic moment when you first feel the lil' ripple that is the baby letting you know that it is really there. There is the wonder you feel when the doctor confirms a heartbeat. And there is the growing intimacy and closeness you feel toward your favorite man who is hopefully sharing the feeling of this time with you. BUT, lest you assume this is a tract to convince you that this is "the most beautiful time of your life," let me hasten to assure you that there are a few problems. One occurs when you first try to button up your favorite blouse and there is a stomach there for the first time. There are more and they come in stages. More on all of this later . . .

APRIL 10, 1974
Just a brief note to say that last night about

9:30 after a hearty meal of two egg rolls and some shrimp fried rice, the lil' baby moved for the first time!!! I felt it and Michael could feel it, too. It was really hip. Felt like a little stretch was going on in there. Like a slow lil' poke in the stomach. It really was such a positive feeling. I feel very good right through here about the whole thing. I think things will work out and we will all kind of mesh together and it won't be intrusive at all. Hooray! So let me note this for the baby book: April 9, 1974; felt first real movement. Right on, baby!

APRIL 11, 1974

News flash! Today, Dr. Borders heard a lil' heartbeat from the kid. It was really nice. She also showed me the birth film, which was quite a freakout now that I'm actually pregnant. It was positive, but scary with all the blood squirting out and stuff. But it was a real ad for natural childbirth. The woman in the film was drugged and didn't even see anything! Her husband left her alone and she and the baby didn't even deal with each other for a good while afterward. It was sad, but hopefully we won't have to deal with that. I intend to have natural childbirth! Dr. Borders also told me that I am gaining weight too quickly and should be careful so

I won't get fat. I am on an immediate diet! Would you believe cottage cheese for dinner? I am serious! I am not about to gain forty pounds!!

APRIL 19, 1974
I don't know if it is raging hormones or what but I am in a foul mood. I feel fat and gross and icky. And I have four more months to go! I must also confess that as opposed to my very positive feelings of about a week ago, it has occurred to me that I don't even want to have a baby. I almost started crying when I saw the Mexican dancers at the park today. Slender and limber and dancing. I wanted to be dancing, too, but I felt like a tank! Ick. I hope this mood passes cuz I am being a real bitch. What can I say? I want to smoke a joint, but I am afraid of rearranging my child's lil' genes or something, so I won't do it.

God! What a terrible day. Now I am going to a reception with Shirley Franklin and my hair is all cut off and I feel like a pinhead blimp. I think I look like one, too. Shirley will be beautiful, of course. She can't help it. Henry Kissinger is supposed to be at the reception tonight. I think I will stick my tongue out at him or something disrespectful. Anything to purge myself of this bad mood!

APRIL 22, 1974
Just a brief lil' note since it is time to go home for the day, thank god! I am feeling very good and not at all as rotten as I was last week. I do think, however, that raging hormones are not always just in the mind. It is real! I have felt really bitchy several times for no reason. I am therefore making a concerted effort to overrule my hormones and be Miss Sweetness and Light. Thinking sweet thoughts to have a sweet baby! The kid is moving all over the place, too. It is a real trip. A nice, positive feeling. If this is pregnancy, it ain't too bad at all. Hopefully, child rearing is as much different from what people tell you as this pregnancy has been. Peace!

MAY 16, 1974
Had my first fall yesterday. What a trip! I was walking down the hallway at work and kablam! I fell flat down. Not flat, really. Actually I was rather proud of myself for falling gracefully. I kind of settled down on the ground with my skirt intact all around me so no flashing of the panties and I said "Oh!" in a very ladylike way. Immediately, I

was surrounded by about ten people who were semi-hysterical. They kept saying things like, "Lie down!" On the floor? Or: "Get an ice bag!" To put where? I kept waiting for somebody to say, "Boil some water." It was a real trip. But they finally had Walt Huntley lift me up bodily and carry me to my office. He was pretty cool about it since it was kind of embarrassing. "Just put your arms around my neck," he said, and stood up easy as you please. When Michael got back to the office, he said, "What happened to you?" I told him and he was pretty cool, but I think he was worried and he told me to stay home the rest of the week. Now when we go up and down the stairs he takes my arm and stuff like he is serious about helping me so I won't fall, which is nice.

But anyhow, I am really big now and have experienced a feeling I didn't think I would. That is, when I go someplace without Michael, I feel self-conscious about being pregnant. I can't quite figure out why, but I do. I think some of it has to do with the fact that I didn't realize how pregnant I was until about a week ago. I was walking with Michael and I looked in a plate-glass window and saw myself and couldn't believe it. A stomach!! What a shock. I don't know why I didn't think the sideways view would be that different, but I was shocked. I looked huge! Sometimes I feel like people are uncomfortable around pregnant women because they are living proof of the sexual act! Well, sorry to tell you, but it's true. We made this baby together! If it hadn't been for us, it never would have come into being.

So, three months to go. I wish peace and health to this lil' kid. I want it to live forever and be perfect. Isn't that a burden to put on a baby who is as yet only six pre-natal months old? Ha! Already a pushy mother!

MAY 17, 1974
And today I am alternating between a kind of soft euphoria and a deep sense of dread at the thought of having responsibility for this lil' baby. I am getting so big now. I almost always feel awkward and off-balance. It's strange. Here's another tidbit for those who have never been pregnant: if you're a good mother and take your pre-natal iron like you should, you will have green shit for the duration of your pregnancy. I learned that from Kris who answered my question about why just cuz you're pregnant even the color of your feces has to change. Total disruption of normal bodily functions. This lil' baby does not play! Six months along and I start to worry. Will I be happy staying

home all day and not working? My mind puts me in that role and some days I like it and some days I feel like I'll just go mad. Some days I can't even think of what records I would like to play if I was home alone all the time.

I'm so huge. We're going out tonight and I want to look decent. I remember when I had a twenty-two-inch waist! Ah, sweet mystery of life!

MAY 30, 1974

The books do not lie. The last trimester is a bitch. Cheryl said that after her sixth month, she got "bored with her body." I am not bored so much as rather frightened by its seemingly independent growth and expansion. It seems to be trying to put itself further and further away from any semblance of the me I was used to. I begin to despair of ever having a waist again. Is this only vanity? I don't know. I think it is more of the same feeling that I had when I first started showing. That is, a weird feeling that your body is betraying you. When you get fat, you get on a diet and lose the weight. Not when you're pregnant. You can diet all you want. Lil' X is growing and thus your abdomen is growing, too. It's strange. I take a longer time to get dressed these days. I feel fat in everything I put on. I am trying to be cool, but I have three more months and I can imagine that early August is going to be a pure bitch. But, the baby is kicking and seems to be doing okay. That is positive! Somehow when I feel dissatisfied with my own body, I don't associate that with the baby. It is like the baby is in there and cool and this body transformation doesn't have anything to do with the kid at all. It's so weird. Intellectualizing on all this shit doesn't work. There are so many gut feelings (no pun intended!) that are hard to put down on paper. It's hard to sort it all out. But, I feel better when I at least try to write about it. Lord knows I am already a fat pregnant lady. I don't want to be a whining one, too! Better to whine on paper and then get up, get out, and smile for the people!

JUNE 3, 1974
Officially into that final and most difficult trimester. Almost time for the kid. But this is basically another entry about the things the books don't usually tell you about. Seems that all the uglies wait until the end. Just when you are getting the most weight gain because the baby is starting to pick up weight (until now it is you who has been gaining; the kid only weighs two pounds at

most!), you also find that your skin is beginning to break out in earnest. Not an occasional blemish, but a real case of teenage acne. And then your hair grows faster, but more unevenly and you feel heavy, awkward and generally fat/fat/fat. Note: Arms seem to be the most precarious part of my anatomy right now. They feel really chunky and sleeveless dresses are absolutely required in Georgia in the summertime. Help! But the skin problem is really a bitch. All that stuff about the glow of motherhood? It's just teenage acne back to haunt us!

But, Dr. Borders heard the baby's heartbeat today and said it is really strong. According to the kicking I've been receiving, it is a linebacker for the Green Bay Packers. I am uglier, but in a mostly positive mood. Thank heaven for that!

JUNE 9, 1974
And for the first time, a new feeling emerges with great intensity and strangeness. I have felt glimmerings of it before, but last night it came up with a whoosh that almost freaked me right out. We went to a party. I found myself the only pregnant woman there. It was quite strange. I felt that embarrassment again, surrounded by so many flat bare midsections and halter tops galore. It

was like I was some kind of throwback to a time when people had children and I had been suddenly transplanted into an environment where I had somehow made a ghastly mistake and was being pitied by the new beings who would never be so stupid as to be caught in the round fix that I was in. The voices were condescending. "Oh, this is your first. When is it due?" "You look so cute pregnant!" "I see what you've been up to!" A lot of chuckling and rolling of the eyes. I felt embarrassed. At one point, I almost started crying. It was not at all positive and I felt like I was really in a hostile environment. Not that I had bad feelings, but the people there were sending out really bad vibes. It seemed almost like they resented me. I have felt strangeness like that one or two times alone in a store. People stealing glances at you and stuff, but that is more curiosity on their part since pregnant women are rare enough to be checked over for weirdness of shape, etc. But these sleek young folks were just kind of sneering at me over their Chablis. Maybe that is all pregnant paranoia, but it felt real just the same and it was a real drag. "After six months, you get bored with your body," said Cheryl. Maybe so, but you sure do feel protective of its contents!

JUNE 24, 1974

Went to see Dr. Borders today. She is really a whirlwind. You wait three hours to see her because she's at the hospital delivering somebody else's baby and when you finally see her, it is all "Hi/how do you feel/glad you lost some weight/etc." But it was a positive visit on account of the little new nurse says I have lost two pounds. I don't believe her. I think she is new and therefore doesn't know how to work the scale. My own scale doesn't reflect a loss and my own ballooning body doesn't reflect anything but the Rubenesque proportions common to pregnant women who are bearing down (no pun intended) on their eighth month. But I did not intend to tell Dr. B. that her nurse was not correct! That is the first positive weight thing I have had for weeks!

What is happiness? Losing some weight and being commended by your obstetrician! Doesn't take much . . .

JUNE 26, 1974

As the time draws nearer, I am becoming ravenous again. Just like the first four months. I am starved all the time. I really don't need this since I don't want to blow up like a balloon in the next eight weeks or so. It is so weird. I haven't been hungry like this for many moons and now . . . Otherwise, I'm feeling fine. Legs get tired sooner, but otherwise fat and well. I was thinking about it today. If the delivery goes as well as the pregnancy has gone, I've got it made!

JULY 14, 1974
About four weeks to go! I feel good, but awkward and heavy. I have gained two pounds in five days and now weight 127, which is a drag, but I figure with Ma here for a few days some weight gain was inevitable. I will have to watch it. No point in getting all the way to the end and fucking it up. I am so ready for the baby to come! Ma says she had easy labor both times and I am not anticipating any great pains and writhing around no matter what Scarlett O'Hara had to deal with trying to bring Melanie Wilkes's baby into the world after Prissy confesses she "don't know nothin' 'bout birthin' no babies!" I have my natural childbirth class tomorrow. Ravana Mokner is the teacher's name and she is a pure crusader to her heart! But that's okay. I am looking forward to tomorrow's class. I figure once she shows me the breathing, I'll be ready. She really is such a determined advocate of Lamaze. Almost like you imagine an early women's libber would be. An

advocate for women!

JULY 18, 1974

I am really very anxious to have this baby. I am looking forward to the whole thing. I feel positive today although it is hard to sleep because of the weight shifting involved. I mean it is a major deal just to turn over. Huffin' and puffin' and then finally, plop! I'm over! Rather like a turtle for real this time. Ma says labor is a snap. Five hours was the longest she was in labor and it wasn't bad. It was good to get such a positive report from her. People are always anxious to tell you horror stories. I'm not scared, which is pretty incredible. I, the ultimate chicken, am looking forward to seeing how my body deals with the whole thing. I figure since I did modern dance so long and was good at it my body should be able to do this natural thing. I mean, how natural is Martha Graham technique and I mastered that, didn't I?

It's a good day and I am happy/happy.

JULY 28, 1974

Well, we're coming into the home stretch. No pun on the bane of my existence, stretch marks either! We went to the big Andy Young fundraising dinner Friday. I was going to wear one of Shirley's chic maternity hand-me-downs, but decided my morale deserved a new dress. I found a beautiful silky long thing with a lil' matching wrap. Really roomy and pretty and — wonder of wondrous morale builders! — a regular (as opposed to a maternity) size 5!! If you don't think that made me feel good!! At the dinner, folks kept complimenting me until I felt positively un-fat! Funny though, people are always surprised to see a pregnant woman looking good — makeup, some style, etc. I've seen a lot of really pulled-together pregnant women and why not? Seems to me this is the time to put your best belly forward!

The nursery is all done save for curtains and a mattress for the crib. I find myself going into the room mentally conversing with the baby. I guess that is my maternal instinct dropping down on me! I have laid out the clothes the baby and I will wear home from the hospital. I hope the baby is healthy and happy. I think half of having a good pregnancy is having a good husband with a positive attitude. They gave me a shower at work on Friday. We got so many nice gifts. The baby will be well dressed for the first six months anyway!

AUGUST 5, 1974

Ma and Henry came through on their way driving to Mexico. I was hoping the baby would be here, but no luck and they had to go on. Ma said if I have the baby while they're in Mexico, they'll try to come back through here on the way back to Idlewild. She doesn't want to waste long distance charges calling from Mexico to find out about the baby, so we worked out a signal. She'll call collect, person to person for Frederick Douglass. If I've had the baby, we'll accept the charges. If I got no news, we'll say Frederick Douglass isn't here. We both found that really funny!

AUGUST 6, 1974

The ninth month and all they say is true. The baby is due technically on the fifteenth, but according to Dr. Borders it could come "any day now." The lil' thing has dropped into position. Its head is engaged and we are waiting only for the signal from the gods that it's time to proceed. All is in readiness for the baby. Oil bought, diapers ordered, basinet borrowed. Here are some bad things: legs tired; back ache; stretch marks galore in spite of liberally applying "mother's friend." A weird in-limbo feeling is the worst. We are saying things to each other like: "This weekend we'll do so and so, if we're not at the hospital." The baby looms before us as an almost reality. The kicking is more forceful. The contractions are more assertive.

I feel that half the ease of my pregnancy has been due to my own desire to fulfill our shared ideal of a casual, pretty, working, pregnant woman. It's almost a status thing to not fall apart in front of my friends and co-workers. I want to appear to just breeze on through. Ha! Ma called this morning on her way to Mexico. The operator said it was person to person for Frederick Douglass. I said Mr. Douglass wasn't here yet, but was expected any day. Our code is in operation!

AUGUST 7, 1974

It is a real trip. I feel that I might be in labor. I have been cramping and feeling constipated all morning and on to the afternoon. I would be so glad if the baby was ready! I just feel ready for it to be here. Fingers are crossed. That is the trip of the last few weeks. You are just READY to have the baby. Come on. Frederick Douglass!

AUGUST 9, 1974

"Are you still here?"

If I hear that question one more time, I

may scream! The best answer I've heard from a pregnant woman is, "Oh, no! I've had my baby. I'm just carrying this one around for a friend!"

I was so pissed at the doctor's office because I gained four pounds in two days! I am always hungry! The baby must be gaining weight hand over fist! I just want it to come! This waiting is a bitch!!

AUGUST 15, 1974
Well, only three more hours and my official due date will have passed. We are so ready for the kid to come on out!

AUGUST 16, 1974
A word of encouragement from the mayor:
"Pearl — Be strong. We all love you and you are and will be the boss of your department. Maynard."
At this point being "the boss" is the last thing on my mind!

AUGUST 16, 1974
Daddy is here staying with us. I think he's a little nervous about me still hanging around, but what can I do? He keeps saying he understands I want to do natural childbirth, but not to be too proud to ask for some drugs if I need them.

I asked Dr. Borders about upper-thigh-joint cramps. "Don't worry," she said. "It's just your bones separating to make room for the baby."

Yikes!

AUGUST 17, 1974

I am really down. I just had a brief crying jag and now I'm trying to explain to myself exactly why I'm so blue. The main culprit, I think, is the infamous "due date." You should never, ever tell anybody what date the doctor gives you. It's just a guess! It's not binding! Ma called again from Mexico, but I have no news for her. "Mr. Douglass has still not arrived."

The baby is moving all over the place, so I'm sure it's healthy. Just not ready to come out yet. Which is cool, except that I am ready and folks are pressuring me like I have some control over when the kid decides to arrive.

I wonder how big the baby is. I wonder if I'll be able to handle labor without drugs. I know I haven't practiced the breathing enough! I wonder if the episiotomy hurts. I wonder if the stitches hurt. I wonder when I'll be able/ready to go back to work. I wonder if they'll keep my job open for me. I wonder if my body will be soft and hideous after the birth.

I wonder a million things.

At the park today, Emma was teasing me about being a good feminist because I stayed at work so far into my pregnancy. I laughed and said that I had stuck it out for so long that now I couldn't take any maternity leave as a matter of principle. And that is partially true! I am all psyched about proving that I am not sick and do not need accommodations of any kind. But the truth is, I'm really tired! It's hard to get comfortable to sleep. Hard to eat. I cannot imagine infant care can be harder than late-stage pregnancy, but that may be ignorance talking.

AUGUST 21, 1974

It is only 8:30 a.m. and already I have added some drama to the day. Michael and I were walking in to work and I tripped on a rock and fell right down. It was really scary. I tore a big hole in my stocking and skinned my knee, which was all bloody! What a sight! A weeping, bleeding pregnant woman!

Michael picked me up, gathered up all my stuff that had gone flying and took me home. He cleaned up my knee and told me I should stay home and take it easy. He's right. The fact is I tripped on that rock because I couldn't see over my stomach! It's time for me to sit my ass down. The baby gave me a few reassuring pokes to let me know it was okay!

AUGUST 30, 1974
She's here! Deignan Njeri Kristin Cleage Lomax! Our daughter was born this morning at 10:37, weighing in at a solid 7 lbs. 11 oz. When Dr. Borders held her up, she was so tiny and blue! Then Dr. Borders says, "Cry for your mama!" and the baby takes a big breath and cries. The blue goes away and she's red. They wipe her off and wrap her up and hand her to me and she is awake and looking around at everything at ten minutes old! Babies of drugged mothers don't do that!

I love that she was born on Kris's birthday! Everything went great. I'm exhausted but hyper as hell. Michael did great. He was right with me the whole time. Dr. Borders was wonderful. All the breathing and natural childbirth stuff really works. I didn't have any drugs until she had to sew up my episiotomy. I was so excited I was telling jokes and laughing. "Dr. Borders," I said, "did you know that in some cultures they bury the afterbirth in the yard outside the house?" "Well," she said, stitching me up

107

like an efficient little tailor, "we don't do that at Holy Family Hospital." That cracked me up. She's so serious! The mayor announced Deignan's birth on the radio this morning and then came by to bring flowers and offer congratulations, which impressed everybody at the hospital. Daddy brought me a picture of the new *Playgirl* magazine with Jim Brown's naked photo in it. "Just put this where the nurses can see it," he said. "You'll have more helpers coming in than you know what to do with!"

I'm so glad she's a girl! All the traditional ways of telling whether the child you're carrying is going to be a boy or a girl (hang a needle on a string and see if the point or the eye turns toward the mother; rest a needle on a saucer of water and see whether the point or the eye turns toward the mother, etc.) said she was a boy. I was going to name her Langston (after Langston Hughes) Albert (after my dad) Lomax (after her dad). But she's a girl! So her name is Deignan (a Michael family name) Njeri (because I wanted her to have an African name) Kristin (because she was born on Kris's birthday) Cleage (after me!) and Lomax (after her dad). When I wrote the name on her birth certificate, the nurse said, "Well, I guess you can't have any more children." That freaked me out. "What?" I said, and she laughed. "You used up all your names on this one, didn't you?"

Welcome to the world, little baby! We've been waiting for you!!

AUGUST 31, 1974
It is 6:15 a.m. and they have brought my daughter back to me for another feeding. Her color is getting more even and less blotchy. She has nice lil' ears and big eyes and wrinkled little old man hands. She is very cool, doesn't fuss. She has already discovered her thumb and sucks it with a vengeance! My mother used to tell me that when I was born, she could hear me coming down the hall in the hospital for a feeding because I was sucking my thumb so loud!

SEPTEMBER 1, 1974
This morning when they brought Deignan to me, she was wide awake and smiling. I made my first maternal sacrifice by turning off the air conditioning so the baby would not get a chill although it means I will smother all day. Still no sign of postpartum depression. I hope I don't get it when I get home.

I just thought about the Lamaze books

showing the mother eating a lollipop while she's in labor. I sure as hell didn't feel like eating a lollipop during labor! My concentration was really poor. I started out so off the rhythm that I never caught up until the nurse came and helped me calm down. We didn't practice enough, I guess. I'm not sure but I wonder how many folks really have a lollipop experience as opposed to the hard, hot, bloody, frantic, gritty experience I had. Natural childbirth at its finest!

Even as we were leaving for the hospital, Daddy was still saying, "Don't be too proud to take something for the pain." But I didn't have to! I did get kind of dramatic toward the end and call out, "Help me!" a couple of times, but I figure that's to be expected.

Kris and I were talking about the weird feeling it gives you of being a part of a continuing cycle from the slaves and the masters to our recently compiled family tree to the Africans before that on through Nanny and Poppy, Grandmother and Grandfather. It's like you have added your own bit to our family to keep it going and be sure it survives. Like Jilo and Ife and Deignan become a part of all those other people that had to happen before we/they could happen. It is hard to talk about this stuff without sounding corny as hell, but it's all about LIFE!

SEPTEMBER 4, 1974
A car from the City Hall Motor Pool pulls up in the yard and a messenger gets out and knocks on the door. When I open it, he hands me an envelope and says, "The mayor would like some help on this speech. Just call me when it's ready and I'll come and pick it up." By the time Daddy got up, I was nursing the baby and working on the mayor's remarks at the same time. Daddy just shook his head. He thinks I'm crazy. Deignan was nursing so she didn't seem to mind. She probably thinks all mothers do this.

SEPTEMBER 5, 1974
It's already Thursday! Tomorrow Deignan will be one week old! So much has happened. I just haven't had a second to write down my thoughts.

Deignan is such a good baby. Michael said he was worried about me having the baby. He thought I might die. The weird thing is I don't think that ever entered my mind. Too busy trying to do the damn Lamaze breathing to think about dying! Worked like a charm.

SEPTEMBER 6, 1974

Deignan is one week old and thriving! I feel good, too.

I haven't had a chance to finish an entry in days. Now it seems like I had a lot to say, but can't dreg it up. I do feel a little over-whelmed. A little insecure. I feel like I have to be super mom, super wife, always smil-ing, cute, etc. I know I shouldn't feel that way, but I do. I'm sure I'll get it together. Good grief! She's only just one week old!

SEPTEMBER 9, 1974

Well, I managed to escape the morning sick-ness, the bad labor, the grumpy pregnancy, only to be betrayed in the end by the classic postpartum depression. I mean, have I ever got the weepies!

SEPTEMBER 10, 1974

I feel so much better today. Deignan slept for four hours straight last night. What a groove!

SEPTEMBER 12, 1974

This is my first day in almost a week when I didn't cry. I'm hopeful this is a sign the blue funk is lifting.

SEPTEMBER 14, 1974

We had our first night out. Deignan stayed with a babysitter and did just fine. That is a relief! We went to a party at John and Lillian Lewis's house with David and Shirley Franklin. I feel a lot better. We are thinking now of me going back to work at the end of October. I don't think Deignan will freak out. I will only be working a few hours a day at first so I can still breastfeed.

I know this for sure:

I have to have my own head straight and my own feelings sorted out or I'll be a rotten mother, wife, person, etc.

If we can find someone we trust to keep Deignan, I'll be back in the world before too long. I feel like my life is sorting itself out again and not racing too fast for me to catch it.

SEPTEMBER 20, 1974

Joanne, also at home with a new baby, called and confessed she is depressed. She seems really out of it. She said she left her six-month-old daughter in bed to cry this morning because she felt like it was better to let her cry by herself than pick her up and let her feel all the tension and hostility in her mother. This from someone who was so dedicated to the ideal motherhood thing that she breastfed only for six months! No water, no supplemental formula, no nothing but Mama. I ain't for that! I feel better about the decision to go back to work. I know I'll feel better and Ms. Miles is great with the baby. And with Joanne as a "role model" for the dangers of being a stay-at-home mom, I know I can't do it. I can't be a full time wife and mother. I think one of the reasons I'm coming out of the blue funk is that I realize it is almost October and I'll be back at work soon.

SEPTEMBER 21, 1974
Nothing prepares you for the total physical dependence of an infant. It is so hard to balance everything. This society gives points for pregnancy and for birthing, but after that, we isolate the mother and the baby and expect them to function the best way they can. It is very anti-family, anti-woman, anti-person!

Joanne is so depressed and isolated, but she is already talking about having another baby! Why?? I think Michael and Deignan use up my quota of love and affection and attention. I really don't think I could handle two kids. But that discussion is a good ways off so I don't have to start worrying about it yet!

SEPTEMBER 22, 1974

Deignan has been kind of sick today. A stuffy nose and congestion. It makes her fussy and sometimes she sounds like she can't catch her breath. Scary as hell! Poor baby. I feel helpless because I don't know what to do for her. Also a bit guilty like maybe I should not have taken her out so early or left her with a babysitter, etc., etc. These feelings are totally baseless, but when a baby is sick, it's a real freakout.

If she doesn't feel better in the morning, we're going to see Dr. Hall!

SEPTEMBER 25, 1974

My days are now defined by game shows and interview programs. By what current champion wins the most money on what stupid quiz program. It's a desire to hear grown-ups talking. I know that's it. Plus, you don't have to concentrate on a game show.

But all that is changing. I'm getting more organized and actually getting significant amounts of work done. And I'm going back to work soon so that will be a good thing.

The baby is still stuffy, but better.

SEPTEMBER 27, 1974

My lil' baby daughter is a month old today.

God! Seems like she's always been here, but also like she was born yesterday. She slept four hours at a stretch last night. Right on, Deignan!

Here's the sad thing. The TV is on so much that I can tell the time any hour of the day by the show that's on. It's my most sustained contact with the outside world. This is my day:

The Today Show	7–9 a.m.
The Phil Donahue Show	9–10
Joker's Wild	10–10:30
Now You See It	10:30–11
Winning Streak	11–11:30
Hollywood Squares	11:30–12
News	12–12:30 p.m.
Merv Griffin	12:30–2
Newlywed Game	2–2:30
Truth or Consequences	2:30–3
The Price Is Right	3–3:30
The Match Game '74	3:30–4
Bewitched	4–4:30
Mike Douglas	4:30–6
News	6

But in two more weeks, Ms. Miles will be starting and I will have a bit more freedom. The trip is I'm already starting to feel guilty about leaving the baby! Life is so complex.

116

OCTOBER 1, 1974

A memory that came to my mind today: I was in high school and we lived on Oregon, corner house. One night I was lying in bed and it was freezing outside but I had the window open anyway and my face was freezing, but I was warm otherwise since I was under blankets, quilts, comforters. It was snowy and pretty and so quiet and still. I remember that quiet so clearly. And I was thinking to myself, "I hope I have an interesting life." So far, so good!

OCTOBER 5, 1974

Read another article where the woman was trying to be funny by saying this:

"Love for your children," she wrote, "is nature's way of keeping you from smothering them."

We've got tickets to see Stevie Wonder! Can't wait.

OCTOBER 8, 1974

Stevie Wonder was incredible. I was screaming, jumping up and down, clapping. He sang for two hours and talked to the audience a lot, but not too much. He was really cool and funny. I loved him to death! Anyhow, it's good to be alive and healthy and happy again!

So many stories about child abuse on the news! I think during the first few weeks, most parents develop feelings of love for their kid. They feel protective of the child. But if that is somehow short circuited, I know that leads right to child abuse. To have a baby you don't love and want making the kinds of demands that all babies make on you must be pure hell. I think that is the crucial point that anti-abortionists miss. They act like the baby alone has rights! The mother's entire life is changed and re-routed and if she was not ready for it, she and the poor baby are going to be fucked up. Abortion is such a personal decision. How can someone force you to have a baby? To go through labor? To get stretch marks? To have milk come into your breast so the baby can be fed from you? To have to get up every two hours all night long? A fertilized egg cannot feel at the early stages. Why are its rights supreme?

OCTOBER 10, 1974

Henry Miller is on television. Poor man is being interviewed by Merv Griffin, who is being so goddamn condescending, like because ol' Henry is old he's sort of feeble-minded. He is calling the man "Mr. Miller" and ol' Henry is calling him "Merv." Henry Miller seems so nice and relaxed and real. I remember when I was little — junior high school maybe? — I would sneak and read the Henry Miller books my mother had. There is one scene in *The Rosy Crucifixion* where one man and two women are having sex. They all three fuck each other all over the place and at age thirteen, it was the height of decadence. The pages almost steamed. If I had known what masturbation was, I'm sure I would have engaged in it!

There is another scene in the book where he uses a friend's bathroom and her toilet is stopped up and when he flushes it, his turds flow out everywhere. He is, of course, horribly embarrassed. I thought that was funny and real and well written. Anyhow, Henry Miller seems to like himself and to be a good person.

I've decided to splurge on Leontyne Price's *Madame Butterfly.* It's a three-record set, but I really want to hear it. I remember Ma playing it so loud when we were growing up that we could hear it through the windows when we were playing handball against the house. Everybody else on our street was playing Motown, but my mom was blasting Leontyne Price pining away for Captain Pinkerton and when he comes back he brings that horrible English wife and Butterfly kills herself. Terrible pain, but such beautiful music!

OCTOBER 11, 1974

Deignan is six weeks old today! A shared milestone for mother and baby. We are now officially ready for the world. She is lovely and healthy, but she is sleeping now and I'm fretting because she's been asleep almost two hours and I am thinking all the morbid thoughts about crib death and stuff. I have peeked in on her twice and am resisting the impulse to go in and feel her back to see if she's breathing or make a loud noise to see if she jumps. I remember when Jilo was a baby and spent one night in Detroit with me and I woke up forty times to see if she was still breathing. Anyhow, I'm going back to work Monday. This is our last full day of the initial infant-gets-to-know-Mama period. She smiles when she sees me now and stops crying when she hears my voice. Incredible! What an ego trip!

The sad thing is I'm leaving her for work. I think about how much of her I'll miss. Her first walking? Her first talking? Eating from a spoon? Am I willing to give up all that to go back to work at City Hall? How are you supposed to resolve kids/marriage/

work/sex/etc.? You don't, I guess. You just worry interminably.

I told Ma I would be glad when Deignan was bigger and not so fragile so I wouldn't have to worry about her so much. Ma just laughed and said, "You worry about them for the rest of their lives!"

Can you stand it? All this to insure that there will be someone to take care of you in your old age!

OCTOBER 12, 1974

It is surprising how many things you can learn to do with one hand.

Example #1: Yesterday, I had to dash by the grocery store with Deignan. I slung her across my shoulder (gently!), threw my items in the cart and dashed to the checkout to pay. I even carried the small bag to the car in one hand. Ol' Deig slept peacefully on my left shoulder the whole time.

Example #2: This morning, she wanted some carrying around, so I cleaned up the living room, emptied and reloaded the dishwasher and put two Stevie Wonder albums on the record player, all with Deig in her usual position draped over my left breast.

I read an article that said mothers universally carry their children on their left sides.

The man who did the study was theorizing that this happens so the babies can be near their mother's heartbeat, which calms them and makes them remember their time in the womb. Bullshit! He's never had to function with one hand! I'll bet right-handed mothers carry their babies on the left and left-handed mothers carry their babies on the right to leave the most-used hand free for action. His theory is overly romantic! I wish I could get a grant to prove mine! Women's studies at their finest!

OCTOBER 13, 1974
Back to work tomorrow. Lil' Deig is sleeping. She had her first cereal last night and slept eight hours! We are hoping for a repeat performance tonight. I am anticipating a major attack of the guilts tomorrow. I refuse to succumb. I love Deig and I think she'll understand.

Anyhow, I'm super organized for tomorrow. I finished the speech for Mayor Jackson, laid out all my clothes, got breakfast all together and if Deignan will cooperate, we should have it made!

I still feel a bit apprehensive about going back into the fray, but it's now or never I guess. Whew . . .

OCTOBER 14, 1974

What a day! Went back to work and immediately got totally involved in the godawful office politics. Good to be back at work, but exhausting. I came home to Ms. Miles and a fat, happy Deignan. I miss her when I pause at work and allow myself to dwell on it. I hope I'm doing the right thing. I'm about to take a nap. More later . . .

JANUARY 1, 1975

Well, I damn sure didn't intend to begin the new year like this. I feel like hell. I can't even claim a hangover. I think it is all stress. Michael said 1975 couldn't be as good as 1974 because that's the year we had Deignan. That was sweet. Made me feel a little better.

Anyhow, I have only two real New Year's resolutions:

1. Simplify!! That means everything from money spending to personal relationships.
2. Write!! That is the most important thing! If I don't write, what am I? "A fighter fights; a writer writes!"

So we begin another year. Peace!

JANUARY 2, 1975

This was a pretty good day. Deignan is staying up later in the evening and growing like a weed. We did another draft of the mayor's State of the City speech. It's coming right along.

I have nothing else to say so I'll close. I'm a real bore these days. A whole day of life and this is the best I can do!

JANUARY 3, 1975

It is frightening to see what is happening in this country. The unemployment rate is 7.1 percent and growing every week. People just don't have any jobs. I went to the grocery store this evening by myself and as I was picking up my bags, an older white man came up and put the bags in the car for me. You could tell he was embarrassed to be doing it, but he needed the money. I felt paranoid as hell since he was a stranger, but I gave him some money. He thanked me and walked away. It was sad.

Gerald Ford is a complete fool! He's off skiing for two weeks while Rockefeller skulks around in the background and Henry Kissinger gives inane interviews about nothing ruling out the possibility of violence as we rip off the Arabs and claim their oil as our own. Things are getting worse and worse. How do poor people survive?

JANUARY 5, 1974
Don't have an explanation for the blue funk I'm in. I think motherhood is complex as hell and I don't think you can be prepared for it until BANG! It smacks the shit out of you. I also feel dead-ended career wise. City Hall is a madhouse. I cry every day. In my office. In the ladies room. In empty committee rooms. Standing in front of the mayor's desk being told I am not aggressive enough with the press. That's because I should never have been made a press secretary! I'm a speechwriter!

I think I want to get back into TV anyway. I hate my job. I hate the neverending meaningless paper shuffling. No creativity. No power to the people. Just paper.

I am not writing. I have no discipline! Lord! I feel as bad as I have in a while. Hope tomorrow is better.

JANUARY 15, 1975
I wrote a poem for Deignan. I love her and the poem is good. I am trying to figure out career and baby. It is impossible to have both, I think. The concessions you have to make to motherhood mean the job must take a backseat. I feel old and ugly and

125

mean. Life's a bitch.

Can I get a witness?

JANUARY 23, 1975

The benefit bout between Maynard and
Muhammad Ali was a trip. Big crowd. Lots
of famous faces. Ali; big and fine and ar-
rogant. Maynard; in patterned briefs and a
big white T-shirt, was game, knowing Ali
would never hit him.

The other night we had to go to a meeting at Maynard's house. It was tense. He
never thinks we are doing enough. He is so
good/inspirational with big groups of
people, but as a boss, he's hell! But I'm
learning how to be a press secretary. I'm
now doing daily radio feeds to WAOK and
hope to get Mr. Ware, the publisher, to let
Maynard have a column in the *Atlanta Voice*.
I'm sure I'd be the one writing it!

Here's the poem I ghosted for the mayor
to offer at the pre-fight press conference:

An Ode to Ali
The Champ of the world will soon be in
  our city
And the fate that awaits him is not very
  pretty.
They tell me the champ is Muhammad
  Ali

But that's just because he's never fought
  me.
They call him a heavyweight, but you
  know good and well
When it comes down to heavyweights,
  that's where I excel!
My plan is together, my game is uptight
When I do my thing, my form's out of
  sight.
Dance like a butterfly, sting like a bee
My fists are so fast that they'll dazzle
  Ali!
The Champ may be strong, but he isn't
  all there
If he thinks he can beat this dy-no-mite
  Mayor!
Liston was strong and Foreman was
  tough
But when you mess with the Big "M,"
  the going is rough.

If I decide to just have some fun
I'll flatten Ali in round number one.
If I'm in a hurry and have to get through
I'll win by a knockout in round number
  two.
And this ain't no braggin', but listen to
  me,
If he makes me get mad, I'll take him in
  three.

I don't wanna bore you, but here's just
  one more
I think that for KOs, the best round is
  four.
I don't like to brag but my game is so
  hip
I'll make Ali wish he had passed on this
  trip.
But I'll tell you this, and you better
  know it
I'll face Ali's challenge with courage, not
  fear
Cuz he may be a fighter, but I'll throw
  out this dare
He wouldn't survive for a week being
  Mayor!

FEBRUARY 1, 1975

I keep going through a thing in my head
that I should have known how hard an
adjustment a baby is. But you can't know
until you have one. You can only imagine
and you always glamorize and sanitize how
hard it is. You figure other people just aren't
organized. You assume you will be different.

FEBRUARY 4, 1975

Good day. I am overwhelmed by the beauty
of my sleeping baby. I love her little gold
earrings! Dr. Hall didn't want to pierce her

ears, but he did. I was supposed to go to a dinner with the Diplomatic Corps crowd, but we couldn't get a babysitter, so I'm here with Deig and Michael has gone to the dinner. It's raining and cold enough to freeze later tonight, but I'm warm and cozy.

MAY 30, 1975
It has occurred to me that I have no close woman friends with whom to share confidences, fears, lusts, dreams. I am keeping an entire area of woman thoughts tucked away with no outlet or possibility of exchange!

My job is a real bummer and I can't figure out why. I do know that I am completely demoralized and the mayor's constant harping on my lack of aggressiveness only makes me feel aggressive toward him!

JUNE 7, 1975
I feel that it is impossible to know a man as a good friend for any long period of time without at least considering him sexually. You don't have to act on the thought, but it's there.

JUNE 15, 1975
We went to a Father's Day barbecue at David and Shirley's. There were a lot of people

there and a lot of kids running around and two people asked me at two different times when I was going to have another baby. Total insanity. First of all, it's nobody's business. Second of all, Deignan is only ten months old!

JULY 31, 1975
Deignan is walking like a champ! She started on Thursday. Tonight, Gladys Knight was singing on TV and Deig got up and starting dancing! She was bending her knees and waving her arms and bouncing up and down. She is such a sweet baby. Soulful, too!

NOVEMBER 12, 1975
I have let it be known to Channel 5 that I am interested in joining their team. They seem receptive and I am hoping for an offer around the end of the year. I don't even know what kind of job they have in mind. I just want something that will let me leave Maynard with a hug and a kiss and my sanity intact.

The good thing is I'm writing poems again and they ain't too bad!

DECEMBER 5, 1975
Sunday is my twenty-seventh birthday. It

has been ten years since I graduated from high school. I feel like I have compromised everything I believe and everything I want. I feel like a shell. I am tired of receptions and parties and dinners with boring ass people I don't even like. I want some privacy and some peace and some plain old sleep!

We're going on vacation with David and Shirley Franklin. They're very excited about Brazil. Michael is, too. Me? I don't want to go to Brazil but it's too late to get out of it so I guess I will have to make the journey. Mollie is going to keep Deignan, but it's a long time to leave her and I already feel guilty for being gone so much.

DECEMBER 31, 1975
(Changing planes in Lima, Peru on the way to Rio de Janeiro)
I wanted to write this all down as we went along but it's all happening so fast.

Lima was strange. The guide book says: "Almost half the people are Indian." Ha! They are all Indian. There is a complete shantytown on the roofs of the buildings in Lima. I mean a complete town with shacks, dogs, cats, chickens, etc. Not on the ground, but on the rooftops. Shirley and I could look over from the hotel window and see the people, but they are hidden if you're just walking down the street. Last night, walking back from the restaurant where we had dinner, a raggedy, filthy man came toward us, slipping and sliding down the street. He was zigzagging and holding his crotch and speaking softly to himself. He never acknowledged our presence at all. The town feels angry and hostile. Lots of Indians living on the street. Tiny little babies lying on the ledges and mothers nursing on the street. Chicken frying, little meat pies cooking and churches everywhere. One with a courtyard in front has stalls selling all kinds of religious medallions — even some in pink and blue plastic cases! Every little store has the same llamas and ponchos and touristy junk. Very expensive, too. So Lima was not my favorite town. We only had to stay here because the plane we're connecting to is "twenty-four hours late." I love the way the guy said it at the airport. Like it was a fact; no point trying to sugarcoat it.

We left Atlanta at four this morning. Cold and grumpy. Afraid of flying. We agree not to wake Deignan up to say good-bye, but cannot resist. Last sight of her in her pink pajamas in Mollie's arms saying "by, by." When we finally get to Brazil, it is no better. The people are all beautiful. The cabdriver who took us to the hotel would have been a movie star if he lived in L.A. There are all colors of people here, but the darkest ones are clearly the ones who are doing all the shit work. I hate being in a place where I can't even speak the language. I feel like an ugly American. I am never taking another vacation. I hate the hassle. I don't like eating in restaurants and staying in hotels. And I miss Deignan! I have only liked about six hours of this fucking trip so far. Nothing to do but shop and eat and sleep. You get no contact with the people who really live here so what's the point?

JANUARY 4, 1976

It's complete insanity. The four us spent the morning on a walking tour through old Bahia. At Market Square a sick-looking old man was tied up like a slave. Rope tied through his legs; hands tied behind his back tight. The barker calls for money from the crowd. When enough is tossed into the hat, he gives the sign and the old man begins to untangle himself. I expect Houdini; something spectacular; a blast of Brazilian trumpets and he's free but the point is just the opposite. The performance is watching the agony of him trying to untie himself. He is tied so tightly that he rips his skin off trying to get free! I want to go home!

Dear Mayor Jackson,

I have done some very serious thinking about our conversation last Thursday morning and it is with a great deal of personal and professional regret that I have decided to offer my resignation from your staff. This is certainly a painful choice for me but it is one I feel that I must make in the face of your continuing dissatisfaction with my work and what you invariably call my lack of "aggressiveness." I have performed as well as I could in every task assigned to me since joining your staff. Although I have been unable to remain in the office beyond 5:30 p.m. since Deignan's birth, I have taken work home on a regular basis since I am aware that my job cannot be done adequately during an eight-hour day. I have attempted to organize our department to utilize the skills I have in the best possible way. The point I am trying to make is that I have not taken the position or the incumbent responsibilities lightly. My lack of aggressiveness is, I feel, a personality trait which I am unable to modify significantly at this point, but which does not reflect a lack

134

of commitment, strength or discipline and which I have not found to be a problem in dealing with people professionally.

At this point, however, I do not feel that I enjoy your confidence. I feel that you are disappointed with my overall performance and with specifics which I thought were positives, such as our most recent newsletter. I have no wish to put you in the position of maintaining me as a member of your staff because of any personal affection you might feel for me. I would find that kind of situation degrading and intolerable and I am sure you would not want to place either of us in such an uncomfortable position.

I have also gotten to the point where I am doubting my own competence. I no longer have confidence in my own abilities, even in areas where I know I do high-quality work. This kind of insecurity is due in part to the feeling that all of my work is now greeted with the same kind of conversation we had this morning. I do not think this kind of disintegration of personal confidence is good for me personally or professionally.

Finally, I respect you a great deal. I came to work in your campaign and in your office because I believe, and still believe, in what you stand for and in your commitment to black people and to all people. I do not want to lose that feeling in a messy haze of accusations, explanations and the tears for which I have now become famous. I would like to request two months' time, beginning April 4, to find other employment and help you fill my slot before my resignation becomes final on June 1. It has been an honor to be a part of your administration.

With all respect, I remain, yours
sincerely,
Pearl Cleage Lomax

JANUARY 17, 1977

We went to one of the King celebration events and parked on Auburn Avenue. It is really a different world down there at night. A drunk man walked up the street with us and he was all upset about white folks and the rumor he had heard that the Muslims were going to let white folks join the mosque. It's weird to me that sometimes when the scariest street people stop you they only want to talk about white folks. They are so close to the edge that the struggle is constantly on their minds. Uppermost, even. It was sad, but I wasn't scared like I had been wandering down Bourbon Street in New Orleans and running into drunk people. I don't know why, but I just wasn't. I looked into his face and he stopped being a scary thing and was just an agitated drunk, worrying about white folks. Maybe that's the key. See them one by one, each by each . . .

Anyhow, the script is going well. I feel somehow that my journal always suffers when my other writing is going well. I need to find a balance.

JANUARY 18, 1977

What is the world coming to? I talked to Tom Houck this morning and he said Larry Flynt, the pornographer, wants to buy the *Gazette*! At first I didn't believe him, but he said it's true. "Well, I guess we're out of a job," I said, but Tom said Flynt isn't going to change the *Gazette* staff. He just wants "two or three pages a week for his rantings." Two or three pages? Can you stand it? I mean really, I love writing for the *Gazette,* but I can't work for Larry Flynt! I felt really freaked out about it. I didn't even want to go to the movies and see old Lina Wertmüller's latest. I just went to the Krystal and ate three little cheeseburgers and went home. Weird, weird, weird. I turned in early, but then I dreamed about Larry Flynt getting out of flying saucers all night long and the dog kept scratching to be let out every two seconds. Then Deignan got into bed with us and all in all, it was not a restful night. I asked the editors of the *Gazette* if we were all going to have to pose in the nude when Flynt became the head cheese and they didn't think it was funny at all. Strange things are happening. Flynt is also looking at *New Times* magazine and *Rolling Stone.*

MARCH 4, 1977
Yesterday, I saw a man and his wife screaming at each other on the street. Drunk and crazy, weaving through downtown, sucking on their fingers and screaming, screaming, screaming. I love a sentence like this: "I feel that I must take a lover or go mad." It's a two-part problem: I must take a lover. I must go mad. The two things are certainly not mutually exclusive and perhaps are even complementary in a strange sort of way. My friend Kay and I are constantly analyzing our friendship, ourselves, our men, our lives. We cry at the slightest provocation and shake our heads at the harshness of adulthood. I must go mad. That is so melodramatic, especially from me when it is clearly

138

not true. I will never do anything so decisive and definitive as going mad. I am certainly not Sylvia Plath with the suicide's determination to leave a mark. I am not even Virginia Woolf, loading my pockets down with rocks and wading into the river. I just don't think I am capable of madness. It takes such trust. It takes such a willingness to let people handle it all for you. It is a lot like joining the army, except you are certainly not issued a weapon. But the lover idea obsesses me. I find myself evaluating every man I now meet with this criterion. Will he be discreet? Will he be good? Will he be gentle? Will he understand the fear and the other things I will bring with me? How will he feel about stretch marks and cellulite? Does he care? It is an interesting way to pass the time. No one is immune from the questions. I have ridden the bus and asked myself each question of each male passenger. I am still too traditional to ask it of the women. The Andrea Dworkin *Woman Hating* book stresses the need for androgyny. That is such a wandering from the point, I think. The book is a call for women to love women and we are all shying away from that part of it like new foals.

Kay tells me that one of the best poets we know is depressed because he doesn't have a job. No career. He doesn't need money, but he feels like he should have some ambition in his life. Writing doesn't count. It is not like a painting, he says. You can't hang it on the wall, so it is invisible and can't really be important.

APRIL 3, 1977

Robert DeLeon is dead. He died in Hollywood. Driving a Ferrari. No color given in the report I got, but I would hazard a guess: red. Driving a red Ferrari. He flew off the side of a gulch and down into a canyon and died there of massive chest injuries. Speculation is that means he was impaled on something. The story is almost a cliché. A young, bright, black writer goes to Hollywood, marries a beautiful star and takes on the system. Wants to win it; beat it; be it. Not too long into the battle, he dies. And what a *Last Tycoon, A Star Is Born* way to die, too. I said: "Is there any indication that he drove off the road on purpose? Was he alone?" I don't think my source understood the questions. Suicide or not, he is dead. Alone at the bottom of a gulch. Dead. I remember talking to him in the kitchen at John and Lillian Lewis's house. He was so cool; so smart; so confident. Now dead.

Rest in peace/rest in peace/rest in

peace . . .

At what point do you realize that your parents are old? When they begin to complain about their teeth? When they begin to ask for softer foods and tell you with some embarrassment that they can't really deal with apples anymore? Is that when you know? Is it when you notice that they are walking slower than they used to or that they begin to look like you remember your grandparents looking? How is it that my mother will always be thirty-six years old to me? And my father about fifty? And my stepfather somewhere in between? How do you deal with the death of your parents? I find that when I am with them I am feeling an almost frantic urge to talk and tell everything and then hold them back from whatever I am afraid of. Of their dying? I want to hold them here now and forever. What happens when they die? How do you handle it? Or do you just gradually realize it will come and hope when it does you have prepared as much as you ever can. It's only a matter of time.

But now there is the random violence of the Adams Park killer. Somebody is shooting lovers in parked cars two blocks from our house. We are close enough to that park to hear the baseball games. Who is the killer? What does he do during the day? Last night, lying beside each other, feigning sleep and listening with newly paranoid ears to every sound, every crackle of leaves outside the window, every rustle of the curtains. We take Deignan into bed with us when it isn't really necessary. We feel the need to be close to each other, to cuddle while we listen and listen and listen . . .

MAY 4, 1977
Only a love of Puccini made me brave the Metropolitan Opera performance at the Civic Center. The music was beautiful, but the people were terminally snooty. I went upstairs to the bathroom at intermission and it was full of all these snooty women, waiting to pee. It was so different from the bathroom at the Rolling Stones concert where girls crowded two and three into a stall. Some girls actually peed in the sinks and the trash cans with no inhibitions. Nobody at that concert was dealing with makeup. A few flowing locks were combed, but mainly folks were about peeing and splitting so they wouldn't miss a minute of Mick. This crowd acted like they were in line at Neiman Marcus. No indication that

anybody really had to pee. Lots of repairing of makeup, too, after they did pee. Does peeing adversely affect makeup? I never knew that. I mean, two red stripes on the cheeks and then lots of re-teasing of hair and re-painting of ruby lips and re-lining of tired eyes. I remember the Letty Cottin Pogeibin article about how naked and strange and ugly she felt going out into the street without makeup and how it was one of the last frontiers. How weird is that? The last frontier is your very own face! There was a real snooty woman in a white, off-the-shoulder dress with a tiger printed on it; a dress so tacky I could hardly stand to be in the same room with it much less with its owner. And then there was the woman with the flower in her hair. A real live flower! Everybody was very quiet and very intense. Several women emerged from the stalls where you have to deposit a dime to use the toilet and quickly slammed the door shut behind them to be sure nobody waiting in line rushed in without paying. Would anybody do that at a rock concert? You would be stoned (not in a good way!) for that kind of behavior. You would hold the door open for the next person in line since who thinks you should have to pay to pee in the first place?

No one ever thinks they will have an abortion, but we do. I can't imagine having another baby right now. I am so glad abortion is legal!! I remember girls at Howard having illegal abortions. Then back in their dorm rooms, bleeding and crying. A girl on our floor bled to death in her boyfriend's apartment. Scared to call her mother. Scared to go to the hospital. Scared.

The thing was, I felt very relaxed dealing with the Feminist Women's Health Center. When I told the intake counselor I wanted to have an abortion, she was totally cool and non-judgmental. She gave me an appointment. Kay will go with me. The thing that struck me was how many women were waiting for services that day when I was just scheduling. There were all kinds of women there: young and not so young, black and white, well dressed and down at heel. Some of them had men with them, looking miserable and nervous. Some had women friends. One young woman seemed to be clutching her mother's hand. Nobody was happy to be there. We all feel scared and guilty, but at least we don't have to worry about bleeding to death on somebody's kitchen table!

My wild friend wants me to snort some coke. I don't think I can handle that. As a matter of pure fact, I don't even want to try. "No," I told him. "I'm afraid I might die." He was incredulous.

JUNE 7, 1977

Kay and I are going to see two Lina Wertmüller movies and I am bouncing with anticipation. I have gone by to pick her up and feel a twinge of envy when I see her private office space. I don't go in the room without her and she comes downstairs with one shoe still in her hand. "Did you go in my office," she says. "No," I say, smiling. I understand the idea of territorial imperatives and sacred space. "Close your eyes," she says. I hesitate. I do not like to close my eyes standing up, even for my friends. "Please," she says. "I want to show you something." "Okay," I say, "but if I fall down, that is going to be your ass!" "You won't fall," she says, leading me into the office. "Sit down," she says. "You are right over a chair." The backs of my legs are touching it and a modicum of trust returns. She is not trying to make a fool out of me. I really am over a chair. I sit down, squinting at the effort not to peek. "Now open your eyes," she says proudly. "Open them." I do and I am faced with a huge, wall-sized painting/collage which I know is the portrait that her friend has done of her. It is huge and wild and lovely. It is not literal, but the mouth somehow, without being her mouth, is completely her expression. I am impressed and startled. I tell her how much I like it and get up to take a closer look. It has real feathers and various bits of this and that on it. It is so wild and free that I am attracted to it immediately. It is so sure of itself. I love it! I am jealous all over again. The private office and now an amazing portrait. I tell her she is lucky and that she should write something for her friend about the sittings. That is all a writer can give, which is unfair somehow. We have only words while people who are visual artists can give real images of one kind or another. Words are kind of a sad, once-removed excuse when you get down to it, but we are writers, so what can we do?

We head out to the movies: *Seven Beauties,* and *Swept Away,* both with Giancarlo Giannini, who is gorgeous and whose eyes say it all. Great movies. I want to write about my reactions to both, but Deignan is in bed and she is saying, "Stop waking me up!" so I have to stop typing. One last note, the Domino sugar people have done a women's series with pictures of women on the little sugar packets. What a ripoff! Margaret Sanger on the sugar packets at the International House of Pancakes? Is nothing sacred?

JUNE 8, 1977
Here's the interesting thing about *Seven Beauties* . . . The question at the end of the movie when the hero, Pasquolino, kills his friend in the concentration camp by shooting him in the head is one of honor even in situations of horror and madness. The honorable response would have been for Pasquolino to refuse to kill his friend or to kill his friend and then himself, or to kill himself with the bullet. Those would certainly have been more honorable than his response, which was to honor his friend's request and shoot him in the head. But the beauty of that is that ol' Lina wipes out the validity of that honor argument in the beginning of the movie when Pasquolino kills the pimp to defend his family's honor. Clearly the pimp has dishonored him and his fat sister, but we do not sympathize with his overdramatic response and we find it ludicrous. When he is in jail and refuses to plead insanity at first because of the honor question, we feel that he is a fool. We do not, she will not let us, take the honorable way out of it at the end, when we sit there

screeching that he should do the honorable thing and not shoot his friend, the argument is empty and meaningless because she has already made us admit that honor isn't shit.

It is beautiful the way she structures the movie so you can't get out of it. I didn't see all that the first time I saw it, but then I looked over at Kay and she was all hunched down in her seat crying at the end and said, "But what does it mean? What should we do? Why did he kill his friend? He should have shot himself first!" It occurred to me that not only does Lina make a case for life, and I think she does although I haven't figured out how yet, but she makes a case against honor. Or you as the viewer have already made the case against honor and if you cheat at the end you are doing just that: cheating. The movie is so perfect. All the bits come together and she makes you stand up and deal with what you think, or were forced to think by watching her amazing images. More later on *Swept Away*.

JUNE 28, 1977
Took Deignan to the Piedmont Park symphony concert this weekend and Michael Palmer was directing rather than Robert Shaw. About ten minutes into their first

piece, she turned to me and whispered indignantly: "What happened to the other conductor?" First of all, she noticed that it wasn't the same guy we're used to seeing. And second, she knew what the conductor was and what the word was for him. Nothing short of genius!

JULY 25, 1977
This is my last political campaign. I said that out loud today and I knew immediately that it was true, true, so true. Politics is anathema to any kind of sustained good feelings or creativity. I am going through an incredible period of discipline and work right now and the fucking campaign is diluting it and diluting it with bullshit. Why would they want to start an "enemies file" on Vince Egan? "Where does he work?" they want to know. "What does he do?" Shirley is talking about running for office. "I think I could beat Q. V. Williamson," she says in all seriousness. And Clint Deveaux has his eye on Congress. I want to understand how people begin to decide that they are the ones we need to lead us and guide us and decide for us what we must and must not do. Joan Didion says a writer is always selling somebody out. She is right, of course. Whenever you tell the secrets or remember

149

selectively or recreate a scene that the person in it didn't authorize, you are selling somebody out. But who gives a fuck?

I feel good and I feel like I am writing better and better. Please don't let a dread disease strike me now that it is almost time for my life to cool out.

JULY 1977

Kay's name is in the *Village Voice* from the conference she just went to and we are so proud. Her boss's comment is there, but no name attached. "No name, no money," I tell him. Hollywood teaches you that ideas don't count. "If your name ain't there, you get no bucks." They laugh and I do, too, but we all know it's true.

JULY 27, 1977

On a day too hot for sex or conversation, I am sitting on the top front step, dressed for the weather in a white jumpsuit, calmly smoking a joint and drinking a glass of Gallo burgundy. Stevie Nicks's voice is drifting out through my three front windows and suddenly the heat is no longer an irritation but a thing as natural as breathing and having arms and legs. I remember Spartacus telling the other slaves when the guards tossed them slop to eat to "hold the food in

150

your mouth and smell the smells and feel the heat and look at the horror and let it all get inside you and then swallow it and you will be able to keep it down. You must get it to stay inside you." That is the trick with heat, too. Stop fighting it. It is ninety-nine degrees. "This is rich folk's weather," the man in the barbershop said to James as I waited for my haircut. "Rich folks can lie around all day and not worry about this at all."

JULY 28, 1977
A stoned realization: If women said they were sorry only when we really meant it, most of our conversations would be cut in half.

AUGUST 13, 1977
News flash: Michael wants to run for office. Am I ready to be a politician's wife??

I walk into the barbershop and a drama is already in progress. The place is called the Four Scissors and it is not a chic barbershop at all. It is the kind of place where when James is in a bad mood, you better not get your hair cut short or you will have a plug cut out of the back of it. The waiting bench is almost full but I squeeze in at one end. I notice a fat man asleep on the opposite end from me. He is snoring loudly and his shirt is open to reveal a big fat stomach and his hat is pulled down over his eyes. His snoring gets louder and louder. Finally, people begin to snicker as he snores and snorts and shudders in the throes of a deep sleep, or a drugged one. I'm trying to read an ancient issue of *Jet* magazine. The owner finally gets pissed. "Who is this dude?" he says to no one in particular. Nobody knows. Another snort. The owner walks over. "Hey, man," he says, "you gotta leave. What are you doing here anyway?" "I'm waiting for James," the fat man says, real hostile. The owner looks at James, who continues cutting hair without a word. "You gotta go, man," the owner says. "Sleeping in here, you bothering my customers and it looks bad. Your shirt all open." "Ah, fuck you, man," says the fat guy without moving. "Fuck you." The owner, a slender, nervous type is amazed. "Hey, you gotta get out!" "I ain't goin' nowhere," the fat guy says. The others of us on the bench study our reading material intently, but we are ready to flee if it gets too weird. I feel my heart beating faster. The owner is frantic. The fat man is testing his authority in his own shop! "I'll call the cops," he says, putting a dime into the pay phone. "Call 'em," says the fat man. "Fuck you." A thin barber at the other end of the shop comes alive suddenly. "Hey," he says to the owner, "don't do that, man. If you want him to leave, it's your shop, he gotta leave. But don't be callin' no cops. That ain't 'bout nothin'." The owner agrees in principle, but what should he do? The fat guy is intractable and huge. Finally, the owner says to James, "Tell your friend to get out, James." "Go on, Peewee," says James, without looking up. Peewee stands for the first time and mumbles something else toward the owner. "Look, man," the owner says, "you gotta get out." "Oh, yeah," says Peewee, unimpressed, "I'm gonna get out because he says get out?" "No," the other barber says, "because he owns the shop, man. It is his shop." Peewee seems to have at least some small respect for the idea of ownership. "Oh, fuck it," he says. "Just fuck it." He stands, hikes up his pants and sort of shimmies toward the door. "Fuck it," he says once more in parting.

AUGUST 15, 1977
I am reading Judy Chicago's book *Through the Flower: Struggles of a Woman Artist,* and it is really blowing my mind. It is the most startling book since I read *Woman Hating.* She is really touching on the things that are

in my mind! The conflict between your life and your work; the compromises you make because you want to be taken seriously. The way you downplay your own work because you don't get positive points for doing it. She says that she discovered after some struggle that you can't expect validation from men for your work when your very work itself is a challenge to male dominance. I really want to do movies and I constantly downplay how important that is to me. I don't want to force anybody (except Kay, of course) to deal with it because it is regarded as unseemly or something. I think one of the reasons why I continue to mess around in politics even though it ain't my real work is because that writing is immediately validated. You write a news release and a mayor gets elected. You write his speeches well and some votes are swayed. You are rewarded for that work because it means something to the men who are in charge. Another thing Judy Chicago says is that she had to learn that her husband would give her what he could and when he couldn't give her anything else, she had to be prepared to go into her studio and do her work. Period. Ain't that the truth? I want to paint my office space and really fix it up. I think I will seriously begin that process this weekend. I will make that space usable for the fall. Virginia Woolf knew that without a little money and a room of one's own, a woman is never going to be able to get her work done and have it taken seriously. I haven't gotten deeply into the book yet, but it promises to be a mind blower. Jesus! I said "blew my mind," and "mind blower" on the same page! Ick! Mind rot is creeping in rapidly! What would Joan Didion think?

Note: The funny thing is that some good reviewers criticized Judy Chicago for not being a good writer. She ain't, but that ain't her job! The woman is a painter and an artist, not a writer, but because she's a woman she has to be able to do everything better than best. It's exhausting.

AUGUST 30, 1977
Happy Birthday, Deignan!

AUGUST 31, 1977
At Tom Jones concerts, women throw black silk stockings and lace underpants. At Peter Frampton concerts, women throw teddy bears. Peter catches them and kisses them and gives them a hug and places them atop a speaker. He is a child and they are children coming to see him. Several real live ten-year-olds with parents and a lot of baby-

faced fifteen-year-olds, smoking real dope and drinking real beer and loving Peter Frampton. He is so pleased with being Peter Frampton he can hardly sing. He spends a lot of time begging the audience to applaud. "I'm having a contest," he says, "to find the best audience during the tour. I want Atlanta to be number one! Let's hear you scream! Let's hear you clap," he says, and makes them scream and stop with a raising and lowering of his hand. Slowly up and slowly down. A little faster up and a little faster down. He loves the power and they give it to him without demanding anything in return. The audience is almost totally female, but it makes no sexual demands on Peter, although his tight blue pants and slightly erotic lyrics promise more than he is willing, probably even capable, of delivering. He promises but gives no satisfaction. In place of real sexuality, Frampton flashes a tit. Kay says his hit song is all about a return to the womb and not about sex at all. She is probably right. Walking out through the crowd, a guy grabbed her breast and squeezed it as he was walking by her. What could he have hoped to gain from that bit of macho bullshit? It's such a toxic atmosphere, I shouldn't have been surprised. At one point, Frampton says to the nubile and pantingly virginal audience, "Do you want to get molested? I don't care how old you are!" And they scream their approval. Molested? Molested?? Molested??? "Do you want to get molested? Raped? Cut up? Scared to death? Forced to fuck in the ass? Do you want to get molested?" He is a bad force with blond curls. The opening act was bad, too. They used their guitars like machine-gun penises. They held them to their crotches and then made them sound like they were shooting us. Killing us. And it was a love song! The lead guitarist knelt down and established his guitar as a penis and then masturbated it for us and when he symbolically shot off, he made the machine-gun noise. He shot us and killed us! Women haters! All women haters!

Let this be a lesson: You don't have to accept every free ticket somebody offers you. Say "no thank you," and go home and play your Bruce Springsteen records!

SEPTEMBER 26, 1977
The campaign goes on. I feel like no matter what I do, I end up back working for Maynard! The campaign is totally fucked up. We had three hundred free tickets to a Braves special kids day game and the field staff FORGOT to give them out! The

157

tickets remained in somebody's desk drawer until the game was over!

At a campaign forum tonight, the mayor couldn't make it so he sent Councilman Q. V. Williamson, who is argumentative when people ask him questions and certainly not the best surrogate if you really want to be re-elected. Vince Egan, the candidate of the Socialist Workers party, says: "I think we should tax the rich." And: "When the cops stop breaking into people's homes and start breaking into boardrooms and beating those people's heads for robbing the poor, then I'll believe in the cops." And: "All these candidates are talking about unemployment like it was snow that fell from the sky." All classic quotes, I'd say, but nobody is taking him seriously. He is younger than me and so serious.

SEPTEMBER 30, 1977
So wonderful! Three days in a row of the Alvin Ailey dancers and I can hardly stand it. Judith Jamison tossing her head and shimmying her lean brown hips and winking those eyes at the audience like she is conspiring to do something you want her to do so bad you can taste it. And Clive Thompson sitting behind us last night and talking to Deignan and telling me I have

158

such pretty babies I should have another so they are all in diapers at the same time. And then Deignan telling them she made a Betty Crocker cake and we did it all in the same pan, she says. She was so good. She is reaching a phase where you can take her anyplace and she will be comfortable. I love it! But the Ailey people . . . let me say this about the Ailey people. That move in *Suite Otis,* where they kick that leg out and roll their arms around? Good God! It is so black and George Faison's choreography is so dynamite and the Ailey dancers are so dynamic that they ought to join forces more often. I loved it! I love it! It is so great to see them dance. Tight red jumpsuits and their butts stuck out and Otis Redding singing "I been loving you too long to stop now," and suddenly, Otis never sounded/looked/felt so good. And not to mention *Revelations*! I thought I would die. It makes you feel so good to be alive and so connected and so glad to know what you know and be what you are and black/black/black. And there's ol' Clive with his hands on his hips and that little tight vest and lord, lord, lord. Can you stand it, chile? Judith Jamison lives! "Fix me, Jesus, fix me!"

OCTOBER 1, 1977

Working part-time at the museum is like stepping into another world. Yesterday, we got a letter from a Yugoslavian painter who wants to exhibit at the museum. Even though I'm just there to do public relations work, they give it to me to craft a reply. He says everything in English, but so wrong. It is really sweet. My favorite lines are: "If you would like to contact me later, I shall be happy to indulge your demands in my possibilities." And: "If I can be immodest, I am sure that your public and reviewers would on the same way with the rapture accept my paintings." Clearly, the man is a genius. I don't know if his work is any good, but I would love to hear him talk.

Steve Martin has done an album called *Let's Get Small.* I love the little routine about a drug that makes you get small. He talks about it like it was grass. I wonder how I'll feel hearing that when I'm fifty, which ain't so far away. Will I still think it's funny? Will I still get small?

OCTOBER 4, 1977, ELECTION DAY
5:00 a.m.

I have announced several times recently during moments of either great frustration or great insight that once we get Maynard

160

re-elected this will be my last campaign. When the alarm goes off at 5:00 a.m. and the reality of the darkness and the pre-dawn chill reach me, I am more convinced than ever of the rightness of my decision. "Wake up," I say to Michael. A muffled groan and an incoherent mutter are my reward. My daughter is camped out at the babysitter's until tomorrow. My jeans, a well-worn blazer that I am convinced brings good luck and my most sensible ripple-soled shoes are laid out for me to jump into, even if I'm not fully awake yet. "Good lord," I think as my bare feet hit the cold floor, "Election Day at last!" I stumble to the radio and push the button that brings it to life. Bob Seger is "workin' on a night move," but we've got to get up and greet this busy day.

5:30 a.m.

Our meeting last night included a strict order to be here on time for a 6:05 meeting. We are here. No meeting is in progress or about to be. We slump into silence. I remember the '73 campaign when we were asked to come at 5:00 a.m. and we did and found not only no meeting, but the headquarters locked up tight and the staffer assigned to be there to open it asleep on a table inside in full view of those of us outside, and sleeping soundly, oblivious to our frantic knockings and beating on the windows.

6:20 a.m.
The candidate arrives, startling us to attention with his traditional campaign greeting: "Are we going to win?" "Yes," we respond with a sleepy yell. As a cheering section, we're a washout at this hour, but he lets us slide. We were scattered in small clots around the room, but now we come together for the last pep talk, the last assignments, the final moment of partial sanity before the madness of the day. I notice that the radio is playing Phoebe Snow crooning about her poetry man. I try to make my mind focus on Phoebe for a minute. I take a deep breath, raise my hand in response to a question about who will be doing bus stops, grab a handful of punch cards and dash out to the waiting vans. Our disorganization is still evident. Aaron's pants are unzipped.

9:25 a.m.
Smile. Hand them a punch card. "Hope you'll vote today." Move on. Move on. Smile. Hand them a punch card. "Hope you'll vote today." Smile. Move on. Smile.

Hand them a punch card. "Hope you'll vote today. Can I give you one of these?" Smile. Move on. Move on. It is dark and forty-seven degrees and the people spilling off of the buses gaze at me like they think I am crazy. Why would anybody be dashing back and forth in front of Trust Company Bank at 6:30 a.m. if she didn't have to be there on her way to work? Hardly anyone refuses to take the campaign literature. Some do. They won't look at me and stride off a little faster to let me know they don't want it. I don't press the issue. I don't press anyone who looks hostile either. I don't have time for that. Smile. Hand them a punch card. Move on. I start across the street to hit the crowd in front of McDonald's and pass Councilman Guthman. "Good morning," I say. "Hope you'll vote today!" "I already did," he says, smiling. "Great," I say. Smile. Move on. Move on. The van will be back at 8:30. By then, I have passed out over three hundred punch cards. Michael has, too. We rendezvous on the corner of Edgewood and that other street. We are cold, but the activity and the contact have made it definite. It is Election Day at last! "No thanks," a man tells me, patting the card already tucked into his pocket. "I already got one. From the mayor," he says with a smile, pointing

163

in the direction where I know Maynard is shaking hands, smiling, moving on. "Well," I say, "I can't compete with that." We laugh. It occurs to me that at any other time I would have some apprehension about dashing back and forth through Central City Park in the dark, but today, it doesn't occur to me. The people I pass don't look threatening. Just tired.

10:45 a.m.
My notebook is filling up with things I have to remember: Marc Picard wants a personal interview. Barbara Nevins needs five minutes after the returns are in. Hal Lamar has asked for some private time with the candidate. What were the percentages in the New Orleans primary? Who will handle the credentials for national press? The candidate will vote at 9:30 a.m. Jackie will take care of the calls. Ask Cecilia about a forum. Call Tony about the speech. Call John about the tapes. Jim is already at the Fairmont. Call him first. Peggy answers and speaks in her official voice. "Is that you?" I say. "Pearl, Pearl, Pearl," she says. "Who did you expect?" I dutifully take down all requests, including ones that will take effect after Tuesday. I feel a moment of guilt knowing that I will pass these on to someone else

because at midnight Tuesday, I am no longer campaign staff and the media will have to fend for itself without me for post-election interview scheduling. The guilt passes quickly though. I remind myself they will survive. They always survive.

11:20 a.m.

The candidate dashes with me into a small corner office to avoid the noisy enthusiasm which is reaching a crescendo in the big ballroom. We dial the number at the pre-scribed time. The radio interview goes well, but it is running long and he has other things he has to do. I pass him a scribbled note: *At any point now you can tell him you've got to go, but we'll be calling during the day with updates.* He nods thanks. "Well," he says, "I've got to go now, but Pearl will be calling you during the day with updates." I grin, feeling for the moment like a bush league Jody Powell keeping my boss on schedule.

11:30 a.m.

Paula comes by to crouch in front of my desk. She is excited and her eyes are shining. I am ambivalent. Tired. There is excitement, but mostly paranoia and some boredom. I am folding letters, licking envelopes and answering more phone calls than I care to. I have not confessed to anyone that my own paranoia has reached crisis proportions. What if he doesn't win? I think as I stuff a letter carefully into its neatly typed envelope. What if he doesn't win?

12:30 p.m.
There is a science to Election Day voting patterns that I don't understand. Those around me who do emerge periodically from various cubbyholes looking either concerned, elated or determinedly impassive. I do not question them.

1:00 p.m.
"If they come to pick up credentials before four o'clock, they should just come right up. If it's after four, they will need security clearance," the voice tells me. Okay, I think. One if by land and two if by sea . . .

1:20 p.m.
How is it going? I finally ask. A shrug. Pretty well, he tells me; non-committal. I wonder aloud how anyone could consider voting for Harold Dye. "Well," he says, "people voted for Richard Nixon." A telling point, I concede, and go back to my envelopes. Brick is singing "Dusic" on the radio and

for two minutes and forty-eight seconds while I listen, politics is the last thing on my mind.

9:45 p.m.

The headquarters for tonight is this big hotel. We discover that the hike from ballroom to pressroom is a bit lengthy. I had thought you could go out one door and directly into the ballroom, but we now find you must go down a hall, through the lobby, down an escalator, and through the ballroom to the stage. We are not pleased. "Wait," says a man in a white apron. "You can go this way." And we set off following him through a maze of kitchens, hallways, elevators, linen storage rooms, pots and pans and curious hotel employees who wonder what we're doing back here. I push images of Bobby Kennedy lying on a California hotel kitchen floor to the back of my mind. "We won't bring anybody this way," I say to the others. "Right," they say, as if they shared my nightmare. Right.

10:00 p.m.

The returns are so good, we are slightly slap happy. Rob is grinning and scribbling numbers on a pad. The precincts come in better and better and the euphoria mounts.

Still, it isn't the same as before. There isn't the feeling of having climbed a great distance and finally reached the peak. There is more comfortable security. Pleasant, but unorgasmic.

10:20 p.m.
There is no way to please the media and security. I realize this and purposely fade myself into the back of the controversy. Roy and Tony handle it admirably, although the media people are still frustrated and angry and security is still as immovable as Everest. I clutch my clipboard and remind myself that it is almost over. The ballroom is full of excited people watching returns. One council race or another. The school board. City Council president. Mayor. They all begin to run together and I feel like I have spent my life here, riding up and down hotel elevators, giggling with Rita and comparing staff badges.

11:05 p.m.
"We need to go on down," I say to the mayor. "It is after eleven. If they're going to carry any of your speech live on the eleven o'clock news, we've got to go!" "Yes," he says, "let's go!" And we are off and running, literally, down the halls of this hotel,

dashing to the ballroom. People are hollering so loud I can't even hear the introduction. The victory speech. He's doing the victory speech. I hear it. I believe it, but I don't feel it yet. Am I jaded or just tired?

11:45 p.m.

I am convinced that working for the winner is harder. Somebody has to win and better it is the side I have chosen to be on than the other one, but working for the underdog is a lot more fun. There is the incredible rush of power if you beat them and the enjoyable moral righteousness if you don't. When you start off in front and stay there, some of the edge is gone. I concede that it can't be helped, but working for a sane, unbeatable, progressive, sensible incumbent isn't all it's cracked up to be.

12:15 a.m.

He is talking to the media in a small room near the ballroom. The band is next door playing "Boogie Nights" with a vengeance and it comes through the wall loud and clear, but the mayor is cool, collected and incredibly handsome. I am watching the backs of the media's heads as they ask question after question. "How many white votes did you get?" they want to know. "Are you satisfied? Are you happy? Is this a mandate? What are you going to do during the next four years?" He answers them calmly, but he is tired. Bus stops, motorcades, handshakes. He must be exhausted. I know I am, but I suddenly hear clearly what he is saying in response to a question about getting his voters to the polls on Election Day. "That," he says, "is the Saul Alinsky school of community organizing." Saul Alinsky? My hero, Saul Alinsky? The newly re-elected mayor of Atlanta is quoting Saul Alinsky in the flush of a gigantic victory. I love it! I absolutely love it! It's not enough to make me forget my tired feet, the lost button on my dress, my smeared mascara and my confusion about top dogs and underdogs, but it is enough to make me smile and move on.

OCTOBER 10, 1977
A guy sat down next to me at the bus stop. Tooth missing. Drunk at 11:00 a.m., but gentle. "There will never be kids without shoes as long as there is a nigger like me around," he says. "You are a unique lady," he says. "I like you. I'm going to see the Bruce Lee movie at the Baronet downtown. Want to come with me? I wanna see him do that Kung Fu shit. He's bad! A lady did that

to me last week. Put me into the hospital for a week." He's lying through his terrible teeth. "I don't think so," I say, so he asks for my phone number. When I decline, he laughs. "You don't want to, but you kinda do, right?" he says, and in a way, he was right. Not him, particularly, but that kind of chance encounter is interesting. Gets your adrenaline flowing. If he had not had rotten teeth and not been drunk and the movie had been something other than Bruce Lee at the Baronet, who knows what might have happened? *C'est la vie!*

OCTOBER 21, 1977
Well, well, well. What a bizarre week. More time in black-tie sessions than out of them. Dinner with the German ambassador. Coffee with Prince Charles. What's a poor girl to do? Here's the scene: home of the German consul general. Black-tie dinner for about twenty-five people. The crowd is gathering when we arrive. "Hello," beams the hostess. "Glad you came." We touch cheeks like the good jet setters that we are and move into the living room. Intros all around. A man who is a member of the German Parliament has only one arm and one sleeve that is flapping gently at his side when he moves. He bows from the waist. I meet

this one and that one . . . "Meet Dean Rusk." "I'm sure you know the governor." "And this is Ambassador Whatever." Michael has told me that this man is also a baron. He draws himself up smartly and bends over my hand gently touching it with his lips. What a gesture! At another black-tie dinner a few days ago, I am introduced to a group of five Italians, all of whom bend over my hand and just brush it with their lips. European men have the edge in the hand-kissing department! The ambassador, however, is no sex symbol. He is slightly paralyzed on one side which means he speaks out of only one side of his mouth. He wears glasses that somehow give the impression of being a monocle. My mind adds a cigarette holder, but I am sure that is only my imagination. So many Germans.

So the drinks are passed. The conversation flows and actually it ain't too bad. So we mingle for a while and then proceed to dinner downstairs. Silver candle holders, flowers, beautiful table settings, individual menus for everyone. I end up with a man who does something diplomatic across from me and the assistant consul to Germany next to me. Heavy crowd! The waiters who earlier passed drinks and canapés have now donned white gloves and are pouring the first of three wines, counting champagne, that will appear over the course of the evening. And then the food! Ah-h-h-h-h! The food is incredible! It is so good. First, some kind of salmon thing. Then sherbet with fresh lime to cleanse the palate. Then a beautiful cucumber salad and then filet mignon with snow peas, potatoes and carrots. Then champagne and the toasts to Germany and to Atlanta and to Georgia and all that is good in the world. And then brandied pears with some kind of whipped stuff dribbled over the top. Such food! It was gorgeous. But the dinner conversation was weird and sort of disturbing. A lot of it dealt with the supposed inferiority of the colored peoples of the world. "Ah, those Arabs," says a white American man who seems to be attached to Dean Rusk. The Germans nodded in agreement. "They can't fly a plane," he went on. "Only three Saudis can fly a plane." "Why?" I said, surprised to hear this. Who flies their planes for them? "They just can't learn it," he said. "They don't have the same depth perception as we do." Sound familiar? "Sometimes," he said, "when some of them go to Princeton, they can manage to pass their courses, but when they come out, they aren't like other people who go to Princeton." What he meant:

They're not like us. They're not really people. Let's kill them and take their oil.

OCTOBER 25, 1977

I am moving on the checking account thing. So much is happening. I am afraid to be in charge of my own finances, but I want to. I need to. I am so afraid, though. I know nothing about my own insurance, my own will, my own taxes. It is absurd. Some of the feminist stuff says that bright, intelligent, capable women become babbling idiots when asked about their finances. I want to change all that. Being afraid is no excuse.

NOVEMBER 5, 1977

Here is another note: Last night Fulton County Solicitor Henson McAulliffe raided the Atlanta performance of *Oh, Calcutta!* at the Peachtree Playhouse. The same play that was on Broadway for five years. The same play that has now become a part of American folklore. The same play that doesn't begin to approach the grossness of *Hustler* magazine. That same play was raided. The agents came and took one look at all the swinging dicks and dangling boobies and freaked. "Get thee to jail!" they said, rounded up the group and took them away.

What a fool!

Went to see Linda Ronstadt with Kay last night. Deignan came with us. Linda has the worst opening act on record. Dirty jeans, dirty face, dirty mouth, he is a disaster. "Well," he says, "do you all eat catfish down here?" No response from the bored crowd. "Well, you eat pussy or what?" he says. "You gotta eat something." No response. He was awful. But then we did not come to see him. We came to see Miss Linda and he was only an unavoidable prelude. The man behind me is explaining the scene to a couple in their forties. "Well," he says, "the hippies are all in their late twenties or thirties by now." Kay and I exchange glances. He is right. He is talking about us. He is also talking about Linda, and then she comes prancing out, awkward as ever in tight jeans, great Charles Jourdan boots, a tiny vest, bangles and wild hair with a rose stuck in the side of it. She is pleased and excited to see us, but still scared. She doesn't talk at all; she just sings and her voice is everything. Carefully controlled, but telling it all. She sings songs that every woman in that audience screams for. When she sings the first few notes of "Love is a Rose," we all sing the

175

song with her. We also sing "Blue Bayou," and "Desperado," where in the middle her voice rises almost out of her range in her desperation to be heard, understood, loved. The chorus of sighs from the women there, including me, reflects all the lost loves we ever had. She is so good. She tries to talk a little bit because she has heard that rock and roll stars talk a little, but she isn't comfortable doing it. She tries to dance a little for the same reason, but she isn't comfortable doing it. "She doesn't need to dance," I say to Kay. "She can just stand there and sing!"

The thing that I realize is that almost every song is about love that doesn't work and I wonder why. She has the fame. She makes $60 million a year for her record company. Men masturbate with her photograph in front of them and she sings like the proverbial bird, but she is unlucky in love and insecure about her looks. She feels fat. She feels ugly. She doesn't have a man who loves her waiting backstage. "She needs Jon Peters," I whisper to Kay. "Yes!" Kay whispers back and we nod at each other. Jon Peters. The kind of man the liberated artist woman longs for. He thinks Barbra Streisand is the most talented, the most beautiful, the most creative, and she, the ugly duckling from Brooklyn, thinks so, too. Why can't we clone him and make him come in black, white, Chinese, and sell the motherfucker? Every female artist needs one because the money doesn't matter. Neither does the fame or the rose in her hair. She ain't got a man. Nobody calls her the morning after either. We are all sisters. We know how she feels and we love her.

NOVEMBER 9, 1977

Here is my Americans are killing their children story of the week. There is deadly pot on the street that is capable of killing people. It is yellowish in color and it is only deadly because American narcs sprayed it with herbicides to kill it and it didn't die so now it is on the street with the poison in it and it will kill you if you smoke it. So, there we have it. Whatever it is.

NOVEMBER 16, 1977

Memories of the sixties. Standing up for principles and all that. Being righteously and self-righteously indignant about things that you could have just let slide. And here I am kind of feeling foolish about having done it but really feeling that I caught up with some part of myself that was running down the road and almost out of sight.

So . . . here is the story. I am asked to read poetry for the Atlanta 2000 conference and agree to do it with great enthusiasm. Two hundred fifty smackers and a lot of exposure for the poets. I loved the whole idea of it. James Dickey and Rosemary Daniell on the same program? There have to be fireworks! Their affair is legendary for its drunkenness and its volatility. But then an invitation arrives inviting me to a reception for program participants at the Capitol City Club, which has a history of racist exclusion of everybody but white men. It freaked me out and I called to tell the program organizer about it. He was less than sensitive to my concerns so I decided I would begin my reading with a denouncement of the reception being held at such a racist place. Then that seemed not enough. I mean, am I a child of the sixties or not? So I decided to make a statement about what I felt about the whole thing and then not read at all, which is what I did. My brother-in-law was there and he said he doubts the sincerity of my motives (he is a cynic! he always doubts my motives!) but my technique and execution were flawless. I think I stunned the folks. The audience applauded, so I guess I wasn't too outrageous. Mrs. Seaberg came out afterward and said she understood why I did it and would tell her daughters about what I had done and she hugged me and stuff. Kay McKenzie was fussing about it, but I don't give a fuck! Racism is a drag and will kill you/me/all of us ten years earlier than we should be dying so a white upper north side white woman can't tell me shit about when and how and where to protest against it! I haven't done anything like this in so long it felt weird to me. I was introduced by Congressman Fowler and then the freak (me!) gets up and walks out in a huff. I was proud of myself. The time to stand up and be counted is now/now/now! I love it.

Remember the march on the Pentagon and the demonstration at Howard against General Hershey and even the dorm sit-ins. We were so willing to take on everything. At what point does all that change? At what point does fighting at every point become too bothersome; too time-consuming and too embarrassing? At what point do we become old people and workers and so concerned about all the shit that stops us from living on the edge? Romare Bearden says any time an artist stops living like an artist, he is in danger of stopping being one. Strange to say, but true. I will fight back! I will not be a content, amused thirty-year-old! I will rage, rage against the dying of the light! Dylan Thomas lives!

DECEMBER 15, 1977
This is really a retrospective because I didn't talk about seeing Andy the other day. Andy Young, that is. Former congressman and now ambassador to the United Nations Andy Young. He comes up and kisses me and give me a hug and Stony Cooks does the same and it struck me as so bizarre that I know the man well enough to get kissed. I think of the famous black folks I have met: Rap Brown, Stokely Carmichael, Malcolm X, Martin Luther King, Jr., and Sr., Coretta Scott King, Andy Young and Julian Bond and Maynard Jackson and Coleman Young and Tom Bradley and LeRoi Jones and Ron Karenga and some others I have heard speak but didn't meet, like Eldridge Cleaver. And the poets and writers I've met: Nikki Giovanni and Don L. Lee and Gwendolyn Brooks and Ed Bullins and Ron Milner and Richard Wesley and lots of others during that golden period when everybody was writing poetry, and me, too. And everybody had a poem to scream at the masses to change their lives, and me, too.

I am in love with Joni Mitchell. I don't wanna fuck anybody while I'm listening to her music, though. Her music is too much a part of the revolution for me to want to fuck to it. I just think she is something good and pure sort of, although I know how fucked up and pretentious that sounds! Who cares? If nobody sees these pages but me I can be as pretentious as all hell and it's my own business.

DECEMBER 16, 1977
I'm at Nature's Last Stand, a small health food store. I have gone to get some lunch. It's crowded and I am waiting behind a short, slight white man in his mid-twenties. He looks a little scruffy and takes forever to order his meal. He has a friend or two with him somewhere in the crowd. He looks long at me until I meet his slightly fevered gaze. I smile. A small smile. A stranger to stranger smile. A female to male stranger smile. "Ah," he breathes, "you are so pretty. I feel like a thorn before a rose. You are a rose," he says. Oh, shit, I think. A live one. I damp down the smile a little and look away, but he is undaunted. "Oh, God," he says, "You're so pretty. Please sit on my face." What??? Sit on my face? I think: Did he really say that? A strange man says "Sit on my face," to me in a health food restaurant? Good God! "Oh, my God," he says. "I'm so crude." "That was pretty rough," I say, still

181

looking away. I couldn't believe it. As I was leaving, he said, "Good-bye, my rose. Have a nice day!" Just as polite as you please. "Sit on my face." That takes the cake, I guess.

DECEMBER 17, 1977

John Travolta in *Saturday Night Fever*. From the first frame, I knew the movie was a winner. It showed him walking down the street with his head cocked to the side, tall and lean and fine as you please. Boppin' down the street like he owned it. "In Brooklyn," he says, "they call me a fox." He ain't no lie. The movie was great. Really special and so real. Example: They had him get up in the morning with these little bikini drawers on and reach into the front of them and push his dick down! Can you believe that? And at one point he says to the girl, "I know you think I'm just here promoting your pussy, but I'm not." "Promoting your pussy." God! To be able to write dialogue that real! It sounded just like that character would sound. He told a long story about a man being cemented into a bridge and how the guy fell in and everything. Then he grinned and said, "Dumb fuck." So good. So real. When he and his friends were going into the disco, he asked his friend if he felt sharp and the friend said, "Sharp as you can be without being a nigger." Damn! But that was real, too. I know that is what they'd say. And he was very sexy. I should write a column and say the reason *Saturday Night Fever* will make a million dollars is the location and swivelation of John Travolta's pelvis! Great music, too. Yvonne Elliman can sing her ass off!

JANUARY 12, 1978
Newsweek says the Mae West scene in *Bobby Deerfield* is a must for connoisseurs of embarrassment. That is a great line and they are absolutely right. I think that Al Pacino should have taken out his own series of billboards when the studio put up that shit saying "Al Pacino is Bobby Deerfield." He needed a picture that had him sneering, giving the thumbs-down gesture and saying, "No way, baby, no way." All that shit in that movie about rabbits and stuff. Terrible! Daddy says that driver who got burned on the race track says he is so good because his ass is so sensitive that it can feel the car deviate before his mind even registers it. He said that he thought that's what made him good. The ass as bearer of vital tidings.

Anyhow, I am in a good mood today and we might be going to Aspen for a few weeks this summer. What a trip. I love the Bob

Dylan song where he invites his listeners to be in his dream if he can hang around in theirs. Sounds like a fair trade to me.

JANUARY 14, 1978
Made it through Friday the thirteenth, Hubert Humphrey didn't. He died last night. Strange. It makes me feel sad, although I remember him standing on the steps of the plane leaving Chicago after the convention in '68 saying, "Chicago, my kind of town!" and defending Johnson and generally being The Hump. The man had a lot of guts though to be walking around with the cancer eating him up. He was out there. Good-bye to The Hump.

Here are some quotes I want to remember:

"Who said you should be happy? Do your work."
— *Colette*

"Genius is the ability to recreate down to the minutest detail what you have seen in your imagination."
— *Richard Dreyfuss talking about Steve Spielberg*

I want to finish this script and start working on a treatment for Richard Pryor. He needs a good script so bad it ain't funny. But how can you deal with the black audience in the face of his blatant attempts at crossover? Whew . . .

JANUARY 17, 1978

What a day! I walked into the *Gazette* and discovered they actually have sold the fucking paper to Larry Flynt. Larry Flynt! I couldn't believe it. It is weird. They asked me how I felt about it and I said, "Will I get a raise?" It was funny because Paul Hemphill walked in a few minutes later, was hit with the news and asked the same question, "Will I get a raise?" I said, "Ah, Liza, we, your writers, are such an altruistic bunch. Always concerned about truth, honesty, First Amendment and will we get a raise?" I told them I thought they should write an editorial about no demands being made of the writers and then publish a shot of the writers, all nude. I thought that would be great.

Another subject: I think I'm in love. I'm not sure yet if it is Steven Spielberg or Richard Dreyfuss or sweet-faced François Truffaut, but it is definitely a case of love. I saw *Close Encounters* again today and, Jesus, I was so high coming out of there I thought I'd start floating away of my own accord. I love it. The hand signal is: one, like stop; one flat one, two squeeze into fists and one sideways fish hand. And the music and the skies opening up. Maybe the thing I like is it looks like God is coming out. Who knows? I just love it.

I keep thinking about Larry Flynt owning the *Gazette.* I know politics makes strange bedfellows, but I don't think I can be in bed with Larry Damn Flynt.

FEBRUARY 8, 1978

David calls from L.A. last night. From the fucking airport. Just arrived. I got on the phone. It's midnight. I'm nervous and begin to bitch. "Why are you calling so late? Don't you know we're sleeping?" etc. "Hush," he says, "if there is anyone in the world you wanna talk to, it's me." He is right, so I quiet myself. I read the script, he says, you have earned my respect, my affection, my love and most importantly, my money. It's really good, he says. And he is pleased with how technical it is. He loves the camera shots. "The dialogue is great," he says. "It gets into Howard University ethnic near the end, but it is all good. Only minor changes . . ." Only minor changes! He is really pleased and I can tell. I make a few comments, but mostly I feel like saying:

186

"Really? Really? Really? Do you really think so?"

Well, lah-dee-dah! I am gonna make a movie and write a novel and everything!

FEBRUARY 26, 1978

This morning, we saw a big roach in the kitchen. "Kill it," I say. "I don't kill roaches," he says, "they have powerful karma." "Roaches," I answer, swatting at it with my house shoe, "are the only creatures on earth who have no karma whatsoever. Who ever heard of roach karma? In fact," I continued, "God doesn't even admit to creating roaches. He looked up at the nasty little things one day and said, who created this motherfucka?"

We found that extremely humorous. Roach karma at 7:00 a.m.

FEBRUARY 27, 1978

Just a note: Talking to the Writers' Guild about contracts the other day and it was such a hip, supportive conversation. At the end, the guy said: "Good luck. I hope your script is another *Rocky*. No! I hope it's another *Star Wars*. *Star Wars* made more money." How hip can you get?

FEBRUARY 28, 1978

There is something depressingly, distressingly adult about drinking coffee in the morning. Something that disturbs me about buying a newspaper, tucking it under my arm and then sitting down for fifteen or twenty minutes and reading the paper while I drink a cup of coffee. It is so grown. So adult in the business world. So in the rut routine. Maybe I ought to drink herb tea or something and read *Rolling Stone* in the morning. That might mellow me out a bit more.

MARCH 6, 1978

Some unidentified and not-yet-in-custody white man shot Larry Flynt and the prosecuting attorney in the pornography case while the two of them were walking out of a cafeteria to go back to court on the last day of the trial. Flynt is in critical condition and the lawyer is in satisfactory condition. Larry Flynt was shot in the stomach and the lawyer in the arm. It is scary to think about it, man. Killing people about pornography? Shooting folks because of publishing naked people and fucking people and stuff? Who gives a damn about pornography? Is it a capital crime? This country is getting so scary. It is getting so scary. People are all nuts and shooting each other. What is happening? I hope he pulls through. You can no more blame the porno mags for Son of Sam than you can blame the Beatles for Charles Manson. That is all Atlanta needs, to be the town that shot Larry Flynt.

MARCH 7, 1978

There is so much on my mind. Is pornography a capital crime?

Yesterday. Made a wild turn into the health food store and jumped out to go in and get a salad for dinner. Sitting at one of the umbrella tables out front was the guy who manages the Band of Desperate Men and a rather ethereal-looking young blond woman. He asked if I had heard about Larry Flynt. "Isn't it horrible?" I said. We talked about it a bit and then he introduced her and she turned to me with a very blissed-out look. "Well," she said, "it is horrible, but all the violence . . . he is so out front and so energetic . . ." I kept waiting for her to say "bad vibes," but she went on. "That is why people react so strongly. That is why he got shot." She shrugged. "It doesn't have a lot to do with what he stands for. It is just that energy. Like look at the presidents who got shot," she went on. "Hardly any of them were the ones that needed to get shot." She never changed expression as she talked. It was weird. I keep waiting for someone to say "if you live by the sword, you die by the sword," but so far no one has.

Dropping off my copy this morning at the *Gazette,* I walk to the door and look dead into the face of a giant, uniformed guard. He had probably been there all night. "I just want to drop off some copy," I babbled, shocked to see him there. Violence is everywhere. So scary.

But peace is everywhere, too. Allen Ginsberg was on Dick Cavett last night and he was so good. I was stoned, too, but that may not have a lot to do with it one way or the other. He was talking about Zen meditation. "You do it with your eyes open," he said, "you do it with them open because you are not trying to close your eyes and fly off someplace and be god. You are seeing yourself as part of your environment and not fighting that. You are accepting it. So," he said, "you keep your eyes focused, but not fixed, and your back straight and relaxed and you breathe very slowly, aware of what your body is already into." Sounded groovy to me. And I intend to start doing it this afternoon. And running, too. I am too freaked out and too weird. I need some kind of internal cool-out thing and I think yoga or Zen or jogging or something would be good for me right through here. No better way to start than to start, I guess.

Ginsberg also read some things about how the FBI was fucking with the New Left and new black political things. Really scary because you remember all of it and remember saying, "That's probably the FBI," but not really believing it, although you knew it was true and it was! It was all true! All those agents and stuff were really agents!

D.C. next week. Things I want to do in D.C.: see Karen and A.B. See the White House Press Room. Go to Georgetown. Go over to Howard. See a movie or a play or something. Rest and cool out. I was listening to Allen Ginsberg after reading the *Rolling Stone* stoned, and I kept getting these *On the Road* fantasies about taking the train. Ol' Jack Kerouac on the way to D.C. I am weird, there is no getting around that.

APRIL 13, 1978
I feel productive again. I feel energized. I feel inspired. Columns and usable phrases are banging around in my head again. The drought is over! Thank you, Jesus! Could it be Meat Loaf who brought an end to the drought? Could it be Miguel Piñero and

Short Eyes? So much energy in both those things. So much energy and outrageousness in Meat Loaf. So much craziness. Will he live to be thirty? Does he care? It's not that you can't trust anyone over thirty. It's just that they are different. I am different, but I cling to the trappings that make it more the same. The music. The styles. I don't know what the end will be, but this week, I am energized and ready to roll.

Meat Loaf has as much energy as Bruce Springsteen. He used to play with Ted Nugent. Gonzo is right. The man is a Hunter S. Thompson on guitar and just mad as a hatter. I loved it. And the people sitting next to me asked me if I got high and proceeded to share with me a joint of some of the best dope I've had as a freebie. Can you beat it? Not with a stick, my man. Not with a stick.

APRIL 20, 1978
Coming to work this morning and they are playing nothing but Beatles on 96 Rock. I knew every song. Words, music, place in history, intro. I love it! A whole generation following them down the yellow brick road. What now? Maharishi? Smoke some dope? Drop some acid? Sing it and we'll do it, guys. We sure will.

MAY 5, 1978

In Jamaica, they will tell you that Bob Marley talks to seagulls. They will also tell you that he can appear and disappear at will. Perhaps, but it isn't necessary. Toni Morrison says if you surrender to the wind and feel it, you can ride it. You can fly. That may come a little closer. But maybe not. It doesn't matter. Not really. Not really. It isn't necessary.

JULY 7, 1978

Trying to talk to Kay last night about the race thing and realizing how much it is on my mind. I mean, I feel so odd to be behaving so naïvely about it after all these years. It's like I have never really considered race before and now it all seems so bogus and unnecessary. I feel like if people would just stop and look at the race thing, they would say, "How weird! Let's quit this!" Yes, I know all the economic arguments and all the racism-is-in-the-bone arguments and the rest of it, but Kay's mother hated colored folks and voted for Goldwater, but she still hugged me when I got to be Kay's friend. And Kay herself admits that she thinks we are so close so fast because looking at me she didn't have to deal with the race thing because I don't look black and what does that mean?

I told her last night I was going to rent a sandwich sign and go around the country talking to white people who didn't know any black folks to convince them it was okay. Nothing political. Just sit down and talk to them like a friend a while. They would not be intimidated because I look like them and talk like them and they would see how ludicrous all the race stuff is. "Meet the Mulatto," I would call the thing. It'd be great. They would be able to let me know beforehand what they wanted to talk about so I could read up on it if I needed to and be well versed in all subjects. I could solve the whole race thing singlehandedly. It would be a trip. Novel material, at least.

I told Kay how betrayed I felt for liking Pat Conroy and being at his house drinking his peppermint tea and talking to him and liking it all so much and then reading in an article about him that he used to throw rotten watermelons at black folks as a fucking game when he was growing up. Of course, he's different now, but I felt violated because I had trusted him and he could do that to black people just because they were black. Amazing to me. I don't understand it. I swear I don't.

"Meet the mulatto and let your mind be at rest."

AUGUST 31, 1978

So we have come down to it. The writing, that is. I have figured out the format, gotten the characters in mind, located a manual typewriter that I can compose on since it does not proceed at such a rapid pace that it disrupts my rather sluggish thought processes. So we are down to it. . . . I finally came to grips with death the other night. Stoned out of my mind. Sitting on Rob's front porch. Terrified the shit out of me. Don't know why. But then we went to see Fleetwood Mac and I suddenly had the notion that all artists are screaming out against the inevitability of death. I am sure I heard that in a humanities class a hundred times, but never realized what it meant until Friday night. But then today it occurred to me that it won't be so bad when you die because you won't know. You weren't pissed off before you were born because you hadn't been here and you weren't in any form to be pissed off. You won't know shit about it anyhow, so who gives a fuck?

Thinking about death really gives credence to the idea of doing what you want. What, after all, is sixty, seventy, eighty, if you're

195

lucky, even one hundred years? A drop in the bucket. The blink of an eye. So life doesn't matter really because it's all leading to the same place. So be outrageous! Jump out there! What else is there to do? I feel like I came to some acceptance of something, but who knows? Bruce Springsteen probably does. I'll ask him next time I see him. So we have come down to it: writin' and death. Mario Puzo says it is nice to be rich, but can it make him twenty-six and tall, thin and handsome? No. How many houses can you have? Or tennis courts? Or clothes? It's just money and who really gives a damn? Better to just do something so hip and wonderful that you are not forgotten. That people think about you when you're gone. Even just in your family. If you were so loving and kind and stuff that they think about you and talk about you when you're dead, that would be nice. I would like to believe that every time you cross somebody's mind in that way, you would get some kind of touch of life, even though you're dead. Like if you say prayers and bless Poppy and Nanny, they feel it sort of? Weird, but I think it has some merit and certainly is no stranger than reincarnation, so what the fuck? This is a cussin' day. Good day sunshine and here comes the sun.

Another thought is that the fame and fortune isn't what fucks you up; it's liking it so much you get careful. You get scared. You care about mass audience when nobody can sustain that shit. Once or twice, but not much or you're so diluted, who cares? So you have to deal with that. Fleetwood Mac sang one new song. Same concert as a year ago. They've been singing it that way all over the world for exactly one year. How can they? Are they artists or record sellers? Billie Holiday said she couldn't sing a song exactly the same way twice. She doesn't feel it the same way so how can she sing it the same way. Listen to her, Stevie Nicks! Enough! Time to write!

SEPTEMBER 5, 1978
WORRIES ABOUT WRITING LIST
What is the question?
Why am I so tense about my writing?
Okay. What is the answer?
You tell me.
Because:
I am afraid that what I am writing is bullshit.
I am afraid what I am writing is self-indulgent.
I am afraid what I am writing is of no interest to anyone.

I am afraid all of it is poorly written.

I am afraid it is clumsy and derivative.

I am afraid it is embarrassingly bad.

I am afraid it is naïve and boring and stupid.

I am afraid I won't finish it.

I am afraid if I do, I won't have a publisher.

Bullshit. I think I will have a publisher if I finish it.

Why don't you finish it?

Not scared. LAZY. It is not fear. It is not artistic temperament. It is that you'd rather be watching TV or eating or getting stoned or listening to music.

That's partially true. But can't I get high and listen to music and write, too? I promise to turn off the TV and eat after.

SEPTEMBER 6, 1978

Last night I dreamed continuously of Bruce Springsteen as if he was someone I knew. From 2:00 a.m. until 7:00 a.m. taking time to be with him. A strange teenage kind of affliction which I think grows not so much from any appreciation of his physical attributes but from a heated attraction to his energy, his wildness, his commitment to doing it all. Dreamed of him as if he were a

198

friend, a lover, a presence close to me. "Teenage affliction," I say upon rising this morning. "Teenage affliction." But I don't feel that it is . . .

"Well, you know what happened to Pearl, don't you?" they'll say. "She's written two novels and is living with Bruce Springsteen." Ha! A teenage affliction. Onward.

SEPTEMBER 8, 1978
How absolutely wonderful! An evening with no pressure of any kind. No discomfort. No weirdness. Wonderful food. Healthy food, a pleasant child, great drugs and my very best friend. Who could ask for anything more? The phone only rang once and it was cool. What a good day. I have polished the sections of my novel that I want to send off and I will finish the typing on Sunday and mail the motherfucka off to Lippincott. I want them to write and say: "Come up and let's talk and here's three thousand dollars as an advance." I would completely freak out. I wonder if my job would give me a leave of absence. Or a reduced workload or something. Like one day a week or something like that. It's worth a try. Maybe like every Monday all day long. Something like that. Or every Friday all day long. Whatever!

I sent a nasty note to my editor at the

Constitution. It said the following: "Am I to take the deafening silence from you concerning my column as an unwillingness to tell me the bad news or is it true that no news is good news?" I thought that was sorta cool considering he said he'd call me three weeks ago and not a fucking word or sign of any kind.

I think the novel is coming along well. I like reading it so far. I like the way it sounds. I like the distinct difference in tones in the main character's parts and the other parts. That is the hard thing. In *Kinflicks,* the tone is always slightly ironic and in the author/ first person speaker's cadences. I want my thing to be completely naturalistic and straight and more through the characters' eyes; the way they would say things. I think I can pull it off. I need some support money! I need an editor who will make me know it is good work.

SEPTEMBER 10, 1978
Yeek! Talked to Jen last night. She kept calling her baby a leech. She said; "The only time the leech sleeps is when she's got my tit in her mouth. Don't do it," she said. "Don't have a second child. Forget what anybody tells you. I haven't been this tired in my life. The second time isn't like the

first. The magic is gone. You just see the hard work and the frustration of trying to do everything at once."

Anyhow, Kay and I are hanging out again tonight. I think it will be continued fun. I think we should go see Buddy Holly at 4:00 p.m., then go get some Chinese food at six-ish, then go to the exhibition and then to the Rhodes to another movie and then home again, home again, jiggy, jig! I love it. The exhibition is by women artists only. The invitation says: "The Big Peach Shows Pink!" Obscene? You bet! We can't wait!

Tomorrow is gonna be hell. A wedding. A shower. Shopping for gifts for the shower and a birthday party that night.

SEPTEMBER 11, 1978

Kay and I at my house. Laid back on the floor, stoned, enjoying being friends, artists, women. I lean up to put on a Karla Bonoff record. "Oh, no," Kay says, "Not Karla Bonoff!" I have a moment of stoned panic. Doesn't she like Karla Bonoff, I think. Doesn't she know how hip Karla Bonoff is? "Not Karla Bonoff," Kay says again, grinning over at me. "The wisest woman in the world!" In that moment, I know we will be friends forever!

SEPTEMBER 12, 1978

"Well," said the blue-polyester-suited man seated to my left, as opposed to the tan-polyester-suited man seated to my right. "Let's get down to the profound topics. What do you ladies want to do with the rest of your lives?" The woman on his left looked a bit taken aback, but not the kid. "Well," I said. "I'd like to publish a couple of novels, do some more screenplays, direct a movie or two and win an Academy Award." He was amused, but for no good reason. I was serious as I could be. When he realized it, he looked at me in the strange kind of way you do when you realize you are trapped for the evening next to a weirdo, so he turned back to the other woman, who said she wanted to go back to work, but she just couldn't really get up for it because she was so complacent sometimes. "When I look at the kids doing something cute, or when my husband comes home with some big business thing and we're all together, I ask myself, who could want anything more?"

Who, indeed, I thought to myself. Who indeed?

SEPTEMBER 12, 1978

Well, today is the day. I am sending some portions of my novel to Lippincott and to

Houghton/Mifflin. I alternate between pride in them and complete fear that they are the absolute pits. I guess it is better to find out now if nobody likes it, instead of eight months along. I am worried about the sex scene and I am worried about the overview, but both are necessary enclosures, I think. So . . . two dollars' worth of postage. A letter enclosed with each packet that makes me sound slightly crazed and more than slightly insecure and they are off, winging their way to the Big Apple. The dream city. The place where dreams are found and lost. What?? Is Bruce Springsteen in here or what? I figure at the front of my book, I will quote the poem about "The Ceremony of Innocence," and two other musical things: Bruce Springsteen's line from "Adam Raised a Cain," about spending your life paying for somebody's past sins and the old blues line about "what did I do to be so black and blue." Not only touches on the topics of the book, but also shows the pulls of the heroine. The black stuff and the white stuff. God, Pearl, what if they tell you your stuff is good and to keep working and they like it? What if they say they want to give you an advance? What if they say it is the pits and you better go back to writing columns? Risk all, win all!

Saw an incredible movie. Gary Busey in *The Buddy Holly Story.* Absolutely incredible. Kay and I finally went yesterday afternoon. Sat outside in the parking lot and got totally stoned and staggered in to see this absolutely incredible movie. I mean Gary Busey breaks right through into another dimension. He is so good he isn't even acting. He's just doing it to death. You don't realize how fucking good he is until he is off the screen for a second and you realize that everybody else is completely Grade B and he is definitely prime stuff. Prime A-1. Great. At one point, he is sitting down at the table with his parents and they urge him to go to college so he'll have something to fall back on and he says, cool as you please, "I don't intend to fall back." I mean, the man is a genius. There was a scene where ol' Buddy Holly was playing rock and roll and the kids were just flocking to him and it was like they said, "This dude has to be god." And I remember Springsteen saying there was a god and He had told Bruce there was an eleventh commandment but Moses was too nervous to deliver it and that commandment was LET IT ROCK. I mean to say, Gary Busey rocks the entire movie. Great, great, great.

Hopeful note: Last night at dinner, I told Peter White he ought to take his wife and go see Buddy Holly and Joel Goldberg, the president of Rich's Department store, leaned over and said: "Did you see it? Wasn't it tremendous?" I couldn't believe it. I laughed and laughed. I was so pleased. Rave on, Buddy! Rave on!

SEPTEMBER 20, 1978
Went all the hell way back to Perimeter Mall to see *The Buddy Holly Story* again. The movie is still wonderful. The way he walks. The way he talks. Teddy Jack Eddy for president, man! Rave on!

Don't know what the deal is with me. I feel dry on the book and I haven't written shit on it yet. I guess page quotas will have to be instituted or something to insure things progress. Thirty a day is my hope. Last night, I sat up alone, got stoned, drank some Tia Maria and read the *Village Voice*. It was great. Really quiet and nice. Talked to David from California yesterday. He called to say he was going to Diana Ross's opening at someplace or another. Him and Peabo and Stan Lathan and blah/blah/blah. But he wanted to tell me that he had lunch with Stan and Stan had asked him out of a clear blue sky if he had read *Cat's Song* lately. David said no and Stan proceeded to tell him it was wonderful. One of the best scripts he'd seen, etc. David said he told Stan he was going to call and tell me that and he actually did. I felt good, but depressed at the same time. I'm glad he liked my screenplay, but I want to have a project going that is getting somewhere right now! I want an advance on the book or a movie in production. I know that is greedy, but I do want it so bad.

I am sure there is a price. Here is what I think the price is: alcohol and drug dependence. Paul Hemphill told me the problem with being a writer is that you spend a lot of time alone at home; drinkin'.

Mario Puzo says, "Moodiness is really concentration. Accept it because concentration is key to writing." Well, I must be a writin' bitch then because I am one moody muthafucka. I bet I could be a real weirdo without much effort.

SEPTEMBER 28, 1978
There has been some kind of breakthrough here. I'm not sure what. I do know that I was really down; in the pits. Some of it had to do with the campaign. Some of it had to do with the deafening silence from various editors in the New York region. But it's

really a more generalized feeling of being at loose ends. Of not having any direction right through here. Of not going anyplace. Of is this what the rest of my life is gonna be like? That kind of thing. Seemed to break through it last night. Wrote two good columns and just felt like writing was the thing. Not finishing the piece or getting done and moving on, but trying to make the writing different. Trying to play with it a little. Trying to take it somewhere else. Got stoned and played with the words a bit. And liked it. Enjoyed it. Anyhow, thought a lot about relaxing. Saying what you want. Doing what you want. Dressing weird. Whatever it takes. Conceiving of yourself as an artist and trying to stay on that wavelength. Trying to lean all up against the weirdness and nestle in. Hunker down. I am fascinated now with punctuation. Periods. Having words alone as sentences. Single word sentences. I hope the *Gazette* will let me stretch out just a little. I believe in magic, yes, indeed I do.

OCTOBER 2, 1978
Don't think I can write about seeing Springsteen. He was so goddamn wonderful I just don't want to try to translate that energy into words. I don't want to take it the one step removed. I just want to say he is the

207

best that ever did it live and maybe on records, too. But no question, live. The man is a motherfucking star. Kay is in Texas and I told Richard, who was there at the show, too, that we could recreate it for her when she gets back. "She can be the crowd," he said. "And we'll be Bruce." "Right," I said. "She doesn't get to play Bruce."

Here's a bit of Catholic ritual that I thought was incredible. When they realize that the pope is dead, there is a special guy who comes into the room with the body with a special silver hammer and he calls the pope's name three times, tapping his head in a special place with the hammer to see if there are any reflexes. He says: "John Paul, are you dead?" When, presumably, the pope doesn't answer, the guy then takes off the pope's special ring and smashes it with the same hammer. Isn't that a trip? Talk about rituals! Wow!

OCTOBER 4, 1978
What I've been doing is trying to suggest how my mind sees things without spelling it out and it dawned on me that it's poetry. I'm writing poetry again!

NOVEMBER 12, 1978
Ethiopia. A report that a band of monkeys,

crazed with hunger and finding no food available, have begun attacking people and eating them! They have killed two young boys, ages eight and ten, and a grown woman. Killed them and ate them. Ethiopia sounds like hell. Crazed monkeys eating people and the army beating prisoners with clubs made of dried bull penises. Makes me remember that poem about "things fall apart/the center cannot hold/what rough beast/etc." I can't remember the end of it, but it clearly describes this moment. Weird freakish things are happening. Ways of dying that cannot be described. Ways of dying that shame the mourners, make them hide so no one will ask them what happened. The story of that little girl whose father held her up at the zoo to feed an elephant and the elephant grabbed her and stomped her, mauled her, killed her right in front of him. A terrible death. An undignified death. The horror mocked by the weirdness of the reality. Eaten alive by monkeys? What kind of monkeys? Might be baboons or those big ones with the multi-colored asses. They are supposed to be vegetarians, but everything is turning against the natural order of things.

And on my car radio, Mick Jagger is screaming a song: "I'm a monkey man/glad you're a monkey woman, too!" It's on a

Rolling Stones album called *Let It Bleed.*
Now he is barking, yapping as the song
fades out. The end vamp is nothing but pure
animal sounds. "Things fall apart/the center
cannot hold . . ." The rough beast emerges
and we are not prepared to meet the thrust
and we will lose.

NAIROBI, Kenya (UPI) — Wild monkeys
in southern Ethiopia went on a hunger-
crazed rampage, devouring a woman and
two young boys and herds of livestock.
The destruction of natural habitat by a
locust plague and drought this year and
by a guerilla war which has raged in the
area for months may have sparked the
outbreak of "monkey madness." The at-
tacks follow the recent mass migration of
large herds of elephants, also as a result
of the war. Kenyan rangers had to be
called in to shoot and disperse the elephants. (*The Atlanta Constitution,* November 10, 1978)

Monkeys
Because they are facts,
they are presented as if they were
truth. as if they meant
something tangible. something
real. unalterable.

as if they could be understood
the way recipes and comic books
can be understood.
but there is a difference.
we are not talking here
about when to add the sugar
to the egg whites, or the cheese
to the soufflé. we are not discussing
archie and jughead. betty and veronica.
we are talking here about deaths
we have never seen
no slow squirrels squashed in the street.
no errant possums crushed by the roadside
no belly-up alabama armadillos.
we are talking drought and war. famine.
infants dead before their mothers.
stampeding elephants. meat-eating
  monkeys.
the facts are these:
packs of giant monkeys driven wild
crazed by hunger,
plagued by locust, displaced by war,
for the first time carnivorous.
red eyes blazing, scattered over the land in
  packs,
bringing down grazing cattle, small
  children,
women. tearing flesh from bone
before death is final. squealing and fighting
each other. running. loping, unafraid.

terrified. stumbling, running in the night.
we are talking about world's end.
   armageddon. terminal madness.
we understand by reducing it to facts.
   simple sentences.
manageable syntax. boxed wire copy on the
   second front page.
the monkeys now only a symptom, no
   longer a sign.
horrifying, not holocaust. the sky cracks,
   but does not open.

NOVEMBER 27, 1978
Historical note of weirdness: A city supervisor who was not reappointed by the mayor of San Francisco went to the mayor's office today and shot him dead. He also shot another supervisor, Harvey Milk, whom the paper described as a "self-proclaimed homosexual." Mayor Moscone was also once a big supporter of Jim Jones but had denounced what went on in Guyana at Jonestown as bad stuff and tried to disassociate himself from Jones totally. Are these terminal bad vibes reaching up from the grave? From beyond the grave?

What
does
it

mean?

Talking to Bunnie Jackson on the telephone today. An article appeared in the paper this morning about me and Michael asking the question: "Can they solve their individual aspirations and become a successful political family?" We were very honest in the interview and it was clear it was a hard fight to do all the shit we wanted to do. Bunnie said, "Well, I hate to tell you this, but that interview sounded like me ten years ago when I was trying to fit myself into Maynard's political life." A chill went through me when she said that. I knew exactly what she meant. "People," she said, "won't leave you alone. They just won't leave you alone." I know just what she meant.

The question is, what am I going to do about it?

DECEMBER 7, 1978
Well, THIRTY!! There are so few rites of passage anymore. Sexual turning points are now so commonplace it is considered bad form to admit to ever having been virginal and amazed. The birth of children is no longer an experience that all women can share since so many are choosing not to.

213

But turning thirty remains one of the few, one of the biggees, one of the haints! And I arrive here, this day, this morning, feeling relieved, pleased to have made it thus far along the way and completely satisfied with what seems to lie ahead. Let us be honest: The fear is of getting old! Are the breasts drooping? Are the lines at the corners of the eyes and mouth becoming more evident? More pronounced? Does loud music begin to irritate you? At rock concerts will you begin to hear cacophony rather than catharsis? Is Springsteen perhaps not god after all? Will the beloved begin to cast his eye more caressingly after the eighteen-year-olds than he might have done last year or the year before?

Last night, trying to wrap my mind around turning thirty, I walked up on the Big One: the fear of death. Do I really have to die? Of course I do. That is part of the scary thing about thirty. Not only do you have to admit to the fact of it, but you have to personalize the whole thing and admit that the fact — that death! — is eventually gonna creep around to your own back door. So the truth of the matter is, drooping breasts and other physical vanities are just the beginning of the whole sad process.

Whew . . . "Don't trust anybody over thirty!"

The truth is, if I could remain the firm young thing I was at eighteen forever, I would. But if I had to choose between that body and have that same mind or have the body I have now and the mind I have now, I'd opt for now every time! If I can keep that in mind, think how hip I'll be by the time I get to be fifty.

JANUARY 1, 1979
Goals:

1. To lose ten pounds by June and keep it off.
2. To exercise regularly in the morning and run two miles a week.
3. To get back on a regimen of ten pages a day.
4. To try and query one mag a month.
5. To get an agent.
6. To sell two scripts to somebody.
7. To finish a draft of the novel.
8. To complete five short stories.
9. To complete twenty new poems.
10. To quit my job.
11. To revise *Cat's Song.*
12. To go to L.A. on business.
13. To pay all consumer bills.

14. To have my own accounts.
15. To go to New York on business.
16. To have my own place by June.
17. TO BE VERY BOLD.

JANUARY 2, 1979
Watched Ntozake Shange on TV last night. She is wild! It was weird to watch her, but she is totally achieving freedom through weirdness. Little kid plastic barrettes on the end of her braids. Talking a mile a minute. Batting her eyes at Joe Papp. Just a complete wild thing! Something about what she read sounded like Howard University, 1966. I wrote the same kind of stuff. If I work hard, I can be better than that.

JANUARY 4, 1979
Michael is being sworn in as a member of the Fulton County Commission. The room is very crowded. People spilling into the hallway outside and the police officer stops me and then realizes I am a commissioner's wife and lets me pass. They seat me up front in a row with a big "Reserved" sign hanging from it. I am the youngest person in the row by about thirty years and the only black person. He is now a real elected official and I'm sitting here with Deignan on my lap to watch him get sworn in. It feels like a movie.

I don't want to be here. I am nervous. Feel ill at ease. Tense. Michael looks tense, too. Isn't this his arena? Shouldn't it be more fun? Before the swearing in there is a prayer saying, "Thank god for these men and their wives and families who help them. A good wife makes it all so much easier." What is a good wife?

JANUARY 5, 1979
Went to see *For Colored Girls Who Have Considered Suicide When the Rainbow Is Enuf* last night and it was just wonderful. It was amazing. It was all true. It was so good. It was just so good to hear it and see it and talk about it and just know that it is okay. I felt so close to all the black women up there. I felt so close to all the things they said. One talked about having an abortion and it made me cry. "This hurts me," she said. "This hurts me." And I just cried right there at the Alliance Theatre. And the end made me cry again. Latanya as the Lady in Red talking about her man dropping her kids out the window. It was so good and the people didn't know what the fuck they were watching. In the bathroom afterward, one white woman said to another: "I didn't really get offended, but I just got bored."
Sweet Jesus! Bored? They were bored with

one and a half hours of my life! Fuck 'em! Ntozake Shange might not ever do another thing, but this thing she wrote is just incredible. Go, girl! I want her to be rich and famous because she deserves it!

JANUARY 16, 1979

Incredible concert last night. Peabo Bryson singing his heart out. Romantic and cool and fully in control. When he started singing "Feel the Fire," the woman a few rows behind me screamed: "Make him stop it!" As in: It hurts so good. Then Stevie Wonder came out singing as he walked, completely at ease, loving the crowd, asking them for a moment of silence for Donny Hathaway who fell/jumped out of a fifteenth-floor hotel window two days ago. And the Omni got quiet/quiet/quiet. Hear a pin drop quiet. And Stevie singing one of Donny's songs. And saying to the band: "Slow it down. Don't . . . go . . . so . . . fast." He sounded really sexy. Then he made us all sing "We Shall Overcome" for Dr. King and all of us did it, feeling kind of foolish at first and then feeling proud and sad and hopeful, all of a sudden. Singing louder, like we meant it. Like the old days. When we believed all that stuff.

And this morning. Horrible, horrible. I'm

walking to work from the parking lot and a huge wino corners me to tell me that the white contractor he works for would pay me two hundred dollars "to get in your britches." I declined and he was quite pissed off. "That is a lot of money," he said. "Are you black or white?" "Black," I said. "Well," he said, "this is a white man who wants to give you that money. That's a lot of money, girl. You better take it or I'll whip your ass." Realizing he has stepped over the line, he apologizes and walks with me a block or so, lobbying for this to happen. He wants me to call the guy, or let him call the guy and tell him to call me. "That white man saw you," he says to me, "and he said that is the only woman I would pay two hundred dollars for." What a way to start the day! "I'm a drunkard now," he says, "but I used to be a contractor. Just got out the tank yesterday. Give me a dollar to buy some wine." I give him three quarters, afraid not to, and walked on. I realized I couldn't convince him I don't sell it. Not to nobody. No how.

But that was this morning. Last night, I was singing with Stevie Wonder and really believing we could overcome. Had a great moment in the ladies room with a total stranger. We were both stoned and giggling like we had grown up together. "Oh, god," she said, "I gotta pee or else I can't get down with Stevie. Everybody be boogyin' and I'd be sittin' there and people would say, what's the matter with her tonight? How can you sit down for Stevie?" People love him, adore him, and he sends it right back.

Donny Hathaway had drawings of demons and voices in his head that told him to do things before he jumped out the window. He used to talk to the TV and think it was talking back to him. David is trying to deal with the death. Sent a mutual friend to identify the body. "I am ripped," he says after we smoke two joints of good Colombian. "Ripped." "You?" I say. "Not you!" Great concert. Went home happy and hungry. Michael got up and had eggs and muffins with me at 2:00 a.m. Nice work if you can get it.

JANUARY 29, 1979
Speaking of poet Rosemary Daniell, Larry Woods said: "She's a barracuda. She will seduce a man, go to bed with him, and then write about it!"

FEBRUARY 1, 1979
I didn't want to go. I was tired of the idea of luncheons, diplomatic footsie, the whole

thing. "It's history," Michael said. "You should go." Oh, god, I thought. History again! I feel like I am surrounded sometimes by history, but okay. I won't be a hassle. I'll go and . . . surprise! . . . it was wonderful. A Chinese diplomat talked about going on the Great March; about talking to Mao; about the challenges of running a country where there are billions of people. Amazing. And so poetic when he spoke. "We believe that the American people and the Chinese people are industrious and brave," he said. Who could ask for anything more? More on the Chinese later. My mind is jumping too fast.

I am reading Jack Kerouac's *On the Road* and it is wonderful, wonderful, wonderful! Where has he been all my thirty years? I love it! And last night, Kay and I went out and got stoned and went to Peaches, my favorite record store, and browsed around through the records and ate Mexican food and giggled and laughed and talked about old times and went to see *César and Rosalie.* Beautiful, incredible movie about two men in love with Rosalie and what they do about it. The acting is incredible. Yves Montand is wonderful. The young artist says to him: "I love Rosalie." "Since when?" says Montand. "Since always," says the artist. It was great. Rosalie and the young guy were so honest. Never hedged. Always up front. The only sins seemed to be lying and being ordinary. The French seem to take love as seriously as anything else. They believe it is a reason for tragedy and mayhem of all kinds. Americans don't. Love is always sort of a giggle in the American movies. Sort of a leer or something. I don't know. My mind is jumping. No drugs, just excited!

I want to be industrious and brave!

FEBRUARY 2, 1979

I don't know what. I read some more of *On the Road* today in the Equitable Building cafeteria at lunchtime and just freaked. Wanted out so bad! Wanted to be out barreling along, on my way hoboing to Denver. Wanted to drink beer and be Jack Kerouac. Wanted to be a beat poet and grow an Allen Ginsberg beard. Wanted to be LeRoi Jones, only hip colored guy in the crowd. Wanted to try heroin and nod at hip New York parties. Wanted to fuck waitresses in roadhouses and steal cars for joyrides down the mountain. Wanted to just do it/do it/do it! Stop being so respectable, so tidy, so proud of all the wrong things. What do I mean? What am I talking about? Who the hell knows or gives much of a damn?

FEBRUARY 3, 1979
Sid Vicious, the drummer with the Sex
Pistols, dead of a heroin overdose. He who
is accused of stabbing his girlfriend to
death, out on bond, now dead. What is that
about? Sex Pistols. Love Gun. All that shit.
I had a terrible day. I feel so awful doing
this public relations shit all day/all day/all
day long. I mean, I want out really bad. I
think the teaching thing might be the way
to do it, too. I am willing to do that shit as
opposed to the kind of shit I am doing now.
Yuck. My boss was talking shit to me today
and then she started giving me shit about
hours and stuff and I wanted to slap her
face. Tsk, tsk. I need to start meditating or
something.

FEBRUARY 9, 1979
Bob Seger screaming on my radio. Sitting
on the floor, typing away and feeling good
only five seconds after pining away about
the injustice of it all and the impossibility of
love. Know why? I just wrote down the
beginning of a short story that I know will
be good and so I feel better. I don't know
what the hell shape my mind is in, I really

don't. It is all too bizarre to me. It is all too strange.

I love my writing. That is the truth. That is the absolute truth. I want to type so fast the ball falls off this amazing IBM type-writer. I want to sing so loud people think I am crazy. I want to do things I never thought I would ever do.

FEBRUARY 9, 1979
Michael Reagan wrote me a letter. Loved the poems. Said they were really good. That they showed all the stuff I had hoped they did. Pure praise. Henry Miller says that when you are trying to do something beyond your known power, you want immediate acceptance, praise, unqualified admiration. Not critiques, but the cushion of love that says yes/yes/yes! You can do everything!

FEBRUARY 14, 1979
Raining. Yesterday tried to talk to my editor at the *Gazette* and got into a big argument, then realized I didn't give a fuck about writing for them anymore. So I held up an airy hand. "This is so boring!" I said, and flounced out, hoping he wouldn't come after me, which, chickenshit that he is, he didn't. So, good-bye *Gazette*. I was so mad when I left that office and the traffic was

horrible. Then this guy stopped to let me into the line of traffic. He was in the car right behind me; black, about my age, attractive, uniform of a workin' man. At the light, he pulled up next to me and motioned for me to roll down the window. I did and he said, grinning but serious, "Let's go have some martinis." I loved it! I laughed and said, "I wish I could, but I have to go pick up my husband." He shook his head then and said, "You don't sound like you're from Atlanta." "No," I said. "Detroit." The light changed and he grinned and shook his head sadly. "You mean I'm gonna have to go all the way to Detroit to see some pretty girls?"

Maybe he was my Valentine.

FEBRUARY 21, 1979

Why am I thirty and not famous? I read about Michelle Wallace's book and fall into a funk because she's only twenty-six. Is that bogus on my part or what? Yes, I know, but what can I say? It's real! Here's something else that is distressing. I am reading another Jack Kerouac book and it is absolutely terrible, awful, horrible, etc. etc. etc. I mean bad. I wonder if he freaked or if he's like Ralph Ellison and only had one great book in him. I wonder if people are allowed to write unlimited numbers of good or adequate books, but only one masterpiece. That wouldn't be a half-bad rule, I guess. How many masterpieces can a person stand in one lifetime?

MARCH 2, 1979
Spend the afternoon talking to a seventeen-year-old runaway. She looked so young and pasty faced and chubby and sad. Really scared and sad. She talked about violence, incest, all of it in a monotone as if she had told it before and was kind of proud of it; kind of knowing it was so awful that its very awfulness made her special. Even in that negative way. She said her father used to "feel her up" and tell her it was natural and society was wrong and she was just inhibited. She said he used to say, "I'm not gonna fuck you, Tara." Her name was Tara, just like in *Gone With the Wind.* What did her mother think when she was little? What did her mother think when she was just growing up and still new and fresh and all that stuff? What makes it all fall apart? It kind of spaced me out just a bit. Just a bit.

When I left the shelter where I interviewed her, it started raining. I was walking to my car and a guy in a pimp suit popped out of the restaurant next door and said, "You too fine to be walkin' in the rain. Come on in here, girl, and let me buy you a cup of coffee." I wanted to ask him if he ever picked up girls from the shelter, but I knew the answer.

MARCH 22, 1979
New Orleans/The Columns Hotel

There is absolutely no way to describe this place. The letter the folks sent me said it was "New Orleans shabby genteel." What a phrase. It brought to mind Blanche DuBois and Stella Kowalski and the whole *Streetcar* crew. But I figured, how shabby can it be? Well, pretty shabby. I told the cab driver where I was going and he said, "Oh, are they open again?" A dead giveaway. "I hope so," I said, trying to sound cheery. "Were they closed?" "Yes," he said. "Then they made a couple of movies there and I thought it was closed again, but I guess I was wrong." We pulled up and he said, "That's it," and pointed toward a huge white mansion, set back a good ways from the street in a clump of tall trees. No visible signs of activity anyplace. Shadowy and silent and a sandwich sign out front saying: "Open, nightly and residential." Say what? I paid the cab, resisted the temptation to ask him to wait and walked up the leaf-covered front walk, opened the door myself and walked up the shabby red carpet to the front desk. As I got to it, a door on my right opened and a fortyish woman who looked exactly like a Tennessee Williams character floated out in a peach-colored silk wrapper. She looked quite surprised to see me. "Can I help you?" she said. "I wanna check in," I said, not sure I wanted to do that at all, but not knowing what else to say. "Oh," she said and ducked back into the room. A man emerged. He was friendly and I checked in. The inside is all old wood, thick banisters, old wallpaper. "Oh," he said, "they are gonna be wallpapering in here on Saturday. Hope it won't bother you."

"Sorry," he said, "there's no TV. The bathroom on this floor isn't working so you'll have to go downstairs." I am wishing that I had asked the cab driver to wait, but I follow the guy upstairs to the room, tip him for carrying my bag and close the door. The room is dirty; the closet a mass of twisted hangers and everything dark and gloomy. I keep waiting to see a giant, slow-moving water bug. Picturesque, I guess, but I wouldn't wanna live here. Not for three days. I'm gonna try to get changed to another hotel. There's no place to eat in here or close by either. New Orleans and there's no food??

I see the shabby. I'm lookin' for the genteel.

MARCH 23, 1979
New Orleans
Impressions. Time only for impressions.
Have changed hotels. I am now comfort-
ably ensconced in the New Orleans downtown Howard Johnson's. The very same
place where Mark Essex climbed to the roof
and blasted away at people on the sidewalk
all those stories down on the street. I have
just overheard a conversation on the eleva-
tor that reveals to me that the Incredible
Hulk is staying here, too. "The Marvel
comic version," the woman told her friend
conspiratorially. "Not Lou Ferrigno."

The plays yesterday were all awful. One
improvisation wasn't, but the rest . . . Jesus!
This is such a strange, insulated, slow-paced
town. It feels like syrup. I had dinner last
night at the conference organizer's great
apartment in the French Quarter. She lives
with a guy who's gotta be fifty years old or
close to it. He's very hip. We got on the
subject of race and, my god, they were all
so fucking naïve, except him. At one point
he said, "It sounds just like Ralph Ellison's
The Invisible Man." He won the gold star
from me! He was very charming. He made

a water glass sing like a bird. She watches him constantly. I couldn't tell if she was glad we were all there or bored silly. One guy was really into Transcendental Meditation and he kept reducing complex problems of race, class and international power and resources to which countries "felt okay." I mean, he was serious about this, too! He thought I was white. Discovered in the midst of the race discussion that I was black and freaked. Argued it with me and when he couldn't talk me out of it, fell in love. Took me for these fried sugar doughnut things and coffee in the French Quarter afterward then made a mild, Transcendental Meditation hit, to wit:

HE: I'm probably way out of line, but I'll kick myself later if I don't ask.
SHE: What?
HE: How married are you?
SHE: (Smiling with what she thought was compassion and sincerity.) I'm very married.
HE: (Sigh.) Okay. I just had to ask.

MARCH 24, 1979
New Orleans
At breakfast, the man at the table next to me is sitting with his son. He is apologizing

for his behavior when the son, now grown, was young. "Remember how when I used to come home and wouldn't wanna talk to nobody, remember that?" he says urgently. "You understand now, don't you? Now you understand." The son, embarrassment in the set of his shoulders, murmurs his assent. "Remember that time," the father goes on, his voice, more urgent, still rising, "remember that time I came home and it was my birthday and you had a present for me, a St. Christopher's medal and I'd had a bad day and I didn't acknowledge it so well? You understand now, huh? Well, I still have it. I see it every day. It takes some time to understand these things."

In New Orleans, classified ads run thanking the Virgin Mary for her blessings. I saw a man alone at the base of the Robert E. Lee Monument playing a guitar. I saw two men walking together, arms intertwined, in love. I saw a blond man with a hat playing a saxophone in a closed doorway in the French Quarter at 2:00 a.m. The woman sitting at his feet was quiet; still; wide-eyed.

MARCH 29, 1979

Hello, Everybody!
Don't think I am a bore for sending

231

you a carboned letter, but I'm writing Kris, Daddy, Ma and Henry about this, too, and know I won't be able to get it down more than once and wanted all of you to know because it was really wonderful. All month in Atlanta we have had four Italian artists in residence. The project is called "Creative Collaboration," which means they have come here from Italy under a special grant to collaborate with any Atlanta artists that they want to work with. They are: a visual artist, a musician and two theater people. And they are really nice, into what they are doing and very out at the fringes in terms of their work. Avant-garde, whatever that is. Anyway, we had them and their children (a set of twin girls) and wives and some other folks over for dinner. They knew Michael already, but I was just meeting them and I gave the one who is the head of their delegation (his name is Michelangelo Pistoletto! his real name!) a copy of my book because he said he had heard I wrote poetry and wanted to see some of it. So . . . they read the poems and liked them and asked me if I would do a performance piece with them! I was chicken, but really pleased to be asked and said okay. Well, last night we did the piece and it was WONDERFUL. The theater guys had made a musical book. That is, it has about ten pages made of different materials that you can tear, beat on, shake, etc. and it makes noises. He and I and the jazz trumpeter (Enrico Rava) and two local weird musicians sat around in a circle and went through the book first, making noises and tossing pages around and stuff and then they progressed on to their instruments (the trumpet, a cello and a violin) and in between and with and over and under and around the music, I would read my poems. I had chosen some older ones because I was scared to read the new ones in such a weird setting for the first time, but I chose ones that are all related to the street and are all real rhythmic because I knew we'd be doing the music stuff, too, and it all worked! I was sitting on the floor and they were some in chairs, some standing, and we just did it. I couldn't believe it. It was like all the fantasies I've ever had of being a hip, weird, New York freak poet come true and I didn't even feel like I made a fool of myself and had a great time! When I went to talk to them about it about an hour before it was to begin, I was really scared because they kept talking about how I was gonna be like another musician except my voice would be my instrument and stuff like that and I am thinking, "Oh, hell, I don't know how to deal with that stuff," but I just laughed and told them I wasn't sure what I was supposed to do but really wanted to try it and they said just listen to the music and trust us and you'll know when to read and stuff. So I made myself stop trying to get a blueprint for how it was gonna go and just got into it and I read better than I ever have. I played around with the words, repeating them and stuff, and since I was sitting with my back to where the people were perched all over the steps and on this loft thing, looking down on us, I just saw the musicians around me who I liked and trusted and I just relaxed and had a good time. I did all kinds of stuff I have done just acting silly, but never had nerve to do at my readings, which are usually rather chicken whispery affairs. But this time I just felt like I could do anything! I felt like if you just jump out and do it and you are really trying to do something, people won't burst out laughing and say,

"What a bunch of crap." They will like it because if you're any good, it will be interesting. So . . . I am absolutely full of myself this morning, planning collaborations with local musicians left and right and walking about two feet above the ground. Michael and Deignan came and he said he was amazed to see me doing that stuff because it seemed like I was really comfortable and he's never seen me act like that before. I haven't seen myself act like that before, but that's neither here nor there, I guess . . . Deignan had never heard me read and she was amazed. When we got home, I told her it was too late for me to read her a story and she said she wanted to say me a poem, which was cool. So she said this poem she learned in school about three times real fast and then she frowned and said, "I wanna sing it," because at the performance, I was kind of holding the words and sing-songing when I was reading. So I said, "Great," and she did the poem again and she was sing-songing just like I did, playing with the words and repeating some of them and breaking up the lines differently and stuff like that! I was amazed and told her, of course, that I thought she was a crazy in the making and that I was really proud of her. So I'll show you my performance book when you come down and if you get a postcard from Italy, you'll know why.

In love and wildness,
Pearl

May 21, 1979
Passed Jim Ratliff and a girl in intense discussion on the stairs one day. She was saying to him, "If this is a lesson, don't teach it to me now." He was smoking a cigarette; handsome face impassive. He is our very own Dean Moriarty. Mysterious and a little dangerous. Today, I glance out of my studio window and they are standing near the garbage cans. She is on her knees in front of him. He is standing over her. They are talking with some agitation, on her part anyway. His back is to me. He is lighting a cigarette. She stands, still talking. Angry gestures. He walks away. She is fussing. She walks up to him and takes his hand. He drops it. She puts her arms around his neck and hugs him. He stands like a stone, hands at his sides. She drops her arms and steps back, but can't walk away. Still talking; still gesturing. Cigarette smoke a wreath above his head. He turns and walks away.

She watches him and then walks away, too.

This on the same day I saw a woman throw her purse at a man who was walking away from her in the same macho way Jim was walking away. The purse bounced off the man's back, but he never even turned around. "Fuck you, you asshole," she screamed. "Fuck you!" Her child was right next to her. It was 8:30 a.m.

MAY 22, 1979

Feel really productive. Have two short stories growing in my head. "Enough Rope" about the abortion and something about Ratliff and that woman. Worked late last night. It was great. Here is something else to remember for a short story. Went to dinner with two girlfriends I've known forever. Talked a lot about men, and women and stuff. Lots of feminist rhetoric/feminist talk. But we had an attractive young black clearly gay waiter and at some time during the meal, both of them flirted with him in a very obvious way. Why? What is that about? It was strange and depressing. Thirty-two years old, both thinking they are perfect and so far from it. Looking for validation from a gay waiter who is embarrassed by their attention.

I think they are scared to death. Well, I

feel good and I'm not perfect but I know this: I am not scared. I am not muthafuckin' scared.

JUNE 1, 1979

We got our first threatening call last night. 1:10 a.m. Michael got the phone and the man said, "If you run for mayor, you're dead." That was it. We lay there for about two hours after that and just thought our thoughts about it. It scared me. I thought about the Kennedys. I thought about guns. Thought about people hurting him and hurting Deig and me. Having to live with him hurt or gone. It was awful. Thought about changing the phone number, but the cops say keep the number so the crazos can call you and then they can trace the call. It scares me. It scares me a lot. I feel like something is sitting on my chest. I am tense and scared and don't know what to think about all this stuff. "If you run for mayor you're dead." Daddy used to get those calls. He would tell us not to answer the phone. Maynard used to get them. And now Michael. I keep thinking about nothing like that ever happening to political folks in Atlanta and why would he be the first one somebody hurts? And then I just get scared again. Nobody to talk to about it either. "If

you run for mayor, you're dead." For what?
For goddamn what? Jesus!

JUNE 15, 1979
Article about Joan Didion in the *New York
Times Magazine.* Pictures of her smiling,
cuddling with her daughter, cooking. Quotes
about how much she liked the routine of
domesticity. About what a good cook she is.
About how she parties with the biggest
names in Hollywood. About places she
shops. About her distress because her
drapes were pleated and not gathered.
About her making a new set. It bothered
me a lot. Couldn't figure out why. Thought
at first it was because they seemed to be
making her a "woman," not a writer. A
"woman." A domesticated breed. A wife. A
cook. A serene, domesticated pussycat. But
I kept thinking about it last night and it
struck me that her real life seems very far
removed from how and what she writes,
which is not serene, not womanly content,
but extraordinary, passionate, hyper-
conscious, controlled, cynical. It made me
think about the difference in what my mind
says and feels and how I live. It made me
focus on the fact that my writing is getting
closer to how I think as how I live gets
closer to how I think. That is: walking what

you talk. That is telling the truth all the time because if you don't the alien will be on your face sucking everything away.

Can these bones live?

JUNE 16, 1979
The question is, of course, what does it all mean? The answer is, of course, nothing.

I feel myself sliding into an introspective phase. I am glad. It means more writing. It means I am coming out of this monitoring of myself because my personal life is so weirded out. I hope it means I might get back to my fucking novel. It means the spell is broken. It means the weight is lifted. It means something and nothing. Everything and not a damn thing. Ennui on a weekday morning. How weird. It is all so weird. I need another word for what this feels like. I want to hear from a New York editor. Any New York editor! And I want to hear from Ismael Reed and I want to quit my job and I want to write my stories and write my book and see what the real deal is.

Here's the story: a woman watching Ratliff and Angela and all the time having her own affair and it parallels the thing she's watching in some way. In all ways. In no way. I am so weirded out today. Damn sure don't need to be at this job in this mood, but I am being so adult these days. Get up, stockings on, fix breakfast, coffee, lunch for Deignan. I need to get some groceries tonight. A chicken or two for her lunch. Some bread and some more fruit. I can barely get that organized and I have to read in the *New York Times* that Joan Didion is an excellent cook in addition to being able to write her little ass off. I'll bet she's not a good fuck. God! What will the biographers say when they find that one? "Hostility and venom," they'll say. "Nasty and competitive."

Kay and her beau are doing great. She is blooming. Calm, loved, fucked and adored. Can't beat it.

JULY 2, 1979
We are on the way to Martinique for the Cultural Exchange and Arts Festival. The stewardess is explaining how to behave in case of such dire circumstances as water ditching and loss of oxygen. I have just guzzled a vodka and tonic and a Valium and I am very cooled out. I have brought the first three of the *Alexandria Quartet* books to read. Joe Jennings, my favorite saxophone player, will be performing. The musicians from Life Force are on the plane, too. So are Mubutu, the drummer, David and

Shirley Franklin, and some others. It's going to be a good trip. I am looking forward to it, but scared of takeoff. More later.

JULY 3, 1979
Martinique
This place is as different from home as it can be and not be the moon. And not be Siberia. Flowers and French and a rain forest that grows up green and close on each side of the road. Men in tight European shirts and the bars always smell like rum and pineapple. And that rain forest is so close on each side of this narrow, winding, well-paved mountain road.

"I remember this place," David says as we drive past signs saying St. Anne's and Trois Islets. "I remember it," he says. "I know how to get there," but we take wrong turns, stop to open and close the sun roof as it rains and clears, rains and clears. We laugh and suddenly come to a small town and David says, "Yes! It's right up here!" And we climb a steep hill, the car, a Peugeot, protesting, but not fighting back, and there it is! A small place. Black rum in the petit punch. Café Mahogany. The waitress shy and brown and trying to close her lips over teeth rotting away, but we laugh, delighted and amazed that we actually found it.

The restaurant is on the porch of a house with flowers in bloom all over the place, plastic cloths on the little tables and people cooking in a small outdoor kitchen and serving you the food right there on the porch. We drink two bottles of wine and eat grilled lobster and laugh and talk and those flowers are everywhere/everywhere. Our hosts speak no English. We speak no French. There is a lot of smiling and nodding to show how wonderful the food is. We are drinking a lot. We are relaxing. Coming down. Laughing. We all like each other. We are realizing we all love each other. The food is incredible. The setting is idyllic. It begins to rain and Michael runs out to roll up the car windows. We all laugh. David attempts to tell them we want drinks to take out. They giggle. We giggle. Finally, they understand. Café Mahogany it is called and David was right. It is near St. Anne's. We stop on our way back to the hotel and I buy a white gauze dress for me and a plaid dress with a big sash for Deig.

It was a wonderful afternoon. Flowers were everywhere. Now it's time to change for the festival. Perfect day.

The Festival program was wonderful. Joe Jennings and Howard Nicolson and Life Force played and it was so hot, they would wander to the back of the stage while someone else had a solo and wipe their faces with towels. The performance tent was packed and the heat was pulsating everywhere. When we come in, they seat us up front so we can be honored guests. Atlanta dignitaries. I watch Joe and wonder if he would play while I did my poetry and I listen to the people speaking French and looking just like we do. And afterward, some people pass us, knowing we are from Atlanta and that we have been introduced as "dignitaries," and they smile shyly and murmur, *"Bon,* Atlanta, *bon."* We go see Joe backstage and he is dripping sweat and grinning and I say, "Aren't you gonna be signing autographs?" And he laughs. "I should be getting them," he says. Another member of our party materializes wearing a pinstriped suit and speaking in a newly acquired British accent. I want to tease him about it, but he's too far away and the room is too crowded.

We've been invited to a reception at the home of the American consul general and even though I'm really sleepy, we're driving through the streets of Fort de France and arriving at Howard Robinson's house. I'm so tired. He is black and very happy to have us. We drink and drink and they talk and talk. "In order to make Johnson leave the Senate, Kennedy gave him the space program for Texas," says the consul general. Heavy talk, but I am too sleepy. I look out through the porch doors at the pool, the lights of the city, the trees. Always the flowers. I drink more rum. Now they are talking about the CIA so I leave the room and lie down on a rattan couch and sleep. Wake to them still talking and sleep again until they rouse me an hour later at 4:00 a.m. and we find our way home; drunk, sleepy, lost, exhilarated.

The night was wonderful. The day was wonderful. We fall into bed, exhausted. Martinique.

JULY 11, 1979

My mother has cancer. I read poetry last night at Georgia State. After the reading, Michael came back to get me and told me that Ernie called to say the tests came back and she has cancer. She has to go into the hospital on the twenty-fifth and the operation is on the twenty sixth. I called and talked to Kris, who was a basket case. Me, too. I started crying and we couldn't really talk too well, but then I took a Valium and drank some rum and called Ma. Henry answered. She and I acknowledged that I had talked to Kris, knew what the deal was, and then we just talked for an hour. About the movies. About Skylab. About Somoza. Just talking. Just talking fast and stumbling all over each other and talking/talking/talking. I told Michael in Martinique that sometimes it doesn't matter if you're telling the same stories over and over. Most people don't have many to tell. Talking is just a way of having pleasant social intercourse with people and of establishing contact; and concern; and love. And so we talked. And she said, "No, don't come now. I am supposed to rest and get myself together." And I said, "Are you sure?" And she said, "Yes, don't come now." And Henry said something like, "When did she get to be the one to establish when you come?" So I'm not sure what that means. But I am going after she has the operation.

I hope it hasn't spread. I hope they catch it. I hope she is okay. I am so scared, but I haven't even cried. I love my mother. I don't know how to feel all this without just letting myself fly apart and I can't do that. She may be okay. She is not dying. They don't know if she is dying. We are all dying. We are all dying. She has been spotting since December, but wouldn't go to the doctor. Too scared. Scared to know, so she just told herself it was from shoveling snow. Strained herself. Things like that. Eight months of things like that. She has carried on this fantasy for eight months. There must be some relief to having it out; having it said; knowing. Fear, but at last things are happening. Appointments are made. Doctors scheduled.

After I talk to Ma, David calls to say, "You got the job. You are working on *Bustin' Loose*. Richard Pryor, Cecily Tyson, Oz Scott will be directing. You'll be on location in Spokane and you will make six hundred dollars a week." I tell him about my mother and he says, "Oh, my god. Oh, my god. Oh, my god."

True confession: I feel guilty because I think immediately of transferring all this into writing. I think that is an attempt to get some control where there is no control.

JULY 12, 1979

Just talked to Kris. We talked about how hard it is being a grown-up. How scared we are for Ma. And on the radio the Eagles singing about James Dean and the desirability of dying young. My mother is so much on my mind. I mean this: I am always thinking about her. I mean this: I am so scared she is going to die. I mean this: What will I do? What will she do? What can I say/ send that will make it all okay? Nothing. You can send nothing. Last night when Daddy was coming over, I freaked. Took a Valium. Drank two drinks. Floated through dinner, but didn't cry. But later, after he was gone, I smoked a joint and thought about all the women in the family — Nanny, Grandmother Turner and Ma — and their men. And me. And Deignan. And how I felt having the abortion. And the fact that Ma has uterine cancer. Of the womb. Where she carried me. Where I carried Deig. There is nothing for it but hoping she can be okay. Hoping they can do the right stuff and she will come home and be okay. I think about Nanny going through the house looking for Poppy when he died. I think about Poppy, delirious from the wrong medication, walking through the house, calling for his wife. "Where's my best girl?" And how scared Henry must be. And how scared are we looking into each other's eyes and realizing the day would come for us, too. And no bribes, no logic, no preparation prepares you for it. When Poppy died, Ma crying at the cemetery saying, "I just can't leave him here! I just can't leave him here!"

JULY 13, 1979

I did well yesterday, but last night, I just started crying doing the damn dishes. I felt like I couldn't deal with everything, but I did! I just washed my face, finished the dishes, bathed Deig and put her in bed. Then I smoked a joint and calmed down a little. I organized Deig's dolls in the toy box and then went to sleep. You know how people will say somebody slept "the sleep of the dead?" That's how I was sleeping. Woke up exhausted anyway.

JULY 18, 1979

Just read an essay by Alice Walker in *Ms.* about having a kid. About women artists having a kid. Yes, she says we should, but only one. It was so good. It was about children and mothers and white feminists and racism and it said all the things that I have just been realizing. That white women can't be your friend because they haven't read the books. Because, dammit, you don't exist for them. Because they don't know who Zora Neale Hurston is. Because they won't read *The Invisible Man*. Because they just don't know anything about you and it fucking never occurs to them to find out. God! The piece is so true and so well written! She said all the right stuff. All the true stuff. She needed to say more about kids, but she got off on a lot of other feminist things which are important, but I wish she had talked more about kids. I wish she had talked more about why have one at all. She talked about the myths and about how hard it is. God, she is such a good writer.

JULY 18, 1979

I will not forget what I was wearing the night you told me my mother had cancer. I will not forget the white dress I wore for good luck. I will not forget the blue Colombian shoes I wore for security. I will not forget the gambler's earrings I wore for luck. I will not forget your face, your eyes watching me for a reaction. I will not forget the coldness in my stomach, hearing how calmly I questioned you about how you knew and where the cancer was. I will not forget that the first image that I had was of the thing bursting from that man's chest in the *Alien* movie and thinking of the cancer that way. Inside, eating/eating/eating at my mother. I will not forget the cancer is inside her where I was inside her. I will not forget it. I will not forget calling her and both of us in pain, but talking about other things, pretending we weren't talking about love only. Only love. I will not forget what I was wearing. I will not forget trying to find the way out of that building at Georgia State. I will not forget reading that night, my mouth so dry. I will not forget what I was wearing.

JULY 19, 1979
Of all the things I have done, I have only once felt like I betrayed the female ancestors. Only once. And that was when I had the abortion. I felt like they wouldn't be able to understand how I could, or why. But I also felt like they couldn't understand my circumstances. Times too different; demands too different. So I apologized to their spirits and veered off the path long enough to do what I had to do. I think I could convince them to forgive me.

JULY 19, 1979
Feel so strange. Have been reading old diaries and then journals. Don't know what to say about them. They sound just like me now. The questions and the answers from the past are surprisingly similar to my questions and answers now. But they sound so radical. They sound so black. That girl

would never . . . I mean never . . . have married a white dude. She would never have kissed a white man. She would never have fucked a white man. She was so, so correct. Little Miss Perfect, the woman who does everything right and with determination, even run the revolution. It makes me feel weird though. To read it now.

I wonder why I always find jobs that make it necessary for me to get up before noon. Don't know. I am blocking in my writing. Haven't done anything serious since we left to go to Martinique, which was several weeks ago. I don't know why. Ma, I guess. And the movie coming through and just tired. Just drained. I don't know. I am so intimidated by the novel. It is so much in my mind, but I can't get it on paper. And I am not quite sure why. Scared it won't be good, I guess. Scared I will get rejected with it. Scared I can't finish it, even if I do try and work on it and stuff. How about those page quotas? How about ten pages a day? How about five? How about two? You just ain't even tryin' anymore. That is the truth.

I am also convinced that I have cancer. God. I don't know. I really don't know. Where am I?

JULY 22, 1979

Riding down I-20 and Michael tells me Minnie Riperton died just like David said she would. Of cancer. Breast cancer. My mind fills up with my mother. Cancer. Minnie sings "Memory Lane," and now she's dead with that lil' high, baby bird voice. Cancer. We're always breathing it.

JULY 23, 1979

Ultimately, you see, you have to do it alone. Dying. Facing the pain. Here is the truth. I don't wanna go to Idlewild and see Ma. I don't wanna organize it and face it and handle it and be in charge of it. I don't wanna have to reassure my mother; mother my sister; and wander down the dirt roads, all teary and nostalgic. That is so mean, but it is true. I don't wanna do it. Not interested in it at all. But I gotta go. I will go. Have no choice, really. So there it is. There it is. Two weeks only. And the drive to Grand Rapids or the flight. And the whole thing. I love my mother, but I'd rather pretend. That's she's okay. That I can help. That I can share it. I guess she would, too.

JULY 24, 1979

"I am getting ready to go to the West Coast to make a movie," I say to my mother. "I don't want to fly, but I can handle it. If I don't fly, I will get a bus or rent a car or something! Richard Pryor is in it." I know she likes Richard Pryor; feels protective of him because she thinks he sees the truth so clearly it will surely kill him. "Be sure you get enough rest," my mother says. "And don't forget to eat your vegetables."

I feel like everything I am writing is shit. I feel like pretending to be a writer is a good way to get to do what I want, which is not to work too hard and make a lot of money. I don't wanna write novels. Too hard. I can't think of why anybody should read the drivel I'm writing. I can't think of why or who or how. I can't string it all together. I might just do little sections and then let them get together the best way they can. Can't I do the connecting tissue later?

Then I read Gayl Jones's *Corregidora,* and I say, "Damn, Pearl, that is her first novel." It is real. It is black. It is so good. And I think my writing is so glib; so slick. I am depressed. How can I get to Detroit to see my mother? I don't wanna go. I don't wanna drive. I don't wanna do any of it, but I will. I have to.

SEPTEMBER 5, 1979
And tonight, my friends, I find in being

254

black a thing of beauty.
— *Ossie Davis, in* Purlie Victorious

Yup. I do. I had an "I love myself and I love living in Atlanta" attack walking down Walton Street. It was brought on by nothing at all, but was quite a rush. Tonight, we are having dinner with Tony and Cede Ames and Richard Avedon. My friend just freaked when I told him that. "You are so lucky," he said. "You are so lucky." I feel lucky. "This will break you," David says of my working on the movie. Not in the sense of breaking me down, but in the sense of bringing me to the attention of those who can make things happen. I sure hope so. I am ready, willing and able to be broke!

SEPTEMBER 8, 1979
When he was young, Bob Dylan sang about things outside. Now he sings about the things inside. Inside is scarier.

SEPTEMBER 18, 1979
Beatles on the radio singing "I Am the Walrus." I'm wearing my purple Seattle Sweater. Jeans. Pink socks. Filled with indecision/love/fear. Here is something I want to remember. Deig and I stopped in at the French Bakery in Buckhead to get some

croissants and ate lunch there. We saw a lot of white people. Driving; sauntering by with leather hats and ice cream cones; shopping; talking; holding their kids. In the time we sat there, maybe an hour, I saw four black people. They were doing the following things:

A white uniformed black woman, dressed like a nurse, pushing an old white woman in a wheelchair carefully to the curb, opening the car, half lifting, half helping the woman into the car.

A middle-aged black woman with her hair tied up in a bandana jiggling a fussy white baby on her hip while the mother, clad in a white tennis dress, stopped at the door of the car to speak to a friend. Finally done, she opened the door and got into the front seat, leaned over and opened the backseat door and the nursemaid and her charge got in for the ride.

An older black man, maybe sixtyish, sweating and grooming the lawn of a large house in a neighborhood full of large houses and well-groomed lawns.

A black man around fifty, uniformed chauffeur, including a cap, gliding by in a long blue Cadillac; not a limo for hire, but a private car. He was merely waiting for his employer to be through so he could glide

256

the man to his next destination.

That's all the black folks we saw. It made me think of Countee Cullen's poem, "Incident" where the little black kid goes to visit relatives in Baltimore and a little white kid sees him on the street and calls him a nigger. The last lines: *"I saw the whole of Baltimore / from May until December / of all the things that happened there / that's all that I remember."*

That's the way I felt about lunch in Buckhead. The class and race distinctions are so present and unapologetic. *That's all that I remember . . .*

SEPTEMBER 18, 1979

Terror. I feel terrified. I am reading through my old journals from two years ago and I am saying the same things now. Worrying about time to write. Worrying about losing myself. Two years and more of this! I feel like I am not writing. I feel like I am not doing much except marking time. The questions are still these:

1. What do you want?
2. How badly do you want it?
3. How bold will you be to get it?

Until you answer these, it is all bullshit.

257

SEPTEMBER 18, 1979

I hear the artist whose studio is next to mine at the Forrest Avenue Arts Consortium talking to someone in the hallway. We are friends, but he doesn't knock like he usually does, so I assume he's with a stranger. I know the hall smells of marijuana. I am guilty. I have been smoking in my studio. We all do it. My eyes may droop, but my spirit flies! I hope it is not an official stranger. Someone coming to look at his photographs for a possible sale, or talk to him about a grant to support his work. I don't want them to think we're a bunch of stoned hippies. We are serious artists. We just smoke while we work. The radio is up loud and Bob Seger is singing about being a travelin' man, but I rush to the typewriter and begin typing this. It is a ruse. A reason why I have been smoking. Why: An artist needs to remove the censors that plague us and drugs are a way to do that. You hear me typing, don't you? I must be working, right? It may seem like I'm just in here, smoking dope and making a collage and haven't written a word all morning. But what the hell? I am what I am. And sometimes life is pretty damn fine.

SEPTEMBER 24, 1979

Melanie is in the hospital for some tests. She sounded pretty cool, but it is scary shit. Ma is in Detroit for radiation therapy. Cancer/cancer/cancer. It is all over and always scary.

But my screenplay is gonna be good. I believe this: I believe that we are in a revolution. I believe that women are changing so rapidly that it is hard to keep up. I think that we need new rules; new ways of dealing with each other; new models; new options; new LITERATURE AND ART!!

SEPTEMBER 27, 1979

Nancy Marshall and I are visiting photographer P. H. Polk in Tuskegee, Alabama. His house is large, but broken up into studio, rental room and his own space. His house is on Washington Road, named after Booker T. Washington. That's fitting since Mr. Polk was the official photographer at the university for many years. Nexus Press is going to publish a collection of his work and I will be writing the essay at the front of the book. Nancy is the editor. I've seen some of his photographs, but I've never met Mr. Polk. He greets us at the door and ushers us into his crowded house. He has two big fish tanks with collages on the back of

259

the glass. The pictures are from old magazines and not his own work. In one of the tanks are a pair of small plastic skeletons that constantly sit up and lie back down when jets of water jiggle them. It was really hot in his house. He is at least eighty years old and was really pleased to see us. He drives us around the campus and he's driving real slow, like Poppy used to drive. He actually smashed right into another car's bumper as we were leaving the parking lot, but he didn't even notice it. He told me he liked my hair. I think he thought I was white, but he saw my afro and then when I said I had gone to Howard and lived on Chestnut Street in Atlanta, I think he knew I was black. When we got back to the house, he offered us a drink and we accepted. He walked over to the dishwasher and pulled it out and in the rack where the dishes would go, he had a full bar. Bottles of liquor, cocktail glasses, etc. You could tell he thought that was pretty cool. Me, too. I am really looking forward to writing about him. He has a million pictures and a million stories. He came across a really beautiful one of his ex-wife and he said, "She tried to put me in the ground, but she didn't." Sounded like a blues song.

SEPTEMBER 28, 1979

When Nancy and I were going to Tuskegee to see Mr. Polk, we took the wrong freeway and so we ended up in Birmingham, but it was okay. The ride back was kind of a drag because it was raining and the freeway was full of trucks and stuff, but it wasn't too bad. She and I talked a lot about marriage and privacy and space for yourself. She was married before and said she just isn't sure she wants to give up her own private space again. I know the feeling. I like her. I think she is a good person. I find myself liking the word "womanly." She's like that. Sounds strong and firm and feminine without being soft.

SEPTEMBER 29, 1979

Dear Pearl,

Just a line to let you know I have made it in good shape through the first week of treatment. Only problem so far is attitude: who needs it? I received the surprise box and I LOVED IT! You know what I like. I used to go crazy about every three years when you all were little and buy a box of three bars of Yardley's lavender soap. Now, I am sitting here after bathing with the sandalwood you sent and I feel utterly spoiled, which I always love, but especially NOW! I never had Roger & Gallet soap before — only read about it in the Horchow Catalogue — but I love it. Love you for thinking about me. LOVE YOU ALL!

Have to stop and eat dinner. Wish you all were here. I cooked roast chicken and dressing and only the two of us to eat it. Write when you can.

Love, Ma

SEPTEMBER 29, 1979

I can't seem to get anything done today. I can't keep my mind on anything. Yesterday, I felt myself getting into classic campaign mode. The classic hyper running all the time, eye twitching, stomach in a knot campaign mode. And this isn't even about a candidate! This is about a sales tax! I consciously tried to slow myself down and take a few deep breaths. I used to be the serene one in the campaigns. People would marvel at how calm I stayed in the face of one crisis or another. Maynard's second campaign is the first one that really beat me down. I closed my eyes and tried to put my mind somewhere else, as I tried to figure out what it is that gets to me now that didn't use to. I think the basic thing is just that now I know that all of it is hollow. All of it is just posturing of one sort or another. Righteous indignation. Outraged moralizing. Sublime contentment with "the world's next great city." All the ideas that I used to help craft so carefully for the TV cameras; all the catchphrases and buzzwords that I would write into speeches seem shallow and absurd in the face of what I now know to be true. In the face of how little change really comes about. In the face of the strange missed connections in the people who present themselves as whole and become the leaders. The first black ones. The chosen few. The talented tenth. It just seems pathetic and silly to me. And being caught up in it, writing for it, thinking about it, is such a waste of energy and time. Enough! End of the whine.

SEPTEMBER 30, 1979
Here's what I am thinking about with the P. H. Polk essay:

The thing that struck me as so amazing about the pictures he took was the absolute, smiling, all American-ness of the black folks who came into his studio, hair waved to the bone, cheeks powdered, vests festooned with chains and fobs, dressed to the nines in the latest fashions, wanting to have their pictures taken. Smiling and smiling and smiling into the camera. What was going on up the road in Tuskegee? How many people were lynched during the years he was taking those smiling group portraits? What about the syphilis experiment with one hundred black men in Tuskegee who were never told they had it so the doctors could study their deterioration. Still smiling. What about finally getting the right to vote in Tuskegee and black folks refusing to elect other black folks because they didn't want to practice "reverse racism." And what that means is anybody's guess. And still smiling. And Booker T. and DuBois arguing about everything and the black middle class in Tuskegee sending their children north to boarding school, away from the dangers of Alabama, and still smiling.

What I want to talk about is Polk himself as an artist, as a black artist, living in a place like Tuskegee. I want to think about him living and working there with an eye to James Baldwin's quote: "To be a Negro artist, one had to make oneself up as one went along." I want to talk about Tuskegee as an enclave of black folks trying desperately to make a haven for themselves. Trying to be Americans. Trying to pretend that all those dresses and finger waves and Shirley Temple curled children had anything to do with who got lynched and why and where. I want to look at the progression from the noble "peasants" that Polk photographs so carefully, to the students at Tuskegee, to the middle-class people of the town. Exactly the progression Booker T. was looking for; hoping for; praying for; crawling on his knees to funding sources for. And what difference did it make? I want to look at those pictures and think about Kathleen Cleaver coming from there. And Sammye Young, Jr., killed by police there; a child of the black middle class who got too radical. I want to think about my father saying America practices a doctrine of black inferiority and the madness that results from us accepting that, too, even while we are smiling. Rambling. Just thoughts. Looking at those photographs of all those beautiful women and tiny children and remembering my grandmother saying when she used to mind her uncle Victor Tulane's store in Montgomery, the white salesmen who came in would make off-color remarks to her. "I would just purse my lips and look north," she said.

Dear Pearl,

Have heard various reports of your filmmaking experience — from your own cards and letters to us; from Kris by way of your letters and from Barbara by way of letters to your father. Am eagerly awaiting firsthand accounts whenever. Meanwhile, I know you are keeping notes on everything. I am most intriqued by your statement that you are "learning as much about yourself as about filmmaking." Anyway, remember what you told me — soon it will all be behind you, so hang in there!

Well, praise be, tomorrow should be the last day for this part of my treatments and maybe we can go home for two weeks. It's like the last day of school. I've been so patient and "good," but now I'm just WILD to be finished, done and AWAY!

I finally got into Jackie Susann's *Once Is Not Enough.* I think I see why you said don't play her cheap. She is one of the most economical writers in terms of establishing character and moving plot forward. She seems to know exactly where she's going next and gets there neatly with a minimum of wasted motion. My biggest problem at this time in trying to write is knowing where I'm going and how best to get there. And I'm talking simply about plot as in Susann or in Barbara Cartland or Frank Yerby. Not style or creativity or anything but plotting. Susann's characters are poor; thin and stereotyped. Her style is non-existent, but she moves things along. All for now. Love, love, love. Take care of yourself and hang in there. Don't forget to eat your vegetables!

Ma

NOVEMBER 20, 1979

A lame Hollywood rap:

"Hey, Red! I think you got possibilities. Not only those eyes, but I checked out the 42Ds and booty for days. I know you have some paper. Take down my number. I wanna take you to another level. To the next phase. What's wrong? Don't you like money?"

How can anybody possibly live in Los Angeles?

DECEMBER 1979

I'm watching *Hud* with Paul Newman and Patricia Neal and Melvyn Douglas. The dialogue is great. The father is dying. Hud is trying to hit on the housekeeper. The housekeeper is trying to resist him.

HUD: You don't go shootin' all the dogs because one of them got fleas.

And:

THE HOUSEKEEPER: I was married to Ed for eight years and all he was good for was to scratch my back when I couldn't reach it.
HUD: You still got that itch?
THE HOUSEKEEPER: Every now and then.
HUD: Well, you let me know when it hits you again and I'll see what I can do.

And:

HUD: Women just like to be around some-thing dangerous sometime.

And:

HUD: You not lettin' that little ruckus we had run you off, are you?
THE HOUSEKEEPER: Fast as I can get a bus ticket . . .

■ ■ ■ ■

THE JOURNALS:
1980–88

■ ■ ■ ■

THE EIGHTIES: A QUICK OVERVIEW

I got tired, okay? I got tired of all the badasses being white girls. White girls were telling everything, left and right, confessing to being lovers, lesbians, punks, freaks, dope fiends, murderers, sluts, geniuses. The white girls were emerging as complex mirrors of the unique wonderfulness of being a woman in America in the twentieth century. *(Thank you, Jesus!)* But where were the black girls except behind the eight ball? And it didn't seem to matter who was writing about us. The story was always the same. Finally, I just got tired, okay?

I got tired of us always being dumb and country and raped and cowed. Or raped and ennobled. Or raped and loving it. Or raped and crazed behind it. Or the ones that start off with promise and then punk all the men off before Chapter 3. Or the ones that start off okay and then make the girl fall in love with an evil, wisecracking quadriplegic who wears berets. Or the ones where the neighborhood guys take the character with the complicated sexuality and rape her brains out in the alley so hard her stockings stick to the pavement and her brains turn to jelly and her pussy breathes indignant fire and makes a weird rainstorm the next day that nobody can quite understand. I got tired of it.

But the white girls had the bases covered. Some of them were beautiful, but political any damn way like Gloria Steinem. Some of them were punk and don't give a fuck like that woman in the *Ms.* photo with eighty earrings. The damn white girls had Anaïs Nin and Simone de Beauvoir and Mary Gordon and old priss head Jayne Anne Phillips and Miss Assembly Line herself, Joyce Carol Oates. They had acid-tongued Fran Liebowitz and Simenon's ill-fated daughter, Marie, and his wild-ass wife who only appears in his memoirs as *D.*

There were so many hip white girls around. Not just the writers, either. Look at the love affairs they get to have in public. Jessica Lange projecting Hepburn and Monroe at the same time and snagging the Pulitzer Prize cowboy hisself, the old motel man, Sam Shepard. This after we had already had to live though her mind-boggling fling with the beloved Misha. *What the fuck do they talk about?* How perfect they are? How beautiful and well-behaved their kid is? I've read the interviews. I've read how the kid, aged about three, wanders around posh restaurants while her famous mother and her famous mother's paramour make *goo goo* eyes at each other. I've read how she climbs into the proffered laps and coos something precious and then hops down and toddles off, a vision of blond perfection. She probably never even wore diapers. It never stops. They've got Joan Collins as the perfectly evil Alexis Carrington and Linda Evans as the beautiful, but slightly stupid, Crystal Carrington. Villains and virgins. Queens and demi-goddesses. The white girls had a representative that went to the head of every class. Diane Sawyer even gets to sit with the big guys and *60 Minutes* ratings soar. Score a big one for the blond white girl! Give her a raise, too! And give Jane Pauley one, too, so she won't feel bad. And what the hell can we do with Phyllis George, the ultimate white girl gone mad? Hire her, too! What the hell? What the hell, indeed.

I just got tired of it, okay? White girls are not the only ones living interesting lives.

These pages are my proof.

What to give the girl who has everything?
  "A pet man."

Just figured out I like working in the morning now. I will do it. Get to work at noon and work till 5:30. That would be cool. I think that will help me find my writing rhythm.

Talking to Daddy. And I said: "I think I'll make it because I've got discipline and skills." And he said: "That's not the most important thing about you. You've still got an imagination. You're still animated. Your face is alive." And I felt it, too! Alive and well! And I feel REAL.

I can always disregard people's advice on the basis of their difference from me. "He's a white man." "He's a black man." "She's a white woman." Do I have no black women friends because I don't want to hear the truth?

JANUARY 10, 1980

I have no doubt this is the generation that see God.

— *Bob Marley*

Got a letter from Bruce Talamon, mailed from Orly Airport where he was catching a plane to West Africa to photograph the Bob Marley tour! Go, Bruce!! "If you don't/you won't!"

JANUARY 14, 1980

I stand at my sink, washing dishes and wishing I was Ntozake Shange. Wishing I had the nerve to plait my hair and wear plastic clips at the end of each braid. I find myself boring. Trying to be Ntozake and Romy Schneider and Jeanne Moreau. But actually possessive, insecure, frightened.

JANUARY 22, 1980

One of the characters in Pat Conroy's book tells a woman that as far as men are concerned, all a woman is supposed to do is "be adorable. Everything else is gravy."

Gravy?!

At the door, my friend says to me: "I think you are a good woman. I think you're undeniably special. I think you're divinely

275

special and any man who has you is a lucky man."

Do all lovers with spouses pretend the mistress is "special"? I think that's part of the contract. Otherwise, we have to admit it's mostly just sex. And gravy.

JANUARY 24, 1980

Another plane. Another departure. More rewrites are pointless. The movie is terrible. It cannot be saved. Not by the director. Not by the producers. Not by the mad genius of Richard Pryor. This movie is fucked.

I realized this morning that I am making my living writing. It just kind of dawned on me in a real way as I trudged down the long, mural-less corridors of LAX. As many Mexican painters who live in L.A., how can they have a whole complex without one mural? Have they never heard of Diego Rivera? But in spite of the artless surroundings, I was at work. I am what I have been saying I am: a working writer.

Walking through the airport, past the Pro-Nukes activists with signs saying: "3 Mile Island is safer than Ted Kennedy's car." And: "Nuclear plants are built better than Jane Fonda." Along the way, I got stopped by a black Hare Krishna guy. He had a regular haircut and he was very pleasant.

We walked and talked for a few minutes and he gave me a big, fat, beautifully bound, fully illustrated volume about Hare Krishna. I gave him a couple of bucks, but I know that book cost a lot more. He seemed pleased with the exchange and wandered off toward the Pro-Nukes crowd.

The studio teamster who drove me to the airport said he used to sleep so heavily it took him almost an hour to wake up. "I learned how to do it when I was a kid," he explained. "My parents screaming and fighting all the time. No kid wants to hear all that."

The lesson: Nobody has a normal childhood.

JANUARY 25, 1980

Re-entry blues. Dexter Gordon is on the radio playing a song called "I'm a Fool to Want You." I don't want to campaign. I don't want to hear about the campaign. I don't want to talk about the campaign. I'm so tired of politics.

Q: Why am I so blue?
A: Because I'm not writing anything of my own.

JANUARY 28, 1980

On my way to lunch, a black cat started out in the street in front of my car. I thought: "Oh, shit! I don't need no fucking black cat to cross my path today!" So I blew the horn really loud and scared it back up on the curb away from in front of me! I take that as a sign.

Went to three political parties today like a good political wife. Enthusiastic people at each stop. The thing is, I want him to get elected. I just don't like being part of the process. As we got ready to leave the last party, a woman patted my arm and said brightly: "Good-by, Peggy!" Uh, huh. Peggy. Right . . .

JANUARY 30, 1980

David comes over to tell me they're drawing up a writer's contract for me and that I need to go back to California next Thursday. They still think they can save this movie! I don't think so. Richard Pryor is crazed and everybody is afraid of him. They can't do re-shoots of anything because he won't show up.

But it pays so well! That's how they suck you in. It pays SO well. I may get a writer's credit if I do enough on the rewrites to qualify. Is this "My Big Break"? "My Shot"?

At what?

Deignan has decided her pretend name is Lisa Lomax.

FEBRUARY 2, 1980

Just saw *Peppermint Soda,* a really wonderful little French movie. A first directorial effort by a thirty-year-old woman. I really liked it. The people seemed so real. I sat behind two French women who were actually speaking French! That made it fun. Sort of like being in the place where the movie was taking place.

After the movie I went next door to the cheese shop and bought a loaf of French bread. The owner asked me if I was French! I wanted to say, "Oui, oui!" but I restrained myself!

FEBRUARY 4, 1980

I know we are not going to make it. I think he knows it, too.

I don't want to feel crazy and unhappy.

I want to be writing.

I want to be myself and be clearheaded and strong and beautiful.

I want to make myself as perfect as I can be.

I want to make myself as wondrous as I can be.

I want to be free.

FEBRUARY 7, 1980

Michael is in a runoff for City Council president. He got 27 percent of the vote. Marvin Arrington got 35 percent. The runoff is going to be hard, but win or lose, I think the poor showing was a moment that changed him. A trial by fire. In public. Bare feet on hot coals.

I leave for L.A. late tonight. I'm exhausted. Have been up with the campaign for days. I want the runoff to be over so we'll know what is what and who is who. Whew . . .

FEBRUARY 14, 1980

Back from L.A. and already feeling guilty. Can't do enough. Ever. Michael wants me at the campaign. Deignan wants me at her school. I feel torn. Like I'm deserting my husband and not being much of a mother either. I have to get organized!

FEBRUARY 18, 1980

Election Day tomorrow. I am dreading the outcome. Should I stay or go?

FEBRUARY 19, 1980
3:45 p.m., Campaign HQ

I feel like a bitch because I am hating being here at the HQ so much. I am hating listening to Michael calling people and saying who he is and asking the folks if they voted and if they "took care of me." He says: "Thank you now," at the end of every conversation and his voice is thick with determined cheeriness. I feel like a bitch because this morning when he came out of the voting booth with a barely awake Deignan in his arms, he brushed the curtain away and said to her, "Smile, baby." And he said it to her on the way into the place, too. "Smile, baby. They are going to take our picture." And she shook her head "no." I feel like a bitch because I know I haven't done enough for his campaign. Flying back and forth to try and fix a movie that can't be fixed. Now here I sit writing a draft of a concession speech, "just in case."

I am so down. "What did I do to be so black and blue?"

FEBRUARY 22, 1980

I am here in my studio, trying to work. Michael is at home recovering from the loss of the election. He is depressed, but I think he is mostly just glad it's all over. I am, too. We

281

had a great conversation yesterday about everything. In the midst of, in spite of, everything, we know each other. We love each other. We have survived the election. What comes next is hard to say.

FEBRUARY 27, 1980
Bob Dylan on the Grammies. Tuxedo and ravaged face. Singing his Christian songs and smiling. At the end, the crowd stands; stomping, screaming, cheering, whistling at him. And he, still smiling, thanks God for the small award they press into his hand.

Rosemary Daniell wants to tell everything. I have figured out how to excuse the bad writing. It is not a book that is concerned with the smoothness of the prose, the clever juxtaposition of words on the page. It is a communique from the front. It is a battle plan. She is trying to warn the rest of us about the dangers she has seen. And she does that. She talks about all of it: mother/ father/sister/lover/women/men/drag queens/ violence and guns shoved up this opening or that one/always being scared of the wildness/always waiting to be raped. She can't slow down long enough to make sure the prose is memorable. She's trying to tell us where the land mines are. If I knew her number I would call her.

Chip Epstein pedals his bike out of the parking lot outside my studio window and I remember the day he responded to a question about whether or not he had licensed his two-wheeled vehicle by saying he had "poetic license." Kay and I delighted at a musician who could make a writer's joke. And Janie perched on the roof her last day here with a paper cutout crown and a fist full of wilting tulips, posing against the bluest sky and laughing while Richard took her picture just like he took one of me the day before I left for Seattle. "You'll look different when you get back," he said. And he was right.

Al Jarreau's song says his woman's got L.A. gleaming in her eye. And Tom Mount, the Universal Studios big cheese, has a Tom Petty record and a Ralph Steadman poster in his great big office and he's such a Hollywood big shot he can come to multi-million-dollar meetings in jeans. No need to dress up just to be an asshole. Working on the movie seems like another life. I take out the crew photo that Bruce Talamon shot in front of that Seattle garage. We all face the camera, but we have been behaving badly and our expressions are blank; noncommittal.

FEBRUARY 28, 1980

I saw Ed Howard and listened to some of the music he's producing. He had an earphone thing that was incredible. You put it on your ears and hear all the separation of the instruments, voices, etc. It was a mind blower, especially since I had been smoking incredibly strong grass. "It's a Walkman," he said. "They're going to be big." "Yeah," I said. "Especially if they give you a big ol' joint when you buy one."

MARCH 4, 1981

Dear Deignan,
  I just read over the note that you wrote me and it made me feel very lucky and very special to have a daughter like you who loves me the way that you do. You are special to me, too. I will never leave you. When I travel, I miss you the whole time I'm gone. I talk about you to people all the time. I tell them all about my daughter. I tell them how much you mean to me and how much I miss you. I'm not ever, ever, ever going to leave you. You are the best daughter anybody ever had and I love you very, very much. Don't worry about anything. I will always love you and I will always take

care of you.

Love, Mommy

MARCH 9, 1980
Richard Pryor is live in concert and a member of the audience blows a party whistle. Pryor reprimands him: "This ain't Kool and the Gang, nigga!"

But they did open the show. There they were on the stage at the Civic Center in their tight suits and white shoes, preening and prancing and crooning about "Ladies Night," and suddenly my mind is back in Seattle, working on that awful movie and we're all waiting because Richard won't come out of his trailer and that song comes on the radio and Kim gets up and starts dancing. When I don't leap up to join in, the director squints at me and says: "How can you be from Detroit and not dance?" I should have said: "How can you be getting paid seventy-five thousand dollars and not direct?"

MARCH 10, 1980
Our receptionist just came in moaning about how she is still speeding from the cocaine she did last night.

"How ya doin'?" I had said as I walked by her desk. "A little hyper," she said. "Why?"

I said, and she put her finger against her nostril and sniffed an imaginary line of cocaine. My, my, my . . . drugs everywhere you look.

MARCH 17, 1980
Driving Deig to school and the black teacher's aide comes out to wave. She is wearing a bright green blouse in honor of St. Patrick's Day. I am drinking Irish coffee for the same reason. Deig kisses me good-bye and runs up to the school. She's wearing green, too, so she won't get pinched. We never did that growing up, but here they do, so green it is.

Got a great letter from Daddy today. Came special delivery to Forrest Avenue to my studio address. He sent the money I had asked to borrow and said don't bother to pay it back. He said: "I'd probably just buy bubble gum with it anyway." Then he said perhaps I didn't need the stability of any kind of romantic relationship as most people did. "You may not," he said. "I didn't. I recall a great sense of relief when I realized it. Perhaps you're like me."

I wanted to say: "Of course I'm like you. I'm gonna start preaching as soon as I finish making movies and write the great American novel."

I love and miss him!

MARCH 29, 1980
I have moved out of the house. There is too much going on to write it all down. I'm staying at Janie's for a week until my apartment is ready, but it was getting too weird for us to be still living together; counting off the days. It was time to go. It is scary to be on my own, but it was time. I can figure it all out. I WILL figure it all out.

MARCH 30, 1980
How do you feel?
I feel tense. I feel scared. I feel weary. I feel exhilarated. I feel disbelieving. I feel depressed. I feel anxious. I feel strained. I feel like I am holding in a huge fit of tears and sobs and racking noises and trembling. I don't know if I can absorb it all. I feel pushed and pulled. I feel cruel and selfish and willful and wild. I feel deceitful. I feel alone. I feel abandoned. I feel foolish. I feel like I can't trust anybody. I feel like someone is after me. I feel like I am still not good enough. I feel like I am still not determined enough. I feel like the issues are too complex and the time is moving too fast. I feel like I am nobody's mother or wife or daughter or child. I feel like I don't really like anybody

and people who like me don't know me because I'm always lying or withholding or editing.

I am so scared.

APRIL 1, 1980
Sitting here, watching Deignan laughing at Daffy Duck on TV. I always liked Daffy more than Donald Duck. Daffy is so competitive and neurotic, two qualities guaranteed to warm the cockles of my heart! I went to the grocery store this morning. I had budgeted $20 and I spent $19.48! I'm sticking to my budget. One more small step in taking control. No! You already have control, remember?

APRIL 2, 1980
Morning. I'm still at Janie's for another couple of days, but I've made peace with all the dolls and puppets that are everywhere, gazing around with their pup eyes. I have brewed some Sleepy Time tea in a saucepan since I couldn't find a teakettle and now I'm sitting at an oval work table looking at her great backyard out the window. I'm thinking about what it will feel like to be in my own place; how many peaceful mornings I will have.

I have just figured out my budget, which I

had been afraid to do for fear my money was short. Turns out that if I can raise/earn another two hundred dollars, I am okay through the end of June! I know I can scare up a couple of assignments that will pay that much.

I told Deig we were gonna get a giant piggy bank and start saving up for a trip to New Orleans. I would so love to manage my own affairs without having to take any money from any men. If any of them pay the rent it starts to feel like I'm a kept woman and you know I can't have that! I think I can write my way to eight hundred dollars a month which is my current base budget. Eight hundred dollars a month. I am so relieved. I feel like I have my money together. My heart and mind are making progress. But on this morning, I celebrate the fact that I am able to support my own damn self!

APRIL 3, 1980
My apartment will be ready next week. Janie's has been a great place for me, but I'm so ready to be in my own place! My current theme song is Elvis Costello: "I can't stand up for falling down."

APRIL 5, 1980

Things are still crazy, but at least I'm not crying all the time and over-explaining everything to anybody who cares to listen. Here's the rub: I thought I would be free immediately, but I'm still entangled, submerged, trapped, sad. I would like to have my own life back! How can I get it?

Take it, fool! Just take it!

APRIL 6, 1980

"Oh, god!" says my friend. "Your new place overlooks the Fox Theater's stage door!"

"Yeah, so?" I say.

"You'll be able to see the stars," she says.

I don't spoil the fantasy by pointing out you can only see the stage door from the back of my building and my apartment is on the front where I can see the glowing blue dome at the top of the Regency Hotel. Too bad. I wouldn't mind spending an evening watching Mick Jagger being whisked into his limo or Peabo Bryson strolling out with a lovely admirer clinging to his arm, or Johnny Mathis, who in my fantasy is walking alone, looks up, catches my eye and waves.

APRIL 8, 1980

Talking about Joan Didion. I said I don't

like her writing as much anymore because the attraction used to be her struggle to answer the basic life questions. That is: IS THIS IT?

It can also be translated as: IS THIS ALL THERE IS?

Joan was not sure and she engaged in the presentation of evidence for both sides; pro and con. She wanted to answer: "No! Of course not!" But the evidence she found — the choices she made — convinced her that, "Yep. This is all there is." So her writing got more depressed. The tension was gone because the tension was in the question. Not the answer. In *A Book of Common Prayer,* she presents the final evidence for the side she thinks wins. Namely, that this is all there is! The character of Charlotte, the weirdo dreamer, who wanted more out of her life, got the following: no husband/no kid love/bad lovers/death of kid/death of lover/own death. Not a very attractive picture. The more passive character, the narrator, is also suffering for the crime of telling what she knows. For her troubles, she gets: a rotten kid/a dead husband/ cancer. She's given up the fight because she thinks the demons won. She thinks she has to settle for the sad, depressing stretch of meaningless days heading for a painful death.

Joan! Don't do me like this! Don't you know it ain't over till the fat lady sings?

Fulton Superior Court
Final Judgment and Decree

Under consideration of this case upon evidence submitted as provided by law, it is the judgment of the court that a total divorce be granted, that is to say a divorce a vincula matrimonii, between the two parties to the above stated case upon legal principles. And it is considered, ordered, and decreed by the court that the marriage contract heretofore entered into between the parties to this case, from and after this date, be and is set aside and dissolved as fully and effectually as if no such contract had ever been made or into, and

Plantiff and Defendant in the future shall be held and considered as separate and distinct persons altogether unconnected by any nuptial union or civil contract, whatsoever, and both shall have the right to remarry.

The Plaintiff is hereby restored to her maiden name, to wit: Pearl Michelle

Cleage. Judge Superior Court of Atlanta Circuit.

APRIL 9, 1980

Michelle calls from Indiana to say hello and inquire as to my mental health. We laugh and screech at each other about how sane we are. Then she says she read the poems I sent and she had one question for me: "Do you have a lover?" I said yes and she screamed. "Well," she said, once we stopped laughing, "I guess if I had gotten divorced in the eighties, I'd have a lover, too."

APRIL 10, 1980

My Rosemary Daniell book review came out in the *Constitution* yesterday with a ton of editing! All the political stuff was gone, gone, gone! I was crushed. I went down there today, told them what I wanted/needed if I was going to keep writing for them. They apologized, claimed it was only space that made them edit anything and gave me a free copy of the new biography of Georgia O'Keefe to review. A hardback, no less! All is forgiven.

Some notes for something:

Realism is when you show how what happened looked to any eye that was there and saw it.

Surrealism is when you show how the scene looked from someone's point of view specifically — the person involved or the person watching with acute awareness.

Just got a great letter from Janie about being at Ossabaw Island. Naked dancing on the beach. Fires and sweat lodges. She writes well and the letter sounds like one extended perfect moment. Went to the movies alone to see *The War at Home*. Good documentary about Madison, Wisconsin, anti-war protestors and the national anti-war movement. Made me think about: Jim wanting me to make a statement against the war during my valedictorian speech and me being too chicken to do it; me and Kris at the counter inaugural in D.C.; me and Kris at the March on the Pentagon. When I came out of the movie, they were playing Bob Dylan's Christian album. I liked it, so I went and bought it.

I've finished the outline of my screenplay. On Monday, I begin writing actual dialogue!

APRIL 11, 1980
Here are some new rules and guidelines:

1. You don't have to lie.
2. You don't have to feel guilty for making yourself comfortable first.

3. You can love the people you love with no more need for explanation than that.
4. There is no #4. That's it; 1–3 covers the whole fucking waterfront.

APRIL 12, 1980

An urgent message to one who shall remain nameless.

Home alone listening to Bruce Springsteen and Peabo Bryson. Who else do you know who would spend a Saturday afternoon listening to these two and trying to write the great American novel?

Forgive my crimes, real and imagined, and take me to Paris immediately. I miss you terribly and would love to see you. I am crazy, but you always knew that, didn't you?

Call me. Remember what the soothsayer said.

APRIL 14, 1980

My last night at Janie's. My last night of transitional womanhood. I am moving to my own place at Peachtree North tomorrow. I feel so good about it! Packing up the last of my stuff from the house was hard. Michael and I have been through so much together. When I was leaving, I drove to the end of the driveway, stopped, backed up, kissed him one more time and told him I loved him. Said good-bye.

APRIL 18, 1980
25,000 feet above the earth, Delta Flight 856
On my way to Kansas City. Alone and okay! Had a great talk with Kay when she came over to take me to the airport. I told her I felt like she was the only sane person I know. That is: She is the only person who thinks reality is what I think reality is.

Talking to the men who say they love me makes me feel fragile and feebleminded! Like I don't know what I'm doing unless they tell me, but that isn't true!

Kay says my lover feels powerless because now I am freer than he is. Because now I don't have to be the one who gets up to go home, he does! This is too complicated. I promise to write more tonight.

APRIL 19, 1980
Kansas City
Have done my first presentation in Kansas and been asked to come to Oklahoma to talk to Indians and to Nashville to talk to black folks and to San Antonio just to visit. It is exhausting, exciting, interesting. I've made several interesting contacts here. I just went for a walk with two women and we

talked and talked and talked. Atlanta seems far away. Figuring out the boys seems less important.

My life seems clearer. My eyes can see! I feel better!

APRIL 20, 1980
6:20 a.m.
Went to bed last night at 7:00 p.m. I slept until 8:00, got up, put on my nightgown and went back to sleep. It was really good for me to come here. My relationships in Atlanta are so intense. This has been a good break. A brief respite; leaving today. Life in the fast lane!

APRIL 21, 1980
The day started on an up note. Got Deig off to school and marveled again at how easy the mornings are here with just us. She wakes up of her own accord around 6:30 a.m. We B.S. around, bathe, eat, talk, dress and saunter out the door by 8:10. Now I am waiting for my laundry to dry. Kay and I were drinking wine last night and talking. She said she and June were walking down the street and a redneck guy hooted something suggestive at them and she spontaneously screamed: "Get away from us, you suck bag dog!" We decide it is a perfect

297

feminist taunt.

Still processing the conference. So many different kinds of women. A Chinese-American woman says she and her friends are worried about "raising bananas." That is their equivalent of Oreos for us! The Latina said they call them "coconuts, brown on the outside, white on the inside." It made a great connection between all of us. Nobody respects the people in their group who are just trying to be white folks.

Anita and I had a drink at the airport before we caught our respective planes. She ordered: "red on the rocks." I thought that was cool. Straight Scotch is such a world-weary thing for a woman to order.

I have been working. Completed a treatment for a screenplay and started on another. I had a real breakthrough thought today that makes for a lot more freedom in my work. I think some of it is due to reading about Georgia O'Keeffe. The thing is, I had gotten the priorities fucked up. I can write what occurs to me and if it sells, fine. If not, maybe the next one will. I don't have to merge the creative process and the commercial one. All the creative stuff ain't commercial and all the commercial stuff ain't creative. I feel that I should have known that all along. I am discovering so much. Is

Georgia O'Keeffe an inspiration to everyone who reads about or knows about her, or is she talking just to me?

The true things are becoming clearer to me. My work is opening like a flower.

APRIL 29, 1980
Georgia O'Keeffe wrote a friend to say she wanted more than anything for Steiglitz to like something she did. She began her real work at twenty-seven! That is comforting. I also like the photos of her at fifty-six, seventy-five, eighty-one. She looks so secure. I want that kind of security. That kind of confidence in my own path.

MAY 1, 1980, MAY DAY
There are signs all over town that say: TAKE HISTORY INTO OUR OWN HANDS!!

MAY 5, 1980
Kris calls to tell me that they have bombed the Iranian embassy in London. Killing the Arabs, the Iranians and anybody else around the area. After we hang up, Ma calls to tell me that the cancer has spread. She needs a specialist now and they will go into Detroit on Wednesday to have tests and more cutting. She sounded strained, but resigned. "I

299

have had so many breaks," she said. "I don't expect any more." And she says: "I am trying to live one day at a time." And I tell her that I will come and she says I don't need to. "Not yet," she says, "you don't need to come yet."

MAY 13, 1980

Dear Daddy,

It dawned on me when we were talking yesterday that you haven't seen the recent changes in the novel stuff. It is all changed around. The characters that I know the best and the ones I am most interested in dealing with are the women, so I have changed them a bit. Now both are black, and I'm looking at them. I did a film treatment with them and have been working on dialogues between them (as well as assorted male figures) trying to get to know them better, trying to get them to talk naturally. I think that the other story I was thinking about has some real dangers for me. One is that I will be scrambling around trying to be Richard Wright and the other is that I think I have a lot more new and weird things to say about men and women and the stuff between them than

I do about white folks and black folks. Both problems seem fairly unsolvable to me. Alas! I always thought true love solved it all . . . but the men and women stuff is complex enough without the race overlay that I was trying to give it. Anyhow, I want to send you some stuff so you can see some of my writing. It also dawned on me that you haven't seen anything really but columns and poetry for a long time, maybe ever, and I want you to see some of the newer stuff. It is really strange for me personally right through here. All of the things I thought about writing (like: if you have more time, you write more and better and less inhibited stuff, etc.), they're all true! That is a real relief. Think how depressing it would have been for me to have been spouting all that stuff and then jump out here and find that it ain't true at all! That I do my best work in the midst of confusion and crying and being distracted and depressed. I didn't think there was much chance of that, but it is always a possibility until you see that it isn't true.

What else? I'm also sending you the treatment for the film with those female characters in it. Hope all of this doesn't send you screaming out the door. I have no idea if there is an audience for whatever this thing will turn out to be or if it is really a novel or a screenplay without the pictures, but I think it is dragging me somewhere more interesting than where I was, so I am not complaining.

Consider this: There is a musical on Broadway called *Reggae.* It didn't do too well with critics and stuff the first week so the Rastas who were in the cast started marching around outside the theater with signs that said, "The Power of Jah Will Not Let *Reggae* Close!" Is New York a weird place or what? I miss you a lot. Let me know what you think about my stuff. Should I go back and get a Ph.D. after all? (Ha!)

Love, Pearl

MAY 14, 1980
One of the things about reading Henry Miller is that you begin to think about using all the time you have. About using all the hours of the day as your own. About not going in just because it is nighttime. But there is the problem of company in which to travel. Henry Miller bummed around with drunks and whores and wild artists. He was a large man and unafraid. I am a small woman and

302

terrified.

The music is Pharoah Sanders and brings the memory of The Timbuktu, Market of New Africa, up on Northside Drive, where you could find black books from around the world and where they were always burning incense and playing Pharoah Sanders and Leon Thomas's song "The Creator Has a Master Plan," and Ebon Dooley was the owner, but he was really a poet in disguise and sometimes he would stand in the center of a circle of us and read poems. The memory is of that other brother at The Timbuktu with his hair curling out under his skullcap and his dashiki and the rumors about how badly he treated his wife. And the memory is of Skunder the painter and when he put that bead in his beard and all the guys we knew showed up at the next gathering with beads in their beards. The memory is of Marion Brown the jazz guy and his young wife who was in *Jet* wearing a leopard bikini and who obviously loved him so much but didn't have a clue to what was in his mind. The memory is of going down to their basement in New Haven and seeing Marion's handmade instrument there and Karen asking him to show her how it worked and he did. Found percussion. The music is Pharoah Sanders and Chestnut Street and Karen and A.B. coming by to pick us up for the movies and Karen saying: "That's not a pork chop you're eating, is it?" since all my revolutionary friends have given up the pig. And A.B.'s poem that says: "And Neal/he's so beautiful/I wanted him to shine in the room."

And the memory of all the lovers since. And all the poems since. And all the truths and all the lies and all the change and all the dying and the dying, but the music sounds just the same. Almost. Except I can hear more of it now. I am able to hear more of it. Now.

MAY 29, 1980

The radio news tells me that Vernon Jordan walking from his motel to a meeting has been shot twice in the stomach and is in critical condition. The morning paper carries a column about a Japanese play at the Spoleto Festival that is so dehumanizing and brutal that the reviewer was afraid of it. I don't know quite what to do with any of this information.

JUNE 5, 1980

I have just discovered the only advantage to freelancing. You get to be stoned while you earn a living. Unfortunately, that is also true of rock and roll stars, actors who are lucky enough to be cast in Robert Altman films, Rastafarians, and particularly foolhardy circus performers. I think it also applies to the construction crews that do most of the renovations that I know about. It also applies to artists of all kinds, but since I was talking about freelancing, which is a way of making money, let's leave the art out of it, shall we?

JULY 9, 1980

Dispatch from the PR World:

"Shorty the Clown holding for you on line three," says the receptionist, and Debra, who picks up immediately, is thrilled to find that he brings his own ponies. She is in charge of special events and ponies seem to be a critical element of this one. On line two, a very sugary southern lady on the other end of the phone in "Chall-ston" is fretful about giving me the name of the Junior League president because all she has is the woman's first and last names. She can't locate the president's husband's initials, which is how these ladies like to be

305

addressed, as in: Mrs. H. R. Haldeman, Mrs. R. M. Nixon, etc. I am the freelance nomad, drifting from desk to desk, project to project, client to client. It's cool, cuz it pays my rent. A drag, but the road to self-sufficiency is uphill!

AUGUST 5, 1980
I had another Richard Pryor dream last night. I was in a car in a parking lot, underground like in *All the President's Men,* and he was there. And I saw him and leaned way out of the car to wave and he waved and I cupped my hands and called out "I love you!" And he cupped his hands and called out "I love you, too!" and I tried to get back to where he was to say something else, but couldn't get to him. And I kept hollering things and he kept hollering things, but we couldn't get the car and him and me together.

AUGUST 26, 1980
Polish workers stood in line during the strike to get copies of poetry written about the protest!

SEPTEMBER 4, 1980
Ran into Pat Conroy outside of the Midnight Sun restaurant in Peachtree Center.

He kissed my cheek and held my hand and took my number.

SEPTEMBER 24, 1980
This is what I wanna know: How do you get the people you love and the people who love you to leave you alone long enough to write a book?

OCTOBER 1, 1980
Great call from Daddy. At the end of the conversation, he said: "Well, I've been trying to call you for a week. I'm glad to know you still live there and you're not living in sin." "It's only because everybody I meet is crazy," I say, "and I had one of those already." "There is no time for sinning," he says, laughing. "Time's going too fast. Gotta sin on the run." I agree, laughing, too. "Most of the ones I've met," I say, "on the run is the best way to handle it anyway."

I think that when life is sweet, sometimes it's so sweet I can taste it.

OCTOBER 2, 1980
And what, pray, are you babbling about in your head?

I'm gonna change my vibe. I'm gonna stop being tortured and get mellow. I'm going to vibe everybody to death. I am going to cool out. I am not going to give out no bad vibes and don't want to get none. I am going to leave Mia Farrow and segue nicely into Billie Holiday in her best times. Voluptuous; weird as hell; lovely; womanly; singin' "Miss Brown to You." Not a junkie though. Don't wanna be a junkie, but I'm tired of being Little Miss Misery. I'm reading Daddy King's book and it makes me feel like a self-indulgent asshole. He has been up against the primary shit all his life and his kids got killed and his wife got her brains blown out in church by a fiend and he is still talking shit. After I drive him to a taping of a political spot at a recording studio with orange shag carpet on the walls, he asks me to take him to the jewelry store so he can have a ring appraised that was given to him, he tells me, by a white man who admired his son. I wait in the car and he comes back to tell me it is worth more than four hundred dollars. He is very pleased, but it is slightly embarrassing for me. I don't know why except you expect Martin Luther King's father to be extra-special and have no human traits or monetary desires. I don't know. I remember him talking about his wife as I was driving him home and how much he missed her and still thought about her. He said that he believes they will be

308

together in heaven, and they probably will. In whatever spirit place heaven is, I think true hearts are joined there for always. Praise the lord!

OCTOBER 9, 1980

Last night, 11:30 p.m. I am curled up on the couch, reading about ol' Richard Pryor again and feeling protective and depressed and afraid for him. Knowing what he means about having no self-image. About feeling like he was a piece of shit, and knowing he can't get out of the mess he's in with the people he's got around him. Stuff about being taken advantage of by people who are supposed to be handling his affairs. He asserts his newfound self by buying a two-hundred-thousand-dollar Rolls Royce. But back to the story at hand. The phone rings. I pick it up and it's Coretta King! She wants me to work with her on a slide show. She's been looking for me, she says. She wants me to come see her at the King Center. Amazing. I have just finished reading the Daddy King bio, which was so good, and now she calls me, out of the blue. Only in Atlanta. My first job when I got here was working for her so we've come full circle. "Can you do it?" she said. Of course, I told her, I would be honored.

OCTOBER 10, 1980

I just finished reading the morning paper and this is what I read:

- Another child's body found in Atlanta; still no suspect in custody.
- Someone in Buffalo, New York, killed four black men last month by shooting them in the head with a .22. This month, two black cab drivers have had their hearts cut out by someone.
- Fans rioted at a rock concert by Black Sabbath because the band left the stage after a bottle hit the bass player.
- *Dressed to Kill* is showing for one buck at the Garden Hills Cinema.

It depresses me.

It scares me.

It makes me feel bad about people.

It makes me feel scared for Deignan.

It makes me want to have the people I love around me all the time.

It makes me want the fucking president to go on TV and confess that things are fucked up and help us get out of it.

It makes me wish somebody was in charge.

Where are the adults?

The Honorable Maynard Jackson
City Hall/Office of the Mayor

Dear Maynard,

This is not an alarmist letter, but it is as straight as I can make it because I think you are doing some things that are dangerous for you and for what you are trying to do, and what you have done. I watched you yesterday talking to your staff, listening briefly to the two women who came to talk about Halloween, and then through your news conference and it frightened me to watch you and to listen to you. You are thinking in a fragmented way, and you are talking in a fragmented way. There is not always a logical sequence in the statements that you are making. There is not always a flow of one thought to the other. There is a jump from one thing to another with what you are saying determined only by the racing of your mind. You are not completing thoughts, ideas, sentences, positions. You are trying to say too much and often the result is that what you do say is confusing, disjointed and unimpressive. You are acting in a way that does not reflect who you are and what

311

you are and what you believe.

Yesterday, when you invited the two women who came to City Hall without an appointment into your office to talk about their problems, you made them feel great. They knew you had interrupted a meeting with your staff in the middle of a busy, stressful day to talk with them as soon as they arrived. They began with praise for your handling of the situation at Bowen Homes and then moved on to their suggestions. Almost immediately, you began to busy yourself with things on your desk, jotting down notes (which did not seem to have any connection to their suggestions), shifting papers, taking a phone call and finally, excusing yourself and leaving the room abruptly when the woman speaking was in the middle of a sentence. As you closed the door to go into your assistant's office, the faces of the two women were embarrassed; ashamed of themselves; angry; disappointed. They felt as if they had intruded and were very much out of place. Your staff was also embarrassed, but began to draw the women out and speak with them about the problem for which they were seeking your assistance. The women talked for a few minutes and then rose to leave. As Walter Huntley saw them to the door of your office, one of them said: "We hope you will thank the mayor for the time he spent . . ." Then she paused and the look on her face was proud, but very bitter. "Well, for the half minute he spent with us." A situation where people wanted to talk to you; wanted to touch you; wanted you to help them in a very real way, ends with the women feeling that you didn't have five minutes to talk with them. Of course, the telephone call was important, but so were those women, and you never explained to them why you had to leave the room, or why the call took precedence, or what you were looking for on your desk. Your distracted air changed their attitude into one that does not draw them to you, but increased their alienation from you.

I have no right to say any of this to you. I don't work for you anymore, but I was so worried when I heard you on the radio that I had to tell you how it sounded to me just driving down the street. I was even more worried when I left City Hall so I figured I would try to tell you how it felt to me and you can evaluate what I say from the position of knowing me well and knowing, I hope, my support for your work, and for you, and trusting my loyalty. But I think the people are winning who want to surround you with so many details and so much bureaucracy that you couldn't be the man that people — especially black people! — identified with, and trusted, and looked to for leadership.

Maybe that is too paranoid a theory. Maybe there is no plot on the part of anyone to distract you. Maybe it is just the job. Maybe the system is set up such that it manages to crush the kind of idealism and energy and commitment that you brought into office with you and that I didn't see anywhere around yesterday.

Maynard, I don't know what to suggest. I don't know what your plans and outlines are for the last months of your administration, but I think that unless you can take back your own heart, and your own thoughts and your own instincts and your own mind from the thousands of details and priorities that seem to be jerking you in one direction or another, you will not be pleased with these last months.

Who do you trust? Who do you talk to

about how you feel trying to juggle a thousand things and never getting to finish any of them? We talked briefly yesterday about political families. Who do you talk to about the stress of trying to do your job and also be more than a remote, distracted presence for the people you love?

I don't know if it is good judgment or craziness for me to send this letter to you, but I hope I have the nerve to send it. I wished yesterday when the two of us were talking that I had been the woman I am now when I came to work with you and for you in 1973. I could have been more help than I was, but there is no way to go back to all that. I am who I am now, and you are who you have come to be, and both of us have some edges that we didn't have in 1973 when we were sitting in City Hall Annex, planning your inauguration as the city's first black mayor. I have no real idea of what I can do to help you now, but I think that one of the awful things that happens to "the first black . . ." is the isolation from everyone; the jealousy; the mistrust; the incredibly high expectations of black folks; the hostility of white folks . . . all of the things that separate

315

you from people you trust so you can't find a way to relax and talk about your own reality. And I think that as you stop having the time, or the trust, to really talk to people, people stop really talking to you, even the ones who really care. We begin to talk to each other about you. "How's Maynard doing?" "What do you think about how Maynard's handling this or that?" "Have you talked to Maynard?" We want progress reports, once removed because it is too difficult, or too painful, or too something for us to talk to you.

I'm a writer and I tend to cry and fumble when I try to talk to you about the things that are the most important to me. I seem to have a habit of doing that in your office that I can't quite break! So take this letter for what it is; a communique from someone who cares about you.

Pearl

OCTOBER 20, 1980
Maynard called yesterday in response to my letter. He tried to be disappointed, hurt, funky. I was glad he called. I felt focused, not guilty. He said my letter was this and that, this and that. I said: "I wrote it to get

your attention and I did that, didn't I?" He
had to laugh. "Yes," he said, "you sure did
that."

NOVEMBER 4, 1980
And I find this under my door this morning:

> To: Pearl Cleage, Apt. 14009
> From: Peachtree North Apartments
>   Management
> Subject: Rent Reminder
>
> This is to advise you that you have until
> November 5, 1980, to pay your Novem-
> ber's rent without being charged a $25
> late fee.
>   We appreciate your assistance and co-
> operation in this matter.
>   Thank you.

I would like to burn the edges of this letter
and send it back. I would like to write:
"Fuck off, bureaucratic dogs!" at the bottom and post it back to their office. In an
effort to be agreeable and invisible, I simply
pay the requested rent. Fuck it.

NOVEMBER 12, 1980
I had my first Dance Unit class tonight and

promptly fell in love with Leslie and her method. The class was very peaceful. All about a new way of thinking about your weight and your bones. I am trained in another way altogether. I am trained to stand upright, body at the ready, almost tense. Leslie is fluid; centering. "Relax," she says, "pull your weight down to your feet like water and then send it out through the faucet feet." I love the sound of that . . . faucet feet! "Neck," she'd say. "Head, neck, shoulders, ribs, pelvis, thigh sockets, knees, ankles and out through the faucet feet." She encouraged us to think of our feet like pancakes. "Spread them out," she said. "Those feet have to ground you." It was very easy; slow and fluid. No pain; no stress. "Send it out through the faucet feet!"

NOVEMBER 17, 1980
I am intoxicated with the last week of my life.

My sister writes from Mississippi and the paper she uses is a rainbow. Pink like the sky from my window at the top; then peach, yellow and fading to green; light blue; violent and pale purple. "Remember," she admonishes me, "no matter how hot the chicken gets, it still takes twenty days to hatch an egg." I can't argue that, although what it has to do with me I'm not exactly sure. Yesterday, Deignan sitting in the car, elbows propped on the seat behind me: "Can we do a play on Thanksgiving?" she says. "Me and Jilo and Ife and Ayanna and Tulani? Can we do a play about pilgrims?" It is so close to my own memories of those holiday pageants and I laugh. "Did I tell you about that?" "About what?" she says. "About how we used to do that," I say. "We used to do plays. Me and your aunt Kris and the cousins." "You did?" She wants details. Subjects; actors; props used and sets. Audience response. Costumes. Of course, I remember everything. Those red print/blue print long-sleeved dresses for one Thanksgiving. They came with matching pinafores and were worn with the requisite knee socks and highly polished Mary Janes. I remember using the stage name "Cora" because when we saw *The Last of the Mohicans,* the heroine shook her blond tresses and declared that was her name. I don't remember us having programs, so I don't know why I needed a stage name, but I had one. I remember Deedee and Barbara and me and Kris would eat dinner (which always included turkey and dressing, homemade biscuits, green beans, corn pudding and cranberry sauce), and go upstairs to practice the show. Deedee even wrote original songs for us to sing.

"Can we do one about the pilgrims?" Deignan says. And I say: "Yes. Who else was there?" "The Indians," she says. "The Indians were there first." "Right," I say. "I know the name of the ship," she says. "What is it?" I say. "The *Mayflower.*" I nod. The *Mayflower,* the *Niña,* the *Pinta,* the *Santa Maria* and the Spanish Armada are my favorite names for ships in history. They're really the only ones I know, except the passenger-filled *Titanic,* but Shelley Winters's presence in the movie of the same name is probably the only reason why, so it probably wouldn't count for the essay question, plus, that was *The Poseidon Adventure* and not the *Titanic* anyway, so what the hell?

What does count? Remembering weather like this one night in Seattle, working on *Bustin' Loose,* standing down there by the cold river, watching stars struggling to be seen above the fake light the movie people have set up all around us and the sound of the water, insistent and unchanging, and too many technicians and machines and exhausted actors, everybody waiting for Richard Pryor to come out of his trailer, and he wouldn't, and we all knew what he was doing in there, and across the river, a line of cars and teenagers watched us and every now and then somebody would scream that we should "get the fuck outta the woods." Blowing their horns, throwing stuff. "This is where they come to fuck," explains Kim. "They're really pissed off that we've taken it over for the night." "If they blow their goddamn horns during a shot, I'm calling the motherfuckin' cops," says the assistant director, but I don't remember if he did.

You're getting distracted.

I know. I'm happy. It all counts. I think it all counts.

NOVEMBER 19, 1980

I just re-read some of my journal from this day a year ago. I was sitting in L'Ermitage, eating cheesecake, smoking dope, mind full of champagne at the Polo Lounge, limos to the airport, movies. All that bullshit, but I thought I was flying. Talking about feeling free. An *Esquire* article about women having affairs with married men says women always feel the men open us up and we open them up. We believe their wives drag them down with small babies and loving arms and the very things we offer any husband we ever have.

NOVEMBER 23, 1980

It is only 12:20 p.m. and I have the rest of the day to myself. Or, if I want company, it is available. But I want to be alone with my own damn self.

I just had a Ry Cooder attack and had to go get the record of "Down in Hollywood," and put it on. As I carefully removed Puccini from the record player, I realized that the western music psych is so complete that I handle my classical albums (all three of them!) much more carefully than I do my other music. The music I like the most! I throw Springsteen around like a Frisbee and I like him a lot more than *Madame Butterfly.* It is a psych! "Serious music" is more valuable. You gotta have some dignity about handling that music! Don't fling the record around like it was ORDINARY ROCK AND ROLL. My friend calls from the health spa and is pleasantly surprised to find me home. Delighted is the better word. He says: "I just called to tell you like Eddie Kendricks says, I love you so bad." And I just laugh. I didn't even give the required, "I love you, too," in response. I just want to receive.

NOVEMBER 23, 1980

I am rearranging my apartment. When I told

my friend that I had taken down the poster of Romy Schneider, he said good. He was agreeing with my action, but he sounded relieved. Like he hadn't dug it all along or had the right to pass judgment on my progress. Shit. He has nothing to do with it. I just figured I knew what Romy had been trying to tell me. (That is: Feel no guilt and tell the truth.) Now I needed to learn what Georgia O'Keeffe could tell me. How to be an artist and a woman. A woman artist. The poster of O'Keeffe has colors red and green and blue and purple and is an abstract of a labia and vagina. Pussy. A pussy poster. It looks so sweet and mysterious and private and inviting that you just want to lean over and fall into it. It looks spooky and sweet. It looks like a woman and it is so beautiful!

I remember seeing *César and Rosalie,* and Rosalie had gotten pissed off at her two lovers and she is packing to leave the summer house where they are all on vacation. And her mother comes into the room and says: "Rosalie, this is not the answer." And Rosalie, eyes clear as glass and that ol' square Romy Schneider face betraying not the slightly speck of tension or uncertainty, Rosalie turned to her mother, lovely hands suspended in the midst of the task they were performing, and said: "What is the question?" That is as good as that scene in *The Wild One* where somebody asks Marlon Brando's character what he's rebelling against and Brando, in full juvenile delinquent sneer says, "Whatcha got?"

NOVEMBER 26, 1980

I feel terrible. My stomach is one big cramp. My worries about taxes and financial matters are escalating. I feel abandoned after realizing that neither of my lovers is available to me, even in a crisis, because they are married. I don't know what to say about that. I like living the way I'm living, but when I get sick or my funding gets shaky, I feel alone; vulnerable; desperate; frightened; isolated.

DECEMBER 4, 1980
12 a.m.

It's within the first few minutes of December 4 and I don't have to go to bed at all if I don't want to. I went to see Bruce Swartz at the Center for Puppetry Arts and sat there next to Janie and thought of my "puppetplay" in new terms. Felt good. Felt freer. Felt the weight of the Mardi Gras beads around my neck. And it is good.

I think this: I think it is about seeing and feeling all you can. The rest of the shit is just random and you can't control much, but you can BE THERE. You can see and feel and touch what you can. And that, I think, is about it.

There's almost a war in Poland. There's a joint in my ashtray. Food in the kitchen. Bill Withers singing with Grover Washington on the stereo. My child is asleep in the next room. I'm drinking Pernod and eating Cheetos. Did I die and go to heaven?

I am going to New York on Sunday and coming back Monday because the Philip Morris people requested me. Because of the stuff I said about women when their guy was here. They are paying my way up there to talk about WHAT I THINK so they can use it to sell cigarettes. This relationship will never work.

DECEMBER 16, 1980
Approximately four hours after lunching with my first real New York editor. From Harper and Row, no less. This guy wrote me a letter once, three years ago, and asked me if I had any interest in writing a novel. "No," I wrote back. "I'm not writing one." He was at Lippincott then. "Why?" he said. "You should." "I will," I said. Just like that. So a long time later, I sent him some pages. Not good stuff yet, but some pages. Now,

he's in town. I go to lunch with him and he is a bit restrained. I wait with bated breath. So he tells me that I am a good writer, that I "probably have a novel there," but that I should be more "traditional in my form." "Uh, oh!" I said to myself, remembering what I learned at Philip Morris yesterday about not all New York people being bright and creative. I think it also holds true for publishing.

Slow down!

Okay.

What did you learn?

1. I learned that I can articulate why I am doing my book like I am doing it. For example (the best one):

   He says: "you should work in a more traditional form to keep the reader interested."

   I say: "well, the thing is, I don't wanna write that way. It's just boring to me. [I REALLY SAID THAT!] and I want the form to reflect/suggest the subject matter because if," I said, "you write in a traditional novel form you are making the reader anticipate some kind of traditional conflicts and traditional solutions or wrap-ups. I don't wanna do that. I wanna suggest from front to back that all this shit is unknown and weird to me and I don't know the solutions. I sort of just want to raise some of the questions, you know?" He didn't get my drift.

2. I learned that I can't count on white male editors from New York to understand my vibe or appreciate it.
3. That I need an agent.
4. That this is gonna be hard.
5. That I better finish the mutha or no one will know what it's about till it's done.
6. That I better hustle.
7. That I am smarter than a lot of people in publishing, too.

Such arrogance from you! Finish the book, genius!

Okay. I will.

DECEMBER 30, 1980

At dinner with some married couple-friends who are trying not to choose between us now that we are divorced. There was an asshole lawyer there. He got into a long tirade about the status of women and I thought I was gonna have to kill him. Such gems as: Women who get beat sometimes like it. And: A lot of women just want to stay home and take naps instead of working. Yuck! We got into a discussion of *The Story of O* where a woman allows her lover to deposit her at a castle where she is ritualistically spanked and tortured for his sexual satisfaction. By the end, she's walking around naked on a leash, wearing a feathered owl mask on her head. After the conversation moved on, he mutters to me: "You should go to that castle, Pearl." I let it slide. Who wants to talk about a weird S&M fantasy book with a sexist asshole? Such exchanges are not required.

Going there in the first place was just an attempt not to be a recluse. That was a mistake. They ain't my kind of people. The hostess said: "I don't care if people wanna be gay, but why do they have to swish their hips?" Say wha-a-a-at? Boring, backward people. They don't have to worry about choosing. I'm done.

DECEMBER 31, 1980: NEW YEAR'S EVE
Didn't think I'd make it, but here I is, black-eyed peas and collard greens cooking on the stove. Feel good/look good and John and Yoko on the stereo singing "Give Peace a

Chance" on that lil' forty-five record that
Michael bought for me at the Yale Co-op
that summer of 1969 just before we moved
to Atlanta. My, my, my . . . the end of the
first year of the next decade. Ronnie Reagan on the front of *Time* magazine looking,
as Phil Garner said, "Like an old boy, no
good attached." And John dead in front of
the Dakota and, oh, lord, am I ready for
1981?

What it mean?

What it look like?

It mean everything/and nuthin'.

It look like diamonds.

Good-bye, John, take care of yourself.

Good-bye, Henry.

Good-bye, Jean-Paul.

Blessings on Yoko and Simone.

Blessings on Bob Marley and wishes that
he will make it over.

And peace.

And peace.

And peace.

JANUARY 1, 1981
12:02 a.m.

Well. There it is, 1981. I made it. Here's my
list:

1. I want to write more systematically.

329

2. I want to learn to "play to my strengths" professionally.
3. I want to make more money.
4. I want to allow my real persona to come out more.
5. I want to fuck only when I want and be able to still my mind and get off when I do.
6. I want to finish my novel and find a publisher. (This should be number one!)
7. I want to crack public radio (nationally).

JANUARY 5, 1981
My first patron for my solo performance at Nexus! Zaron calls and says he will pay for two hundred invites! That is twenty five dollars! Whoa! I love it! It's funny that we met each other so long ago that night in Princeton and just clicked so easily. Now he's living in Atlanta. When we met, I was married. Now he is! But he can still be a patron. And he is! I feel so-o-o-o-o-o good!

JANUARY 6, 1981
Some notes for the show at Nexus:

1. Reading is PERFORMANCE.
2. The worst thing a performance can

330

be is boring.

3. Being timid leads to rapid, whispery readings and the appearance of confusion.
4. Being timid leads to boredom.
5. The people who know you want you to break out.
6. The people who don't know you want you not to bore them.
7. The people you like to see perform are both energetic and intimate.
8. Being hesitant and embarrassed puts that vibe on the audience. If you're not sure, how can they be sure?
9. Lovers who come to poetry readings are responsible for themselves. You are responsible only for not being boring.
10. You used to be an actress. Play the part. Flirt with them. Pretend. Make them love you.

JANUARY 11, 1981

I am making my goddamn living writing. I am totally insane about how my work is going to look at Nexus. I think I'll be great. Or a geek. One or the other. And I love it all.

Maynard and Valerie Jackson signed on as

patrons for the reading!

The day after the bad day.

Early morning rising to go do TV chatter. Back to help Deig fix herself a tuna sandwich and play a quick fix of Maze singing about "The Look in Your Eye," dash down Peachtree Street. Kiss Deig goodbye at the school door, dash over to the bus stop. Ride down the rest of Peachtree, hop off in front of the doughnut shop, grab a paper to see what Reagan and Haig are up to, ease into my office, close the door. Sigh. It's only eight-thirty. I've had two hours of sleep, several buckets of tears and am trying to disguise both facts with a little blue eye shadow and more attention to my smile.

Sorry doesn't begin to say how afraid I am that nothing will be the same between us after all the confusion. There is nothing to be said or done to make that go any way but how it goes, and my speech about if it gets too weird being with me should probably have a new chorus or something. Promise you will always tell me how you really feel and don't make me guess. I just wanna know . . .

FEBRUARY 2, 1981

Went to dinner at a great new Chinese restaurant. Great food. Talked a little, but enough, and it was easy and relaxed and cool. Then to *Rockers,* which was incredible. All those Rastas and ganja and music and them walking like they are dancing even when they are just walking. My, my, my . . . and Peter Tosh so dangerous, singing about being "a steppin' razor," and he sounds like that is exactly what he is.

I wait until the very end of the credits to see that the soundtrack is available on Island Records and Tape. I will get it! Yes I surely will!

And my apartment is so clean and I feel so clean and so good and so full and so rich and can't think of what better feeling I have had in a while.

Peace and quiet and myself to myself.

"I and I."

Dontchaknow?

FEBRUARY 20, 1981

Some people like to do sit-ups in the morning. I like to have orgasms.

FEBRUARY 24, 1981

Went to see Springsteen last night at the Omni. It was great. He sang for three and a half hours and was pure positive, high energy the whole way. Jumping and singing and playing and holding the mic out front. The crowd sang the entire first verse and chorus of "Hungry Heart" before old Bruce even opened his mouth. Rob went with me and we did great. High as dogs. Drinking beer. I got asked to produce ID to buy a beer. We stood on the chairs and danced and sang and shouted and he had binoculars so we could see the sweat falling off the man. He was working so hard! I watched him and I wanted to change. I wanted to be in charge.

MARCH 5, 1981

Do you know about Christo? An artist who wraps things? Walkways, coast lines. Makes fabric fences that run and flutter for miles? He did one in California. Twenty-four miles long. Just cuz he wanted to see it. Thought it would make people look at their surroundings differently. So he did it. He just did the work and did it to death!

The question is: How much stronger do I have to get before I can be free?

I sound like that guy talking to Don Juan. Impatient and scared. But working on it. Always working on it.

MARCH 10, 1981

Well, how weird can your life be, sweetie?

I am at home, smoking roaches with a sterling silver roach clip and getting ready to work on my story after having deviated from my work plan long enough to write my lover a letter claiming true adoration and the phone rings. It's the mayor. I talk to him for a minute and the upshot is he is coming over here and bringing that writer guy, David Lewis, along for good measure. I have burned a little incense. I have sprayed some Lysol and aired out the place as best I can and changed my clothes into a better set of working clothes: orange tank top, purple sweater, green hospital pants, pink socks, black Chinese shoes and my gambler earrings. It is so bizarre to consider my life sometimes. I can't imagine the mayor coming to call on the wild girl. It will be an adventure. It occurred to me that I don't have to clean up my act to impress the mayor or anybody else.

MARCH 24, 1981

Canned and praised in the same breath. Tuesday morning at work. Took the bus down here and am vibing out on the look of downtown. I am very aware of the amount of makeup on the women. The purple eyelids and slashes of red across the upper cheek. Even the cashier at the coffee shop has on blue shadow up to her eyebrows and Liz Taylor eyeliner. Mascara, too. I'm reading Henry Miller. Thinking about Daddy. Going to write him.

So . . . I got fired from the WSB-TV show in the morning. "Cutting back. Changing format. More news. Blah, blah, blah." Bye, bye. Lester Strong took me to his office and told me. Nice gesture. I said, "Well, let me say this. I want to come and work for you. I am looking for a job. I wanna stop writing ad copy." He freaked. Told me he wanted me to work at WSB. Was agitated because they just filled a job that would have been perfect for me. Said he thought I was "a good person and a smart person and a gentle person" and he had a lot of love for me and wanted to give me a job and teach me to meditate. In that order?

MARCH 27, 1981
Of course I'm still stoned.

It's moving day. I've been carrying Henry Miller around as if he was a talisman to ward off bad spirits. Evil eyes. Boring lives. This morning I moved some critical stuff into my new place. Then I sat down in front of all of it, laid out neatly on my green shawl. Smelled the incense. Listened to the traffic and the occasional bird. And read this:

> . . . No one to whom I can communicate even a fraction of my feelings.
> — *Henry Miller,* Tropic of Cancer

First private time in my new space. I hear how loud the traffic is on Peachtree and I panic. Is it too loud? Is it the wrong apartment? Is it too far/too dear/too little/too old/ too unsafe?

It is my own. This is my own private choice. Yesterday, bringing Deignan here, pressing my palms against her child hands. Rituals for good luck. Long life. And her eyes are round and hopeful as the full moon through my window. This is what I have brought in this first load:

Photographs of my father, my mother, my great-grandmother, my grandparents (both sets), my great-aunts (both), my grandfather on the steps of Dunbar Hospital.

The postcard of Niagara Falls, shimmering with the green and pink of artificial and determined spotlights; manlights.

The doll Kris made of me with rosy nipples and pubic hair. A tiny tuck of a navel.

Madam Walker's product publicity sheet.
Candles. Incense.

A book of photos of Georgia O'Keeffe by
Alfred Stieglitz. I open to the page filled
with her breasts and her legs spread, open,
open, open.

The butterfly book I bought in defiance of
budgets.

A bottle of Amaretto.

A pink depression glass shot glass, an
inspired Xmas present from Ayanna my
middle niece, to her cousin Deignan.

The collage Kris made for me.

My green Mexican shawl from Georgetown.

Four photographs of myself: three in my
Forrest Avenue studio and one from Seattle
that Bruce took. Arms folded; face turned
away.

A flea market music box that plays the Viennese Life Waltz while the ballerina rises
and falls and dips and swirls.

An orange paper lantern from Janie on
the road to the other coast.

A blue plastic frog.

A pair of smiling red satin lips.

A travel clock in the shape of a stack of
gold coins.

A set of photographs of me and Deignan
from the zoo photo machine that gives you

four shots for a quarter.

The quilt Kris made.

A snap of Deig at Sweetwater Creek and me kissing that salmon I caught in Puget Sound.

An envelope of letters to and from my lover.

China Men/Don Juan/On the Road/Anaïs Nin photo supplement.

Toni Morrison's *Newsweek* cover.

"Henry Miller" by Norman Mailer.

A Janie hanging charm.

The San Antonio candle.

The plastic statue of the Black Madonna pointing at her baby that I got at the monastery where the peacocks walk around free, tails and all.

The fishing weight from the Puget Sound fishing trip.

A goat bone from the farm.

A shell from Ossabaw.

Postcards of Christo's *Running Fence,* and Dali's *Woman at the Window.*

Scented soap in blue pleated paper with a flowered seal.

Four perfect joints in my green plastic cigarette case from the twenties that I got with Bill that day in the antique place.

Paper.

And a pen.

It's all perfect.

Welcome home/welcome home/welcome home . . .

APRIL 5, 1981
I have friends in Brazil. Leave everything and come with me now.
— *The Conformist*

Why am I not writing in my journal? Because of paranoia about losing the pages? Because of taking another lover on last night? Don't want to see it written down because of the tawdry factor? He was okay, but talks too much during sex, asking about. "What do you like?" And "Isn't this good?" Also gives directions. He needs to cool out a little, but he's pretty okay. Went to Walter Mittey's and that was nice. Jazz in a basement place makes you feel cool, even when you're not. I think this will be an okay friendship, but not a sexual one.

APRIL 6, 1981
I read last night at Little Five Points pub. I was the last one to read. SUPERSTAR ALERT. Faye First introduced me and she was great. "I knew Pearl first in 1974 when we both worked for Mayor Jackson. She was great to work with and she's a great writer.

She can write anything. Etc." Then she finished up and they applauded and I leaped up on the stage and lowered the mic cuz I was shorter than the other people, especially the tall, slender blond before me who swayed her knee-length (!) hair and sang country love songs about *"my man done me wrong,"* to an audience made up largely of lesbians and bi-sexuals. But now it was my turn and there I was; purple jumpsuit, black turtleneck and my silk scarf thrown around my neck. I sat down on the stool and I said, "Flashback! Flashback! Flashback!" and I played with the word for a while. Then I stopped and read "Blue Lights in the Basement," with waving arms and gestures and all that stuff. Making faces and shit. I was having a ball! And the audience laughed and listened and got real quiet. They had talked all through the other performances. Walking around, talking. But you could hear a fucking pin drop. So I got bold. Told them I was gonna read some other stuff and then did the thing about Kris and the Klan guy giving her a ride; some things about Deig and the missing and murdered kids; and they ate that shit up! Gasping and quiet and laughing and clapping. "I will claim myself for myself . . ." I said, and they really applauded me. It was great! I read with expression. I used my arms. I was a fucking actress. I loved it!

APRIL 13, 1981
Love note that cannot be sent:

    oh my love. i am open as a flower.
    with you i open like a flower.
    i am open like a flower with you.
    i open like a flower with you.

APRIL 18, 1981
A ring around the full moon. Two black cats that disappear when I park my car and pass the spot where they were crouching seconds earlier. The only one left is that haughty black cat with white front feet that refused Deignan's offering of milk this morning, turning up a small feline nose as if the thought of drinking stranger milk was beyond its cat comprehension.

Saw *This Is Elvis.* The whole movie is the anatomy of a descent into madness. It starts with the sweetest-faced, most straightforward, funny, sexy singer and it ends with a stoned, doped out, fat, phony, depressed and distressed superstar. The contrast is startling; depressing; genuine. You realize that he died at forty-two and John Lennon at forty. You think about mortality and choices. You think about freedom and power and love. There is a scene where his wife, Priscilla, is clowning for the home movie camera while he stands by her side grinning and attentive. She is dressed in a black bikini and she is sweet and eyelined to the max and a little chubby and in love. She turns to him, smiling, eyes batting, and throws her arms around his neck with great abandon and confidence and sex and hope and trust. It was really vulnerable and beautiful. At one point later, they show him being driven around in a car by his cronies and he is ripped. They ask him something and he says, "How should I know? I was buried in some beaver." And later he says: "That girl last night gave great head," but he sounds like he's doing it to keep an image. Not that he cares or felt anything. At the end, it seems like he didn't feel anything at all. Like it had all been taken away. He tries to do the monologue in one of his songs and it is just painful to watch. He is fat and sweaty and his eyes are tearing up and it is terrible. At the end, they show him singing "All My Trials," and then he raises his arms to the crowd's applause and he has on this spangled cape and metallic belt and shit and he holds out the ends of the cape like diaphanous blue wings. The boy king ascends. On the wings of a snow white dove.

John Lennon says Yoko is his Don Juan. It took them a long time after they met to get together. That comforts me somehow. I feel that I am in the middle of something good and if I can just be cool, it will all work out. John says when he fell in love with her, he knew it somehow was different from everything. It was, he says, "magnificent."

Do people really change their lives for magnificent love?

APRIL 19, 1981
Went to see *The Postman Always Rings Twice* with Jack Nicholson and Jessica Lange. I think it should have gotten lots more good reviews than it got. It is incredible. It is the best fucking I have ever seen on the screen. Very hot. Very intense. Like real sex. It was like the sex in *Luna.* It was recognizing that sex is sex.

My father says sex is something special, off from the rest of life in a world of its own.

Can I get an amen?

APRIL 20, 1981

Cackling and rackling
Messin' and guessin'
On the job Monday blues.

344

Hype 'em up
Send 'em out
Make 'em shout
On the job early Monday blues.
Don't give a damn
I am what I am
Free heart/free soul
Toss the dice and let 'em roll
Satin shoes and Monday blues.

MAY 5, 1981

High in the afternoon. And Bob Marley on the radio singing about love and sex like one must lead to the other and I know I gotta go.

Gotta leave that man alone.

If he can't be with me, let him do without me.

Drunk and high and it ain't even four o'clock in the afternoon. Tsk, tsk, tsk. Bad girl.

Pawn the ring.

Sell the car.

Fuck the house.

I ain't never goin' home.

MAY 19, 1981
Morning: 7:25 a.m.

Still raining outside. Deig eating her breakfast in the other room as I get ready to jump

into the shower and start the day when Al
Green comes on V103 singing like a dream.
And the last time I heard Al Green was with
you and hearing him now makes me remember.

Don't wanna fuss and whine and thrash
around. Just wanna love you and don't
know how to do that without hurting myself.

Al Green on a rainy morning and my
mind is full of you.

MAY 25, 1981, MEMORIAL DAY
I sit here in a blue dress that makes my eyes
bluer. Music on.

I have read some more Henry Miller. And
some more Marilyn French. I feel like I am
just coming out of a real deep cave. Like I
am just beginning to feel what is what.

I am always so scared I won't write that I
don't write. But it is the fear, not the writing that defeats me. Everything is not a
masterpiece.

MAY 26, 1981

If I could tell you
all the things you do
for me, you would not
believe me. if I could

346

tell you all the ways
you make me feel,
you would not believe me.
if i could tell you
how much i do/
how long i will/
you would not believe me.
so i close my mouth
and hope that you can
feel it through my skin
through my hands through my mouth.
Talkin' to you/talkin' to you/talkin' right to
    you.

MAY 27, 1981

Don Bryan from the Just Us Theater Company just called me and said: "We are considering our next season and we want to know if you have a play we could look at." I told him about "puppetplay" and he was excited about it. He invited me to participate in their support group which raises money, etc. I made it very clear that I'm not really interested in raising money. I wanna be involved on the artistic side. "Fine," he says, "why not come and have drinks with us on Friday at the Country Place?" I say, "Cool, I will." I am so excited! It's happening at last!

MAY 28, 1981

There are lots of "special" activities for kids this summer because somebody is killing kids and nobody knows who or why. They're trying to put kids in organized activities so somebody can keep an eye on them. The question is: How come somebody has to start killing kids before anybody coughs up money to do something good with them? Where was all that money and concern and help when they were dying SLOWLY?

JUNE 9, 1981

I read the *Rolling Stone* wrapup of Bob Marley's career (1945–81) and I am appalled at how light the story is. How far from what it felt like to see him live. I remember promoter Alex Cooley sending me a bouquet of Birds of Paradise and two tickets after I wrote a column where I begged him to bring Marley's tour to Atlanta. And I remember sitting in the first row of the balcony at the Fox, watching Bob singing and dancing and swinging his dreads around and thinking I could fly through the theater and settle gently at his feet. Now he's dead at thirty-six. I am thinking of the money necessary to live. I am thinking of the love necessary to live. I am wondering how my lil' life is going. I am listening/

listening/listening for the phone.

JUNE 12, 1981

My faraway friend calls this morning to say
hello and tell me that he is going to the reggae festival in L.A. this weekend, and how
was I, and did I wanna go to Jamaica for
Sun Splash, the big daddy of all reggae
festivals! And I said I was fine, and I would
love to go to Sun Splash!

"Okay," he says. "We'll go."

It is gonna be another traveling year. That
is good. Time is speeding by so fast. The
buds on these trees outside my window are
opening already. It was eighty-five degrees
here yesterday! And now here come Taste of
Honey on the radio singing a Smokey
Robinson tune. I had a good time at the
play last night, but when I came home, I
wept a tiny weep. Lonesome. The wages of
sin.

Bob calls from a phone booth outside the
A&P to ask if he can come over. "No," I
say. "I have my daughter with me." "What
are you doing?" he says. "I was weeping
when you called last night," I said, laughing
to show it wasn't true when it really was,
"but I'm better today." Weeping for one and
teasing another. He laughs, too. He already
thinks I'm crazy; I might be weeping any-

time. It doesn't occur to him to ask me why.

I feel like there are a million options. It's up to me to pick one.

JUNE 30, 1981
One of the reasons why it felt so safe and comfortable at Linda's party is that there were no men present. A few here and there . . . I think two max at any given time and both ho, hum. So I didn't feel the necessity to play the games. I am letting go of that, too. That is: It is very hard to be around men without playing the old games. I have no new patterns with them. One tells me I have on a pretty dress and I immediately evaluate his potential as a lover. I always do that with almost . . . almost? Don't hedge! With every man I meet. I constantly evaluate them as to lover potential. If they don't fail the test outright and immediately (on the basis of no sexual vibe or they are gay . . .) I begin to play the potential lover games with them. At least now, I am more conscious of it so I can try to deal with it. NO! So I CAN deal with it. I will not continue to do it. I think part of it is thinking I need to take another lover. I don't. I like the one I've got. I don't really need another man in my life so I can stop looking around for them. That is a relief,

too. I've got friends and a lover. Let it go at
that. Okay! DONE!!!

JULY 18, 1981

Dear Pearl,
   When is your performance? Where?
What will it cost you? Will you charge
admission? Don't forget to send us an
invitation!
   I quite agree that Kris and Jilo are
making up all this stuff about going to
Norway and are probably hiding outside
the gas station near Mendenhall! I
thought I'd believe it once they were
actually there, but truthfully? I know
they are not in Braxton, Mississippi, but
I don't know where they are! Maybe in
outer space!
   Kris and Jilo apparently do a lot of
walking. Don't you think it's lovely that
she and Jilo have this big block of time
with just each other? Jilo will be a teen
soon — increasingly preoccupied with
herself and her peers and not much time
or wish to be alone with a parent. I seem
to remember that I was not much aware
of my parents from puberty until I was
about thirty. I just had too many personal involvements with growing up —

and I still had a child-parent relationship with them. I could not talk about what was filling my mind and heart at that time, so we went through the well-established rituals and that was it. But I never could have made it through all my problems without whatever they gave me before I was thirteen or so. (Of course I know, too, that I never would have had some of the problems without whatever they gave me!)

Life is weird!

As for Marilyn French, I agree with you about her style — she needs help! Yes — so much of the book was familiar, I'm sorry to say. Do you know you are the only person I know who can talk about women honestly? Henry and I argue and I think Kris thinks both you and I have read too many "feminist books"! I can't get Henry to write what he thinks, but whenever we all get together, I'm sure he'll say it to you.

Haven't read Susan Sontag, but will. Agree with you that when anyone writes about love it is autobiographical or else it is like Toni M. — PHONY. And it shows every time.

Ernie's girlfriend talked to Hugh and Gladys about Deignan. Said how "articulate" she is and how she has such "poise." Such a "little lady." It made me think long, long thoughts about all my granddaughters and about you and Kris, of course. You always, always want what's good & best & right for your child and as long as you can, you try to arrange life so that that's what they get. But oh so quickly you can't arrange and you do what you can, trying not to do too little or too much but wondering, always — what does this child have? Can she deal with this, whatever is happening to her? Is she ready for this? Will it make her grow? (and that always hurts when it is emotional and intellectual —) or will it make her withdraw and choose the "safe path"? How many women of both kinds do you know?

Anyway, I've known since my first visit to see you in Atlanta that you were "stirring," "fretting," "seething," not settled into whatever mold you were supposed to be in. I could see the mold fit badly but I didn't know why or what to do or even if you knew you were in a pattern that was not you. I didn't know WHO or WHAT you were. I had hardly seen you since you climbed on the train the first time, heading for Howard University. We had left the child-parent relationship and had no other.

Well, you say you've learned A LOT in the last ten years. And I've come to know you as I never did in our whole life. How can you "know" a baby? At least, I never thought I could. Love it, yes. Know it, no. Anyway, I know you now (in spite of having to do it through the mail!) better and in a different way — and I not only love you as I have always, I LIKE you, and if you were not my daughter, I would both like and love you anyway. So there!

A word — all these lovely things you have so recently come by with great difficulty; things like personal, emotional strength and freedom and self-confidence sometimes have another side — at least they did for me, and that's loneliness. But at my loneliest, even now, I wouldn't give up one smidge, even if it meant I could tap dance like Sammy Davis. The applause may make you feel good, but when it's gone and you're by yourself, you have to tap dance anyway because that's all you are.

Best of all in the world is: 1. knowing and liking what you are for real — and 2. loving people, however few. And I think 1. has to come before 2. Or does it?

Love, Ma

PS: I shall burn continuous candles and incense for your reading. More love, Ma

JULY 25, 1981

"And you," my friend says on the phone, "your energy. It's like sticking your hand in an electrical socket."

JULY 27, 1981

Phone rings. I answer with a lighted joint in my hand. An old man's voice says, "Hello?" at the same time I say, "Hello?" He makes a little joke and then I laugh, but I think: Who is this? Then he says something else funny and I realize it is Mr. Polk! I laugh and say, "Mr. Polk!" And he says he was in town and was gonna come to my reading, but he had to get back to Tuskegee. I say, "I knew it was you," and he says, "No you didn't. You thought it was JOHN HENRY."

That cracked me up.

I am going down there in September. "Bring a couple of changes of clothes," he says, "and we'll take a couple of pictures." I laughed, but he was serious, so I will. I'll take my white silk dress and the black-and-white-striped stuff. Angel whites and prison stripes.

Soon come . . .

AUGUST 1, 1981

The Jean Harris Reading went great! At least seventy people came! It was standing room only! Maynard and Valerie came. Zaron came and brought his kids. He was sitting on one of the couches and they lay right down and went to sleep. I wasn't even nervous. I felt calm. I felt like I had something to say and a place to say it. I want to remember everything about this so I can do it again!

AUGUST 9, 1981
Montego Bay, Jamaica

(Trying to light a joint in the wind makes me appreciate the stillness more.)

We went there for the reggae. Pulse beating in time to Family Man's bass. Jah Rastafari! I and I. Haile I Selassie I. We went there to listen and try and touch something. There are so many soldiers in and around the stadium, but when the lights go out temporarily, a voice near where we are sitting, cries: "Turn on the lights, mon! The pickpockets are at work!"

(The wind is so high, it threatens to blow

this joint out of my hand.)

Alone in Montego Bay. Smoking dope rolled in Tampax papers. Staring at the ocean. Not pregnant. Ain't got cancer and moving up on that magic number.

(The wind is whistling through the palm trees. I am momentarily startled by the sound of it and by the bellhop and a guest walking by close enough to smell what I am smoking.)

I realize my eyes are swollen from the a.m. weep. A boy rides by me on a two-wheeled bike, or does he disappear and the bike become a turquoise motorcycle? Honda, probably. With enough chest to make it macho and enough speed to make it dangerous.

(I am inattentive. Seduced by my own words on paper and the possibilities inherent in the vanishing bike rider. The wind whistles and blows out the joint.)

I feel different. I am out. In another country. With my own passport. Bob Marley's face and music are everywhere.

We came here for the reggae and they give it to us from 10:00 p.m. until 7:00 a.m., but we woke up to the sound of Miles Davis from the room next door and he laughed. "L.A. Rastas playing Miles," he says and names the tune: "Back Seat Betty." I remember that picture of Betty Carter with black leather hip boots and studded black leather belt and parted teeth and feverish eyes. I wonder if that was what Miles liked about her first. Her teeth and her eyes. The water is so blue I feel like I can fly. I think I can keep up an airplane with the power of the beating of my own wild heart. Such is the power of freedom.

AUGUST 18, 1981
David called me today and wanted me to do some work for the campaign. I agreed in exchange for two tickets to see Miles Davis at the Civic Center. But I went over to the campaign office and it made me feel awful. Uptight. Terrible. Repressed. Distressed. Can't handle it. So, I won't. Miles won't miss me.

AUGUST 20, 1981
I am reading May Sarton, trying to get to Mary Daly and wondering what the fuck is different now than it was in 1979. I am still lonesome. I don't know anything. I feel good in a way and crazy in a way and desperate in a way and pressed in a way and free in a way and all of them together in my head. Drinking Pernod and it's upsetting my tummy. Wanting to smoke a joint and

wanting to be held and wanting some good love/good love/good love.

Is this what the jazz guys mean when they say "nothing changes but the changes?"

AUGUST 25, 1981

Marched into her office, yes I did! And said: "I can't stand it. I gotta go. I'll stay till the end of September, but sorry, nothing personal, but I gotta go." I quit that job! Gave notice. She wouldn't hear it. "You can't!" she said. "We'll lose the account if you do." I didn't cry. "I can't be a straight person," I said. "I can't do it." And I left the meeting. Split immediately. Came home. Took a shower. Changed clothes. Went to an interview for another job that won't drive me crazy and crossed my fingers. I hope they will hire me, but even if they don't, I feel so good. I feel better. I feel freer.

I sat in there and looked at my boss and I said to myself: "You don't have to do this/be here/take this. You can split!" And I did.

SEPTEMBER 3, 1981

"You crazy, girl," said my soon-to-be lover. "Look at that shit you got on your wall!"

"Yeah," I might have said. "Crazy like a fox . . ."

Dear Pearl,

Part 1 — Skip this part if you faint when other people describe their medical problems. I would not inflict it on you but I don't want you to hear it from other people.

They decided against surgery when the last X-ray showed cancer in both lungs, just like before. Dr. Vaugh said considering the total lung space, involvement is very small and we have lots of time to work on it. The problem is to find the specific drug that will destroy this particular kind of cancer. There never was a choice between surgery and chemotherapy. The choice was surgery followed by chemotherapy or just chemotherapy. You never know where the little devil cells are hiding! Surgery would just have removed the ones we know about. Hopefully, they are the only ones, but you just don't know. Methods of diagnosis are not good enough to provide complete information.

So, we're on to the new chemo. For this medication, they insert a small plastic tube in a vein in your arm and attach a small pump to it. For five days

360

the medication is pumped into the vein all day and all night. The pump is powered by a little battery. Once I got used to the idea, the arrangement was not bad. Every day, I went to the clinic to have the pump refilled. They warned me that I might be too nauseated to eat for these five days, especially at first. But I had no problem with nausea at all. But by the end of the fourth day, the corners of my mouth had begun to crack and I had a tiny sore on the side of my tongue. So they took away the pump, told me to use Vaseline on my mouth and gave me some stuff like novacaine to rub on the sore on the tongue. Well, I had a time. My body did not like that medicine. I had such a sore tongue, I could neither eat nor TALK! Talk about supreme torture. Of course, I put everything in the blender and drank my meals and I talked anyway, but let me tell you, a tongue lined with sores on each side is a terrible thing. But they're just about gone. Yesterday, I didn't use the blender and am just about back to normal. It wasn't the worst ailment I've ever had, but it was doubly depressing because it was so unexpected. I thought after I escaped the nausea, I'd have five days on the pump and then three weeks at home with no medication. Well, "life is what's happening while you're making other plans," I guess.

How I enjoyed your call last night! So many good things are happening to you! So EAT! Or you won't be able to enjoy them. The creative mind must have energy and vitality and they require FOOD! I hope we can see each other in October. For the first time when you were here last month, I sensed a little of the nature and extent of the real pain you were going through in your marriage. How complicated it all must have been. Everything must have seemed overwhelming many times. I am so sorry I could not be near enough to help. I think I could have. In understanding yourself, you might have known me better and understood that I was still going through the same process and will be, I am convinced, until I die. There is no solution to relationships so complex and so firmly fixed on both sides so early in life. There is only constant struggle to see, to understand, and to make what changes we can, like you have done in your own life and like you trying to communicate to Deignan what you know so

362

she may have a little head start in working out the same problems in her own life.

Don't you wish we were close enough to Kris so that we could have been there to provide support when she came home from Norway? The kind of support that women can give each other in just talking and listening.

All for now. I've been sipping Asti Spumanti all day so I'm full of good advice! Write me when you have time and don't forget to EAT!

Love,
Ma

SEPTEMBER 6, 1981
Saturday. Sitting outside at Spelman with Deignan. She's flapping her arms around and scaring the pigeons. Another perfect Saturday.

Last night, it was fun sitting in Gregory's, drinking Bloody Marys with A.B. and Shirley and Max Roach. I felt good. The lecture A.B. gave was great. It was about jazz and he talked about not being able to find stuff out about the music because the culture won't validate it. He called it "art music." He said there were anti-jazz societies once. He said they turned a cruise ship around once for playing jazz. He talked about Art Tatum. He talked about Charlie Parker. He said think about where they play the music. In clubs! Around gangsters and stuff. He said they demanded to be dealt with as serious artists. The way they dressed. The way they talked. The way they walked and stood, etc. All these things said they were serious. And Max Roach said they used to have to do tricks with their drumsticks and horns because it was expected; demanded by the club owners. *Art music.*

SEPTEMBER 11, 1981

Dear Pearl,
How is everything? We are okay. My mouth is almost back to normal. Finally read the interview with Sontag that you sent. She said some interesting, isolated things, but nothing new and I didn't come away with any overall philosophy. Don't understand why she thinks rock & roll is so great. Maybe it freed her from some of her childhood hangups so she could experience some feelings she didn't know she had. Will have to get some more of her stuff and read it.
How would you like a bald mother? My hair, three-fourths of it, has fallen

out this past week, so Henry and I cut it, thinking less weight and fewer tangles might save some. Can you see me in a wig? Maybe I'll just make a fashion statement and be bald! Weird! All of it, but I am okay!

Love,
Ma

SEPTEMBER 13, 1981
One:
Sunday morning. I have no debt outstanding. No one who has been told one thing when I mean another. No one who can say, "You said . . ." and I will cringe or cry or rail or unplug my phone or anything like that.

Sunday morning and I wanna sing like Chaka Khan, but am satisfied with my apple-cheeked face in the paper this morning instead. "A Fresh Look At the Deep End," they have titled my column. It makes me feel happy to see it. I am a working writer! My ego sighs and settles and I feel generous and serene.

My friend the artist says, "I'll be free in five years and we can be together." I say, "Hey, don't count your chickens. I ain't got five years to be waiting around for you." And he sighs. It is fall and he is wanting to

365

be in love. Me, too.

I put together a dinner for the object of my affections. "Do you think you will love me?" I say and he says, "I already do that," and spills champagne over my chicken and delicately buttered veggies and it was so sweet and funny that I didn't care and he didn't care. He doesn't get embarrassed so I don't have to. That is the best thing. But this is Sunday morning and whatever may be the question, the answer is nuthin' but love/love/love . . .

Two:

Press the roses.

Save the theater stubs.

Take picture in the Five & Dime.

Tie the letters with pink ribbon and save the carbons of the ones you send back.

Record his eyes; his nose; his walking and talking

And fucking and jiving.

Preserve the artifacts.

Construct the evidence.

SEPTEMBER 14, 1981

Deignan dances around me. I have shown her how to make cigar box doll boats for the bathtub and the water is full of Barbies floating facedown. The only two black ones are still dry in the boat. She has taped a

Love Boat sign on the front of it and they are floating around the other dolls, almost kissing. The woman is leaning over the man. He has on a blue fighter's robe and she has on a wrinkled yellow negligee. I think these Barbie dolls are channeling Tennessee Williams.

SEPTEMBER 15, 1981
List the good things:

1. Just Us Theater is going to do my play.
2. I get to interview the big-time playwright when she comes to town.
3. Topper Carew called me yesterday and today about writing a play about Eleanor Roosevelt and Mary McLeod Bethune.
4. My column has started up again.
5. I've got a good idea for a program at Clark College.
6. I'm collaborating with a dance company on a piece of new work.
7. I'm reading my work in Indianapolis in October.
8. Deignan is very cooled out.
9. I am not falling in love with anyone.
10. MY CONFIDENCE IS COMING BACK!!!!!!

I feel so good. I can't think of one fly in the ointment. Now I feel immediate guilt: Ma is so sick. All her hair out and her standing before the mirror saying to herself: "Cool out. Are you your hair? Are you only your hair?"

But that is not me. I am able to help her if she will let me help her, but I am not her. That is not me.

I wanna have my play done. I wanna make some money on my work. I want Janie Geiser to make me a seven-foot puppet.

Yes/yes/yes! Gotta be/wanna be free.

And, yes, he said. I'm free. Married men always say they're free, but they're talking to themselves and we who want to believe them watch them like what they are saying bears any resemblance to the truth. Sounds bitter, but I'm cool.

SEPTEMBER 16, 1981

Dear Pearl,

What a lovely, spirit-lifting, happy-making surprise to find your letter in the mail today! We didn't ask our post office to forward mail because we don't know how long we'll be here, so it was a complete surprise. Loved the Egyptian card — they had some lovely ideas, like painting people they loved and things they loved on the walls of their tombs. Wish I could tuck my Asti Spumanti under my arm and pop over for some quiche. I remember fondly the one you made when I visited you — the only one I've ever had. Read a good book since I saw you, *Sally Hemings* is the name of it. It's in paperback for $3.25. She was Thomas Jefferson's slave and mistress for twenty-plus years. A really good book with real insight into black-white and woman-man relationships. I think you'll like it when you have time. Henry and I bought WIG#1 today. Very conservative and strange, but I still have enough hair not to wear it, so I won't get my "dreadlocks" wig yet! Did Kris tell you Lucius Lomax was hitchhiking from Georgia to Texas? MY GOD! He came walking up the driveway to visit them; stayed the night; and they enjoyed him thoroughly. He made fun of TV just like they did, she said. Next day, he hit the road.

I see the doctor tomorrow. UGH! But so it goes. Will call you. Keep the quiches coming!

Love,
Ma

SEPTEMBER 17, 1981

Got home and found this on my apartment door:

> Your apartment has been sprayed for bugs today. Mews Development Corporation

I wish somebody would tell the goddamn roaches.

SEPTEMBER 19, 1981

I don't care about famous. I don't care about keeping up. I'm still working on trying to remember how it feels to be free. Or learning it for the first time.

The problem with writers is that it ain't real unless it's on the page.

The problem with leaps of faith is, what if nobody catches you?

My daughter and a friend who is staying the night are dressing up in my clothes and giggling at each other. Deignan puts on a dress I bought to go to Martinique and a purple straw hat I got off the street in Colombia. The dress has skinny straps that fall off of her shoulders so she, primly covering her teeny tits, puts on a pseudo silk blouse I bought in Seattle when I'd been wearing jeans and T-shirts for five weeks and was beginning to forget what feminine felt like.

My daughter's friend puts on the dress I got married in. My wedding dress. It is 1969 short and they giggle at how short we used to wear our dresses. I tell them it was terrible. Car seats would burn you in the summer and freeze you in winter and you always had to worry about not bending over too far. They giggle and say "yuck!" I zip up my wedding dress for the little girl and it almost fits her. She is only seven. It doesn't even drag the ground. I laugh. Childbride/childbride/childbride.

I have been in love before. Would like to be in love again. Would like to give it and take it and share it and make it and the good stuff. But I don't and won't do the whole act the same way again. Too hard. Too hard. Too hard. Too hard. No fun. And I mean NO fun. And no freedom. Not necessarily in that order.

SEPTEMBER 27, 1981

Just finished a speech for Hank Aaron. He's gonna deliver it at the Thankful Baptist Church in Rome, Georgia. I love writing for him. An old-fashioned gentleman. The speechwriting fee will cover my rent so I can stop worrying about it. I can light a joint and listen to John Coltrane on WCLK. The lady DJ tells me that the twenty-third was John Coltrane's birthday and I already knew it was Springsteen's, so how wild is that? Pretty wild.

Pieces of plays and columns and sermons and poems are crowding my little head. I feel great. I feel productive. I am getting ready to make a note about the column about Kay's workshop and then hit a lick at "Eleanor and Mary," for Topper. I wish I had time to go to the movies. Maybe later. I am a WORKING writer! Anyhow, sometimes life is so fine/so fine/so fine.

OCTOBER 21, 1981
Indianapolis, Indiana

Impressions, pleez?

Avery smiling and arriving at my friend Michelle's house, lean and grinning and purple silk scarf hanging around his neck, so much energy the scarf seemed to be streaming out behind him; his coat seemed to be blown open even though the air in the house was still and there was no wind/no wind/no wind. Avery at first glance. His eyes catch mine. "Pearl," he says and strides into the room. "Pearl." And I say, "Hey." And we shake hands and grin and lean slightly against that wind and I say, "It's good to meet you," and he says, "It's good to meet you." And Michelle's house is warm with love and we are surrounded by it, drowning in it, leaning in it. And we scatter. The moment is a good thing and a private thing acted in front of our small group who watch and grin right with us.

I feel an incredible charge. I feel relieved that his energy will give me something to work with during the performance. We can trade that energy; an exchange instead of a transfusion. And so the visiting lawyer and his wife go home with their kids. Michelle's stepsons go to bed and we, the four of us — me, Avery, Michelle, Charles — find ourselves facing ourselves and each other in the kitchen. And we drink wine and breathe and grin and I am sitting on the floor leaning against a cabinet and he is sitting on a short three-legged stool across from me and Michelle and Charles are at the table, grinning and tired. We are all tired. We are all in love with the moment and with each other. The love is in the air and almost . . . what? Shimmering? Palpable? A third eye? Something sweet? He grins and I grin and that wind is still around him. And his voice echoes and vibrates through his chest as if it had so much room and was so comfortable there that it just liked the feeling of bouncing and crashing against all sides to make the echo rich and deep and sweet by the time it becomes the audible sound the rest of us hear. And he laughs and I laugh and Charles and Michelle laugh and we all sigh. It is that wind. We are caught in that wind.

We have to decide about the performance space. What chairs and what windows and how about the sound and it is a long discussion with raised voices, and trust me because I asked you to, and at the end for me, a minute of tears and a relief that I can argue any point for long minutes without weeping at all and that is progress. Feeling some guilt about causing confusion but feeling some strength about the defense of my work. Michelle is talking to Charles. I get up for Pernod and Avery follows me. I laugh and realize he is very tall. I hold the Pernod bottle against me and it is cool and feels good and he is on the other side of the refrigerator door and we talk and talk and talk as if there was no one there but us. And he praises my work in a real way and says it is rare and has vision. All the things I think are true and love to hear. All those things he says and smiles and I smile and pour Pernod. And he says, "Are you all right?" And I say, "Yes, I'm just a crier." And he says, "No, I mean about this, about the performance." And I say, "Oh, yes! I am really glad we are doing this. I think it is important." And we babble and agree with each other and grin and the wind is gone and we are in a small space talking softly and the energy between us is enough to make us laugh and give up worrying and just grin. When we sit back down, he says: "About the transition? I thought I would sing 'Ginji.' " I never heard it and neither had Michelle. The men are amazed. It is a song they think is significant. I shrug. So he says, "How about this then?" And he looks at me standing there on that linoleum floor and recites the most beautiful love poem like he was thinking it for the first time. At the end, Michelle is grinning and I am grinning and he says, "Don't you love to feel that way?" and oh, my, my, that wind! And I say, "Of course I do." What kind of question is that? "I thought of that poem after I read your work," he says. "That's the way I felt. I couldn't write you back because your letter said so much. I couldn't write you back and say, well, yes, I know."

The next day we settle all the space things easily. We all respect and love and wanna work with each other so we do and it is good. Moving chairs and changing light bulbs and sitting here and there to see the angle. Dragging the piano around. Being the stagehands. We did it all and then Avery went to see his dad up the road in Gary. Michelle and I went shopping for some stuff and had drinks at a Mexican place where they were playing Grover Washington's "Winelight" in the bar and Joan Armatrading in the ladies room. I was so happy. I am so happy. And we talk and I have money enough to pay and I love paying. It is a good time and the thought of tomorrow being the day of our performance is so good I carry it through the sudden rainstorm and don't give a damn about getting soaked. We are parked in the lot and we are umbrella-less. Looking at the downpour, Michelle says: "I'll meet you at the car!" and we dash out laughing and it is a wet and special time. And we know it.

The next day we rehearse. Me and Avery and somehow he is even taller than the day before. He's wearing suspenders and his *we are working* face. And we are working together. All business. We are writing and pushing and pulling and organizing and I am listening to him recite the passage from *Othello* where the Moor is making his apology for Desdemona loving him. "I am not a man who makes a pretty phrase," Othello says, and then makes the prettiest phrases ever! Avery says the lines like he's been speaking Shakespeare since the cradle. No

376

pretentiousness. No sham. No cute. Just straight and beautiful and that voice rushing around in his chest and his arms graceful in the gestures of the Moor saying, "I didn't drug her. She heard my words and loved me. Here comes the lady. Ask her yourself." And he stops, turns to me and I realize I am sitting there, open-mouthed at how good he is and he grins. I do, too. He is so good and it feels great to be doing this show together.

And then home and dress and shower and eat two eggs for the protein. Walk around the neighborhood to get my mind set. It is cold and I tie my scarf around my ears, looking and feeling like a Russian peasant woman. Not caring. Avery is working at the glass-top table in the dining room. Upstairs, Michelle is playing Frankie Beverly. Downstairs, I can hear Earl Klugh. Oh, yeah. Time to get ready.

And eyeshadow and perfume between my breasts and in the car and off we go; Gregorian chants on the radio at my ear and writing this now I still feel the nervous stomach that says "performance/performance/performance." And maybe lust. And maybe love. And maybe all and all and all . . .

We arrive at the place and hang out at the library and see people arrive in suits and ties and straight faces. And he and I are pacing and waiting and trying to get ready the best way we can and then it's time and lights out and we face each other, hearts beating and grinning and he reaches down and wraps his arms around me and I hold on to his waist and we hug hard and the energy makes me dizzy. I know there is a wind.

And the show became its own moment. At the end of my part, he enters from the back of the room and calls my name once: "Pearl," and then recites that poem he said in the kitchen while he's walking toward me and I look at him and then he sings to me and we reach out and touch hands and it feels great and I feel safe and he is grinning and I am grinning and we run off to the library and we are laughing and laughing and we run to the cold by the windows and he hugs me again and I hug him again and up against his body that close, I realize I am shaking and we are both laughing with relief. My half is over. Intermission . . .

Then his half. And he does the things he does. He swoops that voice and growls that voice and shrieks and moans and teases and plays that voice like a horn. I am sitting in the back with Michelle and we have already had the "god, he's so perfect, too bad he's married" talk so we avoid each other's eyes. She was amazed at how good he was. The people loved him. I watched him and felt like we had been friends forever; working together.

Then it was over and the people applauded and I went up to hug him and he hugged me, too, tucking me under his arm like a buddy and we're both still grinning. And then we do interviews and handshakes and even autographs and we laugh. We are silly with triumph. Charles is grinning now, too. Michelle and I are delirious with the need to jabber about all this; the need to love the men who did it with us; the need to understand that something wonderful just happened. So we grin at each other and they head off to pick up a bottle of celebratory wine. We promise to meet them at the house and dash out into the cold air. In the car, Pharoah Sanders is on the radio just like it was in the morning and before the reading and now again. Of course, it is a tape, but it has become our theme music. And I am rushing around inside my head trying to figure out how I feel. We admit we wish they would come back. We miss their energy already. We need to complete the circle. And so they return, bringing that wind with them, holding it above their heads and they are grinning and dancing in place like it is already New Year's Eve. But Charles forgot Michelle's Coca-Cola and for an Atlanta girl, that is a serious offense, so Avery volunteers that we will go get some Cokes and we rush back out into the night in search of soft drinks and wanting a chance to be alone in a closed space and think about what we have just done and how good it feels. I have on jogging shoes and purple socks and sweat pants and my football pajama top under Michelle's puffy coat and we both have scarves double-wrapped around our necks like tenors. We pass the market as if it wasn't there. Both seeing it, his foot urging the car past it and I just smile. Neither one of us says, "Hey, there's the market." We haven't had a chance to talk yet, but we don't have the words yet, so we just ride for a few minutes and then he turns around and heads back to the market. We get two six-packs so there is no chance of running out again.

As we climb into the car to head back, he says he used to wonder about that wishing and tossing money thing, but he says he would like to make a wish, so he tosses a coin out the window into the parking lot. He holds out a hand full of change and I reach for a coin. "Do you wanna do it while we're riding?" And I say, "Yes." And we ride and I hold the coin close, try to omit the selfish bullshit that is my first thought and focus on what I really want. Him to leave his wife and babies and run off with me to Paris? Him to be suddenly, magically single and we are never parted again? What? I settle on something that puts my fate in the hands of Don Juan: I hope all that is supposed to happen between us is good and has a chance to happen. I blow on the coin like they do in Vegas and toss it out into the Indiana night and he keeps driving. The windows are open and the wind blows across my face and it is Midwest almost winter so we raise the windows and drive.

And we get home and sit down and drink wine and look at each other and don't look at each other and there is so much to say and no way to even begin to say it. I am trying not to think ahead to edge of morning partings. Charles eats a whole tin of smoked oysters. We eat onion dip. Doritos. Pernod. Champagne. Cognac. And we are silly with exhaustion and triumph. Michelle and Charles go to bed finally and we are sitting alone in their kitchen. "I'm going to stay up awhile," I say. "You go on to bed." What am I hoping for? What do I want? Improvisation. Play it by ear. He is exhausted. He is agitated. He paces the kitchen. I sit on the floor, elbows crossed across my knees, my chin on my hands. I am watching him. He is used to people watching him so he doesn't mind. I am wondering what will happen between us. I remember the sound of the coin I threw hitting the sidewalk and bouncing as we turn the wide corner in the Indiana nighttime.

And he says: "What's downstairs? I've never been downstairs." And I say: "A refrigerator. Extra dishes and stuff." "They ought to have a bed," he says and it seems like a sensible idea. "China," I say. "They have china." And he says: "A bed so that if the china falls it will fall on something soft." I watch him but I say nothing. What can I say to that? "I need to lie down," he says. "Go to bed," I say. "I'm gonna stay up." It is 5:30 a.m. We are leaving at 8:00. He looks at me and I look at him and I feel such an energy and such an incredible loneliness and sense of loss and isolation that I just shake my head and smile and he does, too, and then takes the steps up to his room two at a time.

I sit for a while. I figure no more revelations are forthcoming. I am tired, too. Alone here now. Don't wanna be up without company. So nobody did anything dishonorable. That's a good thing. I take the steps, slowly, listening in spite of myself; fall into bed and in what seems like a minute, no more, Michelle is waking me up and I shower and dress and go downstairs and he comes down, too, and we kiss Michelle since she's not going to the airport and we ride, still exhausted. I am crouched between bags on the backseat of their little gray car. At the airport, everybody gets out. Charles walks ahead of me and when I turn to say good-bye to Avery, he grabs me in a hug and bends over to kiss my mouth. "I'm not going to tell you good-bye," he says, "because we're going to see each other again." "Yes," I say and grab my bag from Charles. "Good-bye." I'm glad we're not on the same flight. Don't wanna fly in that much wind.

I am truly exhausted but not grainy-eyed. The flight is fine. The sleep I get aboard the plane is the finest available and I wake up refreshed and ready. The wind in Atlanta is crisp and cold. I take pictures of myself before and after the trip and compare them: Is this what free looks like?

OCTOBER 24, 1981
I feel connected to every person in the world who ever performed a creative act. I feel connected to every person in the world

who ever performed a loving act. I feel connected to every person in the world who ever performed a sexual act. I feel like Picasso on the beach gripping his child's hand. I am a beautiful woman. I am watching *Taxi* with Christopher Lloyd as Jim the Crazo. His father has died. He left Jim money but they won't give it to him on the basis of him being so crazy. His father also leaves him a trunk. Inside, he finds his father's coat, which he puts on a chair like it's a person. It's a big coat so he must have had a fat father! Then in the pocket of the coat, he finds a tape and puts it on and it's Stevie Wonder singing "You are the sunshine of my life." The most beautifully surprised expression comes over Jim's face and he says: "You like Stevie Wonder?" like he has just realized the most amazing thing about his father. He puts the tape recorder on the chair with the coat and lies down beside it to listen to the music with the spirit of his father. Whew. Is there anything better than being an artist?

OCTOBER 25, 1981
Talking mean to myself:

Shut don't go up.
Prices do.

Take my advice
And shut up, too.

OCTOBER 26, 1981

Raining outside and Gil Scott-Heron on my record player and somewhere in town Mick Jagger is tying his sash and shaking his ass and getting ready. I feel like I need a change. A boost. A nudge. I am avoiding the play like the plague. What is the deal there? Scared of finishing? I don't know. But I need/want to finish it and soon I think I will. I have about run out of excuses not to. And it is raining. I love Gil Scott-Heron. I think about that Conrad Aiken poem Ma likes about Senlin standing before the mirror and tying his tie. The whole universe is swirling around him and he stands before the mirror and ties his tie.

I stop to unplug my phone. Is this journal stuff writing? Real writing?

Relax. Rest. Writing when you can. It's about LIVING, not writing. Remember that! It's about LIVING, NOT WRITING!! WRITING IS A PART OF LIVING. LIVING IS NOT A PART OF WRITING. IS THAT A RATIONALIZATION OR A BREAKTHROUGH?

IS THERE A DIFFERENCE?

Dear Neville Brothers,

This is a fan letter. I don't know if you read these yourselves, or if someone reads them for you, but I'm sending it on anyway. Hope it gets to you.

Halloween. I'm standing in the kitchen of a friend and come across your record. Wonder about the burning gator. "Hey," says my friend, "I got a record you need to hear." "What's this?" I say, holding up yours. "That's it," he says, pleased, and puts it on. And I listened and it sounded so much like New Orleans to me and it made me think about the train ride between New Orleans and Atlanta and Lake Pontchartrain at night, hanging over the side of the train and wondering where the tracks were. Walking through the French Quarter at 3:00 a.m. and there's a guy playing a saxophone on the street and I think it must be a movie set, but it's just New Orleans.

Loved your record. Hope some promoter with sense will bring you to Atlanta.

More please.

Pearl Cleage

Sitting on the floor with a glass of Pernod. On hold with AMTRAK. Trying to make a New Orleans connection for February. Yeah! Wanna go find the Neville Brothers. Wanna hang out and drink wine. Wanna eat and drink and write and what? Don't know but I want to travel more. I want to take trips. Got one for Detroit. Got one to Indianapolis. Gotta get to New Orleans. Gotta take control. What do the roaches know? That persistence pays off.

Today a guy I had just met recently said: "Have you ever made love to a woman?" The fool is trying to hit on me and he asks me if I'm gay! I should have said: "No. Have you?"

Columns Hotel
3811 St. Charles Avenue
New Orleans, LA, 70115

Dear Sir/Ms:
I have stayed at your hotel twice and I like it a great deal. I would like to reserve a room for two weeks in February 1982. The dates I would like to reserve are February 8 through February 20. Since I will be staying for an extended period,

387

I would like to request the large room which is at your immediate right when you come in the front door. It is a large room with a fireplace, two double beds, lots of windows, a large bathroom and a tub with claw feet. Please let me know if I can reserve this particular room. I have stayed in other rooms of the hotel and this is the only one in which I want to spend two weeks. Can you make sure that room is available during that time for me?

Also, please send current rates and I will send deposit, etc.

Sincerely,
Pearl Cleage
Atlanta, GA

NOVEMBER 3, 1981

Dear Pearl,

Got your letter. I wish — how I wish! — that the twenty-first to the twenty-ninth would be good. Actually, it seems it would be the worst if I follow the same pattern as last time. For the week I was on the pump, I just got a little more tired each day. But everything fell on me the week after the medicine, this past week, and I didn't feel human until Sunday when I felt some energy returning and my mouth had calmed down so I could eat something other than liquids.

They are still trying to adjust the dosage. Less this time, but I still react. I am trying to hang in there with this dosage because it is unpleasant but bearable. I just sort of drag around not talking because my mouth is sore. Not eating either, just hanging in there, and that's the way it would be the week you'd be here. I don't need waiting on — I cook and wash clothes and go for a walk, but I'm not what you'd call outgoing. I'm just "laying me down . . . to rise and fight again!" So don't make it that week.

The horrible thing is they might lower the dose again and I might not react, but I don't want them to because it might not be as effective at this dosage. Because it affects me doesn't mean it's also affecting the cancer cells, in which case, I'd be on another medication and I don't know what it would do.

So, there I am: nowhere. And I would be truly depressed if you were here and I were curled up in a corner (dark) in a Martha Graham sack, head and all else inside. Another time will present itself, and it's a lovely thought that you might have come.

We are okay. I am sewing doll clothes for the kids. I plan to make Deignan a robe, too! Don't tell me she has robes! I'm sure she has. I just want to make her one.

Miss you! Love you! Weep (truly!) because your visit can't be this time, but as Scarlett would say, "Tomorrow is another day."

Love,
Ma

NOVEMBER 5, 1981

I feel great. Productive meetings. Deignan cooled out. Went to see a great movie about Betty Carter. Feel my perspective on things returning. Beautiful half-moon glowing gold in the sky. I told a student today: "You shouldn't be so hard on yourself. Praise yourself as much as you fuss at yourself." And I could have been talking to myself. And I was. And I will.

NOVEMBER 8, 1981

Just saw *Body Heat.* People have been telling me to see it for weeks. When it first opened, almost everybody I knew gave me a meaningful look and said: "You ought to go see *Body Heat,*" with emphasis on the "you." So, of course, I didn't go. I was not going to indulge their ideas about who or what I was in such an intimate area. I refused to join the line of people outside the Tower Place Theaters who stepped up boldly and said, "Two for *Body Heat!*" I settled for reruns at the Silver Screen and an occasional midnight concert movie. But in the back of my head, I imagined moving pictures of white movie stars on the wild; fucking and killing their way through an August too hot to remember. I thought it would be a combination of *The Great Gatsby* and *The Postman Always Rings Twice* (1980 version), but it's not. I can see why people like it. I can see why I like it. The problem is the movie continues a grand old American tradition. Whenever anybody is sexually obsessed with somebody else, they have to pay for it. Of course, Mattie doesn't pay, but that is only because she gets to bring in the equally potent myth of the devil woman. Plus, she isn't really obsessed anyway. He is. But I object to the basic premise. Why must obsession/erotic passion/a willingness to drive long distances and take a few risks of discovery in exchange for incredible sex always pay off in death and disaster? Where are the movies where the sexually obsessed live happily ever after, rushing home from work to fuck themselves silly? Or taking long lunch hours at motels near their offices? Where are the movies where the sexually obsessed confess to the husband and/or wife, give up the money, and fuck happily ever after, living as middle-class people, but subsisting on a diet of pleasure alone? Where are the movies where they spend their old age fondling and remembering their twenties and thirties and forties and fifties?

HOW COME SEXUAL OBSESSION IS ALWAYS A CAPITAL CRIME?

NOVEMBER 9, 1981
I would like to have enough money to rent a place without roaches.

NOVEMBER 13, 1981
Friday the thirteenth. Grace Jones is doing a show at the Fox Theater. I'm at the Pleasant Peasant, eating alone, stoned and feeling great. Drinking Bloody Marys like there's no tomorrow. And then walking down Peachtree Street to the Fox for the show. She is wild. She is an artist. Great set. She opens the show singing "Nightclubbing" in an ape suit with a gold tutu! And those red Japanese hats and those spike heels and those cheekbones.

She ain't singin'.
She's reciting her shit like a poet.
She can't sing.
She got no voice.
She got nerve.

NOVEMBER 15, 1981
Sunday nights are the worst. Rolling joints the size of cigars and still can't get high.

NOVEMBER 25, 1981
Well, Don Juan, the path has led me here. Wednesday afternoon. Listening to *Hair* on my record player. My lover coming later. My job quit. Finis. No more. Done. Don't have to deal with it anymore. End of the road. Yeah!

Had one thing hanging over me. Called and canceled it. Oh, yeah! It is all so easy.

And/and/and . . .

Playing "Age of Aquarius" as my first fully free music. Remember Michael leaving my room at Yale and hearing it playing in one of the other dorms. I thought it was for him, but it was for me. Last year, playing John and Yoko and wishing I was anyplace but where I was and who I was and forcing myself to feel it so I wouldn't have to feel it again. So I wouldn't have to do it again. And now. Oh, lord! Oh, lord! And now. I have a proposal in at Harvard. One in to Indiana and one to Detroit. Two teaching jobs and a lover. And I say to myself, why does anybody ever have to know about anything? And the answers are clear, but not necessary. Nothing is wrong. Everything is right. Don't hafta freelance. Don't have to do a damn thing! Yeah/yeah/yeah.

NOVEMBER 27, 1981 (LETTER TO A WOUNDED COMRADE. . .)

Night after Thanksgiving Day. And the question is: What are you doing in the hospital? But you are, so here is the report from my side of the outside world:

It's raining, but the air is very soft outside. My daughter is curled up like a cat watching *The Dukes of Hazzard.* I am trying to figure out what you are doing in the hospital. I'm trying to think of what to bring you to make you feel better. And on the phone you say: "I've gotta shift now. This tube . . . there is a tube in my chest." And you say: "My lung collapsed." And you make a joke about it. But later you say: "Too bad you can't come tonight," and I know how I would feel, alone in the hospital with tubes and wanting to smoke and scared to smoke and so broke and holidays and birthdays and I wish I could come tonight, too. But my daughter is yawning at the exertions of Luke or Bo or whoever the Duke boys are and it is too late to leave her here alone. But I can see you there in a room with somebody you don't know and it is raining, even if the air is soft, and it is the Friday night after Thanksgiving. And so I am writing to you because I can't be there. Because I'm thinking about you. Wondering what to bring you that will make you feel better. Here is what I have decided to bring:

1. The postcard. The thing on the back says it is called "The Dance of Life." I can't figure it out. Is he jumping or flying or falling? And what's the dif? Anyway, I like the picture and hope it doesn't strike you as morbid.

2. The book. Don't know if you saw the movie, but the book is great. Really good, fast writing. Like a good magazine article that goes on and on. No novelist extra stuff. Just the people and what happened to 'em. Wrote a column about it and in case you didn't see it, enclosed it, too. I try to make a case for wildness. I always try to make a case for wildness because it is comfortable.

Talking to myself that way, I mean. Trying to convince myself that it really is Paris if you just concentrate. Anyway, I like the book and thought it might distract you for a while.

3. The disgusting smiley face. Just to keep you aware of the fact that a lame idea like that made millions and smart as we are, don't you think if we can just slow down and try hard, we can come up with something?

4. The anti-smoking button. For obvious reasons. You are the only friend I've ever had whose health worried me. I think it is your eyes. Your heart and your pulse might be okay, but there are still your eyes.

I just opened the door since it is very warm. The air seems even softer. It is not raining anymore. I remember you said you could hear me typing one day when you came to visit. That afternoon you came. That was a nice day.

Peace & love

Soft air outside. Thinking about you. About
some of the things we need to remember in
this new phase. The next time I talk to you
will be the beginning of our outside contact
with the world as a work unit. It is exhilarat-
ing. It is dangerous like everything we seem
to like to do. I wanna risk it. I wanna try
and I wanna win. We need to remember
some stuff. I think some of that stuff is:

That we danced together before we wrote
together.

That we work together by talking and
looking and loving and touching and the
music and the blanket on the floor and the
champagne and the reading and the holding.

That the risks are greater now, and less
now.

That there is a difference between freedom
and carelessness.

The stuff I need to remember is:

To be realistic.

To be disciplined.

To be free.

To be honest.

To be unafraid.

To cross my fingers.

The thing you need to remember is:

397

That I love you and trust you and need you and want you and always will.

Uh huh. Always will.

NOVEMBER 30, 1981
He laughs when I tell him that every time he comes here, I am surprised. That I never believe he will come. He laughs, but it is true. When he steps inside, I can hardly latch the screen and lock the dead bolt. I want to fling myself against his chest. I want to jump into his arms like a child and hold on to his neck tight so he cannot turn his head and must kiss me and kiss me and kiss me . . .

DECEMBER 8, 1981
1:30 a.m.
Just once, I would like to do a reading where at the end I don't come home by myself to an empty bed. I would like to come home and fall into the arms of a man who loves me. Who found himself shifting in his seat while I was reading because he knew me better than the others and wanted me right then, up there in front of the people reading about my only topics: sex and drugs and rock and roll.

Just once.

I would like to come home at the end of

the day and know somebody was coming with me. Just once I would like to have somebody hold me after a reading and tell me I was beautiful and then make love to me and hold me close up against them until we both fall asleep and then wake up in the morning and know they'd still be there and still want me. Just once, I'd like to have that, but this time, I am settling for the knowledge that I did well in front of a larger audience than I've ever spoken to before and that I am moving forward. Last year when the insane guy killed John Lennon after he made him sign an autograph I was there sitting in glass-walled offices, talking to cigarette salesmen about how to sell more poison to women. But this year? No! This year I find myself starting without a shit job (Thank you, Jesus!); a lover whose only fault is his wedding band; a career that seems to be skyrocketing; and a child who is so beautiful and sweet that I can't believe she's mine.

I was talking on the phone with Ma today and Henry picked up the extension and said: "I asked your mother where you came from, you're so strange, but then we saw some pictures of Mick Jagger and I figured well, maybe she's on to something."

Happy birthday, jewel child. You're getting

older and you're getting better. Here's hoping!

He said I know who you are, baby.
    And I said who?
    He said I know who you are, baby.
    And I said, oh, yeah?
    Who?
    So what do you want? Tell the truth.
    I want him to leave his wife and come live with me. I want him to tell his wife he's leaving so he can spend more time with me. It's true. I want love and a kitchen with no roaches and some babies and some hugging and some love and some sweetness and some love and enough dishes and room to cook something and have it smell good in the house and have people I like over to eat it. I want him to have a home with me and not a place to come and go so fast. It is always so fast. Too fast. Just so fast. Ah, it is all so hard.

A touch of ennui. Reading Henry Miller is the best antidote. Good things are happening. But then one lil' bad one is a bummer. That is: went to see Peachtree Press. Big mistake. They are the ones who publish

Lewis Grizzard and the boys and I thought
I might be able to hit them up quick. But
they were so lame and so straight and so
white.

DECEMBER 31, 1981
Zaron leaves a New Year's Eve note at my
door:

> Well, another year buys the farm, kicks
> the bucket, bites the big one, heads for
> the last roundup, goes off to the great
> calendar in the sky, expires. Hope 1982 is
> your year. Ciao, Zaron.

JANUARY 1, 1982
Down with guilt.
　I'm not fucking anybody I don't love.
　I'm not fucking anybody who isn't free.

JANUARY 4, 1982

Dear Pearl,
　Happy New Year! We received the red
book of your Xmas stories yesterday.
First, just wait until your daughter is a
writer and "tells all"! I just wasn't ready
yesterday, but today, I'm ready! I don't
know about guns hanging on the bed-
post, but you are surely not the first

401

woman in this family to go to bed with a gamblin' man.

A little motherly advice: Just whoever is in that bed with you, don't catch anything from them and if you do, see the doctor pronto!

Second, how come the thing you like best about Xmas is lying under the tree looking up through the lights and all? Have you ever heard me say that about myself? Presents, dinners, family gatherings really meant very little to me at Xmas as far back as I can remember. I always like best lying under the tree, looking up. When I was little, no one minded, but as I grew up, I stayed up late so I could indulge alone, usually with Christmas carols on the radio. I guess that's why I love Xmas carols now. They bring back the "under the tree" feeling. I never heard anybody say that but you and me.

Christmas has otherwise meant very little to me. I never understand loads of presents. They always seem to miss the point. And the only really happy sort of Xmas I remember with you all was when we played games all the time and listened to that Miriam Makeba record. Otherwise, Xmas was nice because I didn't have to work; a nice low-key holiday like we had when I was small. There was never excitement at our house, just the usual feeling of peaceful security. Now about marijuana. What does it do for you? Escape? Like wine? Stronger? I guess Kris and Jim smoke it too because when they heard I was sick, they sent me some joints. I still have them in a little vial in case I need them.

Back to the little red Xmas book. I feel like I understand exactly what you mean about still loving someone who is bad to you. Did you all think I knew that when you were teenagers in 1967? Boy, did I! And since then, too, but if the love lasts in spite of it, you don't get quite so "hungry" or quite so "cold." But you can't make love do anything. Lost or not lost. So when you are without it, you'll enjoy all the other parts of yourself and sort of wait. At least I think that's what I did. Did you know that I left your father in 1954 and didn't remarry until 1960? A long, but not unfruitful five years and I wouldn't change them for anything because I learned to depend on myself in a way I couldn't have imagined because I thought I was already independent. I was incredibly green about people and life.

Two more short things in closing:

1. The main objection I have to artificial trees: no smell.
2. Did you ever read a life of Dylan Thomas? I don't think he ever had a Xmas like the one he describes in *A Child's Christmas in Wales* after his childhood ended. You know he finally drank himself to death and not even at home, but going from bar to bar, in Wales, or New York City, or wherever he was, but that poem was an unforgettable Christmas for him and he really wrote it!

I hope your trip to Indiana was good in every way, and your New Year, too, and last of all, I don't know how to say how much it means to me to have the little red book of stories dedicated to me! For me? Wow! Thank you . . .

Love,
Ma

JANUARY 10, 1982
"I trust your judgment." Zaron's response to a question from his secretary as we head out for lunch.

"I could put a pack of rattlesnakes on the table and you wouldn't care," she says.

He does not refute the charge.

JANUARY 30, 1982

Feel good. Feel good. Feel good.

Just got back from *Confessions of a Female Disorder.* A show all about growing up female. And growing into being a lesbian. Actresses on the stage kissing. The lesbian lead very sexy Jeanne Moreau kind of worldly/tough. The bi-sexual heroine was a bit tepid. A writer who opts for a husband instead of her work!

But now Deig is back with me and we're headed out to dinner. We look at the moon. It is new and mist or a cloud fuzzes it in a yellow light. I show her how different it looks from when we looked at it last night. We o-o-o-o-o and ah-h-h and giggle. I tell her the moon has a lot to do with women and she says how. Menstruation, I say, and we talk about periods all the way home. I tell her: "You're usually thirteen, but I was eleven and some people are fifteen or sixteen. It's all normal." We talk about Tampax vs. sanitary pads. We agree periods are a fact of life, but kind of a drag anyway. It's getting late and she dozes in the backseat. I love her so much and she's growing up so fast.

Just finished a book called *The White Hotel*. The writer, D. M. Thomas, lives in England, is English, and moves between his first wife and his second. He is now divorced from both, who live within two miles of each other on the same street. But the book is absolutely amazing. It is a novel that starts with these words:

> I dreamt of falling trees in a wild storm I was between them as a desolate shore came to meet me and I ran, scared stiff, there was a trapdoor but I could not lift it, I have started an affair with your son, on a train somewhere in a dark tunnel, his hand was underneath my dress between my thighs I could not breathe. He took me to a white lakeside hotel somewhere high up, the lake was emerald I could not stop myself I was in flames from the first spreading of my thighs, no shame could make me push my dress down, thrust his hand away.

I want to write a review of it, but the things it makes me consider are so jumbled up in

406

my head and it scared me a lot, too. The woman is being "treated" by Freud for "sexual hysteria." It all stems from her fear of her half-Jewishness. She's afraid her anti-Semite husband would freak out if she had a kid who would be half-Jewish, so she retreats from sex. What he does is make you rethink the Holocaust in very individual terms. He makes the woman so SPECIFIC that you can identify with her through the specificity of your own life. You can get beyond all those pictures of anonymous crowds of faces on train platforms and feel how you would feel if it was you standing there. It's like those pictures of famine in Africa and slaughter in El Salvador. Photographs of mass graves trigger a defense mechanism in the brain that says, "No!" You just can't absorb the information. "Sorry!" And you register it as horror, but not as REAL. As YOU. It is fact, but it is in fact no more real to you than the wild-eyed killers who people the new wave of horror movies that play the most gruesome carnage for laughs. The genius of D. M. Thomas's book is that it allows the reader to spend 220 pages getting to know the most intimate details of the heroine's life and then tosses her literally into the pit of hell where she and her son are slaughtered by Nazi soldiers. The cover shows a blond woman sitting naked in a small white room with three open windows. She is in a rocking chair on a red Oriental rug and her hair is in flames.

One of the most beautifully written and perfectly constructed books ever.

FEBRUARY 9, 1982
Awash in anxiety, I sit before my feature writing class and wait for the clock to hit 6:30 p.m. Another hour to go, but they are writing, so I am cool. But I have two basic anxieties. One is a two-parter; well, both are two-parters, I guess.

1. Fear of VD and/or pregnancy;
2. Fear of no audience and a bad, poorly received show.

You can address the first one frontally by going to the Feminist Women's Health Center and having some tests. Or you can wait a month and see what happens.

The second one you can address by cooling out, practicing, rehearsing and crossing your fingers. You've done the best you can with everything, so just relax. Rehearse and relax. Repeat. Rehearse and relax. Repeat . . .

FEBRUARY 15, 1981

I am drinking more red wine these days. Sometimes I feel like a character in a book.

At a time when Chablis was all the rage, she defiantly drank red because she liked the way it stained her lips, her tongue, even her teeth.

My kinda woman . . .

MARCH 8, 1982

Michael drops Deignan off on his way to a week's vacation in the islands. Deig is wearing an Izod T-shirt and sweat pants. Michael is wearing an Izod T-shirt and wheat jeans. She grins at me. He ducks his head. I pat his shoulder. "Have a good time," I say, and I mean it. Deig climbs into the warm 5:30 a.m. bed with me and we whisper for a few minutes. Whispering as if someone else could hear us. She cuddles against my shoulder and I kiss her soft cheek. "Do me a favor," I say. "What?" she murmurs, eyes wide and deep brown. "Go to sleep for an hour or so," I say. She giggles and dozes. I don't wake up again until the alarm goes off at seven.

MARCH 12, 1982

Sunny Friday. Warm. Sitting down here in my purple shirt. Silver bracelets on my wrists. John Coltrane on my record player and I am beginning to hear what he is doing. Funny that the way into it for me is through the words. What he says in interviews about what he is doing. I need the words to find the music! Good talking with Don yesterday about theater and the things I need to consider for the show. He helped me see that $750 for the puppet is absurd. "This is theater," he said. "It's about illusion."

MARCH 15, 1982

To A Friend Who Is Now a Collaborator:
   Don't know if I will have a chance to talk to you before I leave town and I can't wait a week. I have been thinking about the things you said today about the puppet and money and barter and all of it and I want to say two things:

1. Thanks;
2. You're right.

I am going to try to contact the puppeteer before I go and tell her that it is just too steep. I will talk with her again after I talk with you. I want to talk to you on Friday if you can before we go to the costume place because I think it would be really helpful to me if you could just talk through what you see with me. What you think should happen and how much it will cost and stuff. Actresses/directors/what I need to do/ what you will do/what you SEE. The way we have been going is that you ask me something and I scurry around and come back with something that isn't realistic or even possible. It would be better for me . . . that is, I think I could be more helpful to you and to the production if you tell me in advance everything you know already. Then I will see things more realistically. There's also the money for the musician to think about, too.

I also think I wouldn't . . . wait! Let me start that again.

I also thought about what you said about me saying: "Well, here's a city grant. Let's make a costly puppet, okay?" I don't really wanna spend that money on a puppet. I want to spend that money on publishing something. Or buying time to write something.

I don't know if I'm being clear. I remember telling you once about feeling like I had to apologize to people all the time for everything. It's the same reason I can't barter. I used to feel like people were doing me a real big favor to deal with me at all. That stuff causes you to agree to things that you may think need discussion. It throws the balance off. I don't think that's any clearer, but I don't know how to say what I'm trying to get at.

What else can I confess? Fear of a bad play? Fear of an obscure play? Fear of pretentiousness? Fear of trusting and depending on other people? All of that.

I think you know what you are doing. I think you know a LOT more about theater than I do. I think you know a lot more about theater in Atlanta than I do. I am a writer. A writer very pleased to be having a play done and very paranoid about it being as good as I would like it to be. Yuck. I'm not liking this letter much. All I started off to say was thanks for going through the steps with me.

See you when I get back.

Love,
Pearl

MARCH 20, 1982

First day of spring.

Put Peabo on the box. Roll a joint. Rip the curtains off the windows on the Peachtree Street side windows. The music is alive. The dope is gentle. And the buds are out on my Don Juan tree. I feel good. My house is clean. For the first time in months, I don't feel guilty about anything. I don't know what the day holds, but whatever it is, is all right with me. I feel free! Deig and I went to an opening at Forrest Avenue gallery last night. Good show, but kind of boring. The artist keeps telling me the same thing over and over. I want to know what else he knows!

MARCH 25, 1982

I don't know how it happened. I was talking to my daughter about ol' Herschel Walker, the football star. We agreed he was fine and then went on to other topics. Then she said: "What if you met him?" "Met who?" I said, struggling with double bags of groceries from the health food store. "What if I met who?" "Herschel," she said. "Oh," I said, "Well, I would say, aren't you Herschel Walker?" And my daughter grinned and said: "And he would say, aren't you Pearl Cleage, the famous writer?" And I grinned back. "I would say yes, aren't you Herschel Walker, the famous football player? And he would say, yes, we're made for each other."

And suddenly the groceries weren't so heavy and it didn't matter that she was having Burger King one more time instead of broccoli and meatloaf and a salad and some nice whole wheat bread, and it didn't matter that I can't seem to find the perfect man no matter how many I audition for the part. Suddenly it didn't matter. My daughter thought I was in a league with Herschel Walker and somehow that was absolutely fine with me.

APRIL 15, 1982

Marvin Gaye on the radio singing "Forever." It's raining. I haven't paid my taxes. My mind is alive with ideas. I feel like a Medusa head. I feel strong. I feel like I don't wanna fuck at all! I want all that energy for myself! I feel like I am gaining control of my life. I don't have to do shit I don't wanna do. I am here and free as a bird.

APRIL 25, 1982

To Whom It May Concern:
(In the Event of My Untimely and Tragic Death)

This is not notorized or legal, but it is valid and I myself typed it up. I'm going out of the country for a week. I want to be sure in case anything bad happens that Deignan knows that I love her and will always be with her, inside her heart and brain and eyes and taking care of her and she can talk to me anytime she wants and all she has to do is close her eyes and call me in her mind and I'll be right there. I want her to have all my journals when she is sixteen and she can do with them whatever she wants cuz they are a record for her of me.

I would like my sister to have contact with Deig and for her to spend time with her cousins. I know Michael loves her and will take good care of her just like I would if anything happened to him. She is to get everything of mine she wants.

Deignan, I love you. Be strong.

MAY 7, 1982
My mother died last Friday. I have been thinking about it and I think I had already let her go. Daddy said that when somebody is as sick as she was, it is like they are already in the world of the dead and it is hard for them to communicate with the living. He said that it was hard on Henry

because when she got so sick right before she died, Henry was in the world of the living, but he spent most days in the world of the dead, trying to give Ma the love and support she needed.

I can't write about this anymore.

MAY 13, 1982

My mail is full of letters and cards; condolences about Ma dying. A letter from Henry that makes me cry. It begins: "And I love you, too . . ." Where was it all when she was alive? We could have made it easier. We could have loved each other then!

No. We couldn't. We didn't. She knew it was there. It isn't guilt. It's love. Don't forget it's love. Hank Aaron calls to say he's sorry to hear about my mother and that his brother is in the hospital with leukemia. We all have cancer. But I am alive. I am so alive!

MAY 19, 1982

I spent years around people for whom a lack of knowledge about African political realities of the day was tantamount to illiteracy. You not only had to know the local stuff, but you had to have at least passing familiarity with Sékou Touré, Kwame Nkrumah and Patrice Lumumba. Now, I spend a great deal of time around people who say things like: "You know why you are not supposed to whistle backstage?" And I say: "No, why?" And he says, pointing to the rigging: "You see these knots? They are like ship knots. A lot of old theaters are built like ships, the rigging anyway, so that a lot of stagehands were sailors and they were used to communicating with each other on shipboard by whistling and so they did it backstage and if you were just casually whistling, you might be saying, release that weight, Mac! And somebody'd get brained. See?"

And I laugh. I've never heard anybody backstage call anybody Mac.

MAY 20, 1982

Gangsters
Gangsters of desire
We glide through these streets
Collars up, hats pulled way down.
We are lawbreakers of love
Finding the darkest corners
In out of the way cafés
Drawing getaway routes on the tablecloth
While the car sits out front
With the motor running.
Perpetrators of passion
We meet in secret places
To kiss and press and pant and plot

417

Promising to love each other always
And taping a pistol to the back
Of the men's room commode
Just in case things get tight.
Gangsters of desire
We glide, we glide through these streets.

MAY 25, 1982
Tired of being all things to all people.
Tired of playing nurse.
Tired of playing muse.
Tired of playing house.
Wanna be Grace Jones, so weird and mannish it scares 'em.
Wanna be Laurie Anderson, feeling her way along like a spike-haired blind thang in a white lab coat.
Wanna get harder. Don't wanna see any men.
Don't wanna see any women.
Wanna get into my Self.
Wanna write.

MAY 28, 1982
What a morning!
Zaron comes by to get some papers and smokes a joint and talks about his novel, *Upon This Rock,* a rock and roller's guide to being a black wild thang in the sixties. Bill calls to gush about his latest lover and tells

me the poster should be ready today and the city report we did for money will be delivered today, too. (The printed report will be delivered. Alas, not the money.) And then Rev. Howard Creecy calls to see if I will bring greetings to the women of Mt. Moriah Baptist Church on Sunday. I can't imagine why, but of course I say, "Yes." And I am writing a column that attempts to talk about the Philadelphia 76ers by addressing black female poets. Eat your heart out, Anaïs Nin!

MAY 29, 1982
I find myself in the midst of that thing I have been whining about for weeks and I am terrified in the face of it. A day with no commitments. No lovers due to drop by. No child with a schedule and a yen for the Hello Kitty shop. No missed deadlines. Nothing to do. Nothing to do. Nothing to do.

I feel like I spend my time looking for ways to heighten something. Fucking and not wanting to be fucking is a witness to something. Talking on the phone and chafing at the time is a witness to something. I feel like it is all so stupid.

In *My Dinner With Andre,* the guy says, "It all seems so silly that everybody has to have their little goals, especially when it doesn't make any difference which one."

I keep thinking about that other quote about life being what goes by while we're waiting for something to happen and life being what goes on inside your head all day.

I am not angst-ridden, but I am not happy either. I want to be a famous sought-after writer who makes enough money to buy a large, light, airy house in midtown that has already been renovated. I want to have people over for dinner and buy fresh flowers and decent wine and a good record player and talk all night.

GO . . . FOR . . . IT.

MAY 30, 1982
1:20 a.m.

Spent the evening at Angie and Fred Terrell's. A quickly planned party in honor of James Baldwin. I arrive at 7:00, having been invited for 6:30, and find I am the first guest. I am followed by Carolyn Fowler, who had read the synopsis of "puppetplay" and wanted to know where I got such an idea. It sounded sort of like Ibsen's *A Doll's House,* she said. I don't think so. Nora had thought she and her husband meant the same thing when they said the word "love." She felt betrayed when it wasn't true. The women in my play are dealing with no love, simply protection sought and protection denied. Richard Coggins was there talking about a film he wants to write. I discover that he was at Northwestern the same time I was! I couldn't believe it. So now we can say, "We went to high school together."

I spent a while talking to Baldwin's male secretary, Skip. Lives in Detroit. He was nice. An actor. Gay? I would think so, traveling with Baldwin? Jan was there talking about Andy's office, Shirley's role and David's craziness. It was fun to see James Baldwin himself up close. Those snakey bug eyes. The way he talks so fast. Talking about going to Paris in 1948 because he thought — he knew! — if he stayed here in the U.S. he'd kill somebody or somebody'd kill him. I sat there at his feet and felt like I was in Paris, too!

Baldwin's still holding court toward the party's end and me and Skip are across the room talking in whispers about our work, our marriages, our children, love and life. "Are you hurt," he said to me, talking about love. "Are you in love?" he asked, looking in my face. "No," I said. "No." And when I left, he kissed me on the mouth and took my address, promising to write to me.

Me and Jan and another sister walk outside at midnight and realize it has rained while we've been inside. The air is moist and warm and the sky is clear with flashes of lightning. "It's beautiful," says Jan. "Yeah," I say, "but what do you wanna do on a night like this?" And we all laugh and laugh because it is a fucking night. We all want to go home and fall into the arms of somebody who loves us.

A good weekend.

Stoned on Friday.

Drunk on Saturday.

Stoned on talk on Sunday.

Pretend it's Paris . . .

JUNE 1, 1982

Morning. Airing my diaphragm in my window. It looks like a little flower, sitting there in the sun and breeze. Thank you, Margaret Sanger!

The jive paper has been read. Coffee almost finished. Duke Ellington first and now Miles Davis *Sketches of Spain.* Old records. A big car with a Cadillac horn blows outside my window, but it's not for me. "Your ride is here!" we used to say when parties would be breaking up and fathers would be jockeying for position at the curb to collect their daughters. Nobody wanted their father to come into a basement party where by this hour of the night there was always serious grinding going on, so we'd warn each other. "Your ride is here!" But this is not my ride. Not today.

I am so competitive I make myself sick. Alice Walker on the cover of *Ms.* makes me so jealous I can't stand it.

JUNE 2, 1982

First "puppetplay" rehearsal tonight. I am so excited. The poster is great! The puppet is amazing; beautiful and scary. I love that I had nerve enough to ask David to pay for it and I love that he agreed to do it. I don't have any other friends who can invest one thousand dollars in a piece of performance art!

JUNE 3, 1982

Hey, my love, don't take it so seriously. It's a game. A game. It really doesn't matter. It's a much more fun way to live than writing advertising copy. But it doesn't matter what we do. Not really.

JUNE 14, 1982
Chicago Art Institute

The sign outside the room says, "Do not lean against the gray panel." Okay, I say to myself. Why would I? I walk into a large, white-walled, dimly lit room and there is a large gray panel against the back wall. What is this? I think and walk toward it. There is something eerie about it and I'm walking slowly. As I get up to it, I lean toward it, feeling scared for no reason I can think of and I realize all of a sudden it's not a gray panel; it's a hole in the wall. With some sort of mist on the inside. It's very still in the room and very quiet and I am terrified of that hole. I leave the room quickly. Make a nervous joke to the security guard. My heart is pounding. "It's a hole, yes?" "Yes," she says. "Scary," I say, but I am drawn back. It terrifies me. I leave the room again, go out into the gallery and then back to it one more time. Slowly. I want to put my arm into the space, but I can't bring myself to do it. It is terrifying. It is what I think death is like. Just nothing. Quiet. Gray. Lonesome. Alone. It is terrifying. The artist is James Turrell. The piece is called *Rayna,* 1979. Most effect a piece of art has ever had on me.

JUNE 19, 1982
Wanna be free. Oh, Lord! Yawsah, Yawsah, Yawsah. Wanna be free of niggas with high cheekbones and lies. Wanna be free of old lovers and new lovers and married lovers

and livin' with lovers. Wanna be free of wor-
ryin' about lovers. Wanna find somebody
who can love me and let me love 'em back.
Don't think I will. Don't think I will. Hate
it/hate it/hate it/hate it.

No, you can't come and tape my records.

No, you can't come over.

No, don't touch me.

No, don't talk to me.

No, don't/No, don't.

I'm too fragile.

I'm too crazy.

I'm too wild.

I'm too frightened.

I'm too lonesome.

I'm too hot.

I'm too open/too closed/too outside/too
inside.

Don't touch me.

Don't touch me.

Don't touch me.

Don't touch me.

JUNE 20, 1982
10:00 p.m.
<u>A few words on Feminism and a True Confes-
sion, Not Necessarily in That Order/For My
Friends at Just Us Theater Company</u>
The fact is this: I want to work with y'all. In
order for us to do that as successfully as we

can, I think it might be helpful for me to say the following few words on feminism. The reason I think this is based on the following two exchanges. The players will remain anonymous, but should be easily recognizable.

Routine question: Did you put the posters in the feminist bookstore?

Surprising answer: Say what? I'm not going in there. Forget it. Etc.

And then:

Surprising statement: I don't think it's a feminist play at all. I mean — and correct me if I'm wrong — if it's a feminist play then it would have to be about hating men, right?

Truthful answer: Well, uh, not necessarily.

And one bonus surprising statement: Don't take this wrong, but I think it would be better if you don't say you're a feminist.

Here's the thing:

I am a feminist. I am willing to figure out a way to say that that doesn't frighten off our audience. I am anxious to figure out a way to say that that doesn't frighten off our audience. I am even willing to discuss not admitting to it (but I want y'all to know that is going to take some discussion before it can be settled . . .) but in exchange, I want you to think about the following: Feminism doesn't have anything to do with hating men.

Feminism has to do with understanding power and oppression and control.

Feminism has to do with equality, not sameness.

Feminism doesn't mean unfeminine. Or hateful. Or sharp. Or hard-edged. Or bitch voice/killer eyes/fists instead of open hands.

Feminism is about freedom.

Feminism is about choices.

Feminism is about an end to self-hate and games and pressure and control and roles where you/men get to be strong all the time and we/women get to be weak and helpless and nobody gets to have as much fun as we could have.

I don't care if either of you ever go in the feminist bookstore, but I don't want to feel like I asked you about venturing into a leper colony if I say, "Did you take a poster over to Charis?"

I don't care if we find a new word so that nobody ever knows what I call myself or my writing, as long as we all know what is what and who is who and all of that.

And I really don't care if some people think my work is anti–black men, or cynical and mean and cold and nasty and too personal and all about a certain nameless someone and isn't it terrible how she puts her own business in the street? I don't care about any of that if YOU know that my work is really about trying to figure out why people can't love each other and what happens when they don't and, hopefully, even a look at what happens when they do.

I don't think any of this touches on what I'm really trying to say. In order to make it clear, I wanna start quoting Billie Holiday songs or talking about Georgia O'Keeffe and Alfred Stieglitz and that book of photographs he took of her where she's standing on the radiator naked with that curtain in front of her or how a man who dated my mother once turned to her in horror in the middle of a Saturday afternoon movie and said: "You're not one of those women's libbers, are you?" and she said she was.

It's seeing *A Hard Day's Night* and wanting to be a Beatle that makes me feel I have to explain any of this. It's listening to Gershwin in the park that makes me wanna get it right.

Listen:

I won't tread on the macho that I find around me if you all will just consider the thought that I am a self-confessed feminist and I'm not so bad, so how can you believe what they say about any of it? Don't old people say, "Believe only half of what you see/some and none of what you hear"?

Beware the power of the pup! Luv & Kisses, Pearl

JUNE 27, 1982

Last night I dreamed about the puppet and it had no eyes. It had just the blue velvet but no shiny diamond eyes. And in the dream (which was in color) I was asking someone what happened to his eyes? Where are those glittery diamond eyes?

JULY 25, 1982

This is a rain forest. One night after midnight, I called Zaron to come over and kill a big flying roach for me. I had been hiding from it behind a chair for almost an hour. Kai and Deignan were sleeping in the bedroom and I was paralyzed with fear. When he came, I pointed to the closet door and he opened it. There was the bug on the floor, looking much smaller in the presence of someone who wasn't scared of it. So he squished it, let me look to be sure it was dead and then flushed it.

I had already called Bob for help and he said, no, can't come, gotta catch a plane in the morning. He sounded so sarcastic. So condescending. "Just remember," he said. "You are bigger than the bug." "Forget it," I said. "Never mind." And I hung up.

But Zaron came, saw and conquered!

JULY 26, 1982

Last night, talking and pacing and laughing, Zaron spills a glass full of iced Pernod on my rug. I have already spilled apple juice and water on the same spot earlier that day. He wipes at it vaguely with a kitchen towel and this morning when I sit leaning against the couch to have my eggs, I can smell the Pernod still damp in the design of the Oriental rug. I remember getting this rug in a trade with M. In exchange for the Haitian painting of the animals in the jungle. The plant I have set on the porch is thriving. It is a cutting from the one Nanny had. Ma had to water it after Nanny died. "I was angry at the plant," my mother told me later, "because my mother had paid such a lot of attention to it. I was jealous!" and she laughed. I think of her laughing at herself and I see the plant, stretching out, glad to have been outside in the sunshine and the rain. It's raining so much, every day. We feel like we are living in the tropics. We reach in the closet for our shoes, hoping they won't be covered with soft blue mold.

JULY 30, 1982

Went to see *The World According to Garp.* It

was wonderful. The movie had all the things I liked about the book. Jenny Fields (played by Glenn Close) is beautiful. Sensual. Strong and firm and direct. Her breasts are held out like Amazon armor. Made me cry twice. It's real. It's about life.

"Remember," says the dying Garp to his wife. "What, my love?" she says. "Everything," he says. "Everything."

AUGUST 1, 1982

Out to the linen store. Cap on. Running shoes. Dashing through. Need pillows. "Are you Nikki Giovanni?" the black saleswoman asks and I laugh. "No, but I'm a writer," I say. "I think I've seen you," she says. I tell her my name. "Yeah," she says. "Yeah. I know you." While I am squeezing the king-size pillows, fingering the lace-edged pillowcases, another black woman comes over with a round-eyed kid. A boy. "Are you Pearl Cleage?" she says. "Yes." "I saw your play," she says, "and I really enjoyed it. My son did, too." And the round-eyed kid grins and nods. "Yep," he says. "I did." I am amazed. I laugh. She smiles. "Is it going to be done again?" she says. "Yes," I say. "Just Us Theater is doing it in February." "Good," she says. "Are you changing anything?" "Yes," I say. "I really want to see it again," she says. "Thanks," I say and we smile as they move off down the aisle. I wave at the kid, who waves back. I wonder what he thought the play was about? Two very unhappy women married to a seven-foot marionette. I wonder how his mother explained it to him. Or maybe she didn't have to. He looked like a smart little kid. Maybe he already knows.

AUGUST 2, 1982

I wonder if all of the women who write and who read Anaïs Nin think they are just like her. I am underlining the pages of her diary so frantically I can hardly keep the sense of what I'm reading.

I had two solitary orgies today: a book orgy and a food orgy. I bought fifty dollars' worth of each. Theater books; strawberries and rich, creamy cheese, French bread and a big bag of M&Ms.

AUGUST 8, 1982
8:30 a.m.

Deignan is still sleeping. I slept with her last night. She was so hyper. Really wound up tight as a drum. Talking, talking, talking. But I cooled her down, rubbed her back and listened and she finally went to sleep.

AUGUST 10, 1982

Election night; 10:00 p.m. Michael is ahead by 59 percent over Dodson. I send him a telegram: Congratulations! Love, Pearl.

AUGUST 11, 1982

My friend calls to say she and her husband are divorcing. He's moving out. She says in one argument they had, he said that it was my fault I wasn't famous because I bullshit too much and SMOKE TOO MUCH DOPE! I wonder how I came up in the discussion in the first place. Maybe I was cited as a bad influence. Well, truth is the light of the world . . .

SEPTEMBER 5, 1982

And so at fifteen minutes before the appointed hour, she has perfumed behind her ears, lit incense in living and bed rooms, changed her clothes twice, worried about not having wine and stood on her balcony, hoping he will come early.

Phone. He'll be a little late. Fifteen minutes or so. Half-hour at the latest. Her mind says half-hour to forty-five minutes. She hates the way he sounds. She hates the way her throat feels. She hates the feeling that she hasn't had in the week he's been gone. She is realizing she would rather not. Can't think around him. Can't get any real perspective on the shit.

Don't come at all, she wants to say. Don't bother.

Don't come. Don't ever come.

Buy a big house at the beach. Take her there. Tell her your dreams. Have some more kids. And sneak here when you wanna feel free.

I'm so tired of this role.

I don't know what to do. Do I?

Yes. Tell him no more.

Don't tell him anything. Unplug your phone and disappear. Make him come and find you. Make him? Is this a game? Is this a manipulation? Is it survival? Is it self-preservation? Do you want him? Do you want him? Do you really want him?

"A little late," is all he said. "A little late."

Every minute. Every second. Critical to me. She is embarrassed at wanting him so much that fifteen minutes sounds like twenty-four hours. "Okay," she says. "I'll be here."

But the voice in her head says: Leave now! Go to the movies! Leave a note and split!

Can't stand it. Too hard. Too scared. This doesn't feel like love to me.

NOVEMBER 17, 1982

Behind everything these days is the persistent whine of the woman's worry:

I sure do hope I'm not pregnant.

NOVEMBER 22, 1982

Don calls to say Just Us will schedule my next show for February! Good news/good news/good news!

NOVEMBER 23, 1982

I have been asked to read on a program with Amiri Baraka and Lawrence Ferlinghetti! How cool is that?

I saw Dr. Benjamin Mays in the barbershop yesterday. So old now and fragile. He had to be eased out/helped out of the chair. He had on high-top-old-black-man shoes. Blue suit. White shirt. Neat as a pin. He nods appreciatively at the barber. "I'm going to invent a straight razor that shaves as close as this," Dr. Mays says. Mr. Barlow, our barber, laughs, pleased. Dr. Mays smiles. "They can send a man to the moon. They ought to be able to make a straight razor that can shave this smooth." And he chuckles. Mr. Barlow chuckles. We all chuckle. Everybody has big respect for Dr. Mays. And love. He reaches to the coat rack and pulls a hat off the hook that startles me. Smooth gray Stetson. There are feathers in the hatband and they are spread open. Brown and gray feathers. Eagle feathers maybe? Dr. Mays sets the hat squarely on his freshly cut head. He sits again, folds his arms and legs and smiles at us all watching his every move. He's waiting for his driver. The city provides one now after he got lost on the freeway and drove himself all the way to Birmingham!

DECEMBER 4, 1982

In D.C. at Union Station. Just arrived from Boston for an overnight visit. I find a cut-rate electronics store so I can buy a little tape recorder to listen to music on my train trip home tomorrow. The guy who waits on me is Hispanic, but the place is full of brothers wanting music stuff. I buy the cheapest one I can find, get the batteries, pay the money. The Spanish-accented clerk hands me my change and says quietly, "If you're taking the subway, be careful with this. You know, so many colored guys around, and . . ." I look at him. I consider throwing the bag back in his face, but he stops short, taken aback by the rage and hatred in my small angry face. I slip my arms into my backpack and leave.

On to Karen's house. Her daughters are there with a babysitter. The four-year-old follows me into the shower, talking a mile a minute. She has Deignan's energy and we love each other instantly. Then Karen arrives. A.B. appears soon after. We all hug. They are glad to see me. I am so glad to see them. We talk. They tell me I look good. I tell them I've got a bottle of rare Andre's champagne in my bag for them. We laugh. People drop by. We eat. A.B. has cooked something good. Later, we kiss the girls who are staying with the babysitter and head off to a jazz club. Bad music, but we don't care. We hit Georgetown and get a midnight meal. Back home finally, I fall into bed, full of friendship and red wine.

DECEMBER 5, 1982

I sleep until noon. A.B. takes the girls to the movies. Karen and I talk. I have really missed her! We are thinking about the same things. Trying to figure out the right balance between work, kids, love, family. She is beautiful and strong. Her children are lovely. A.B. thinks she's a queen. She unbraids her hair and blows it out in a cloud around her face. The day flies by and they drop me at the train station. Kisses all around. A porter takes my bags and tells me I am very beautiful and *am I married*? "No," I say, "but I'm in love." "No harm in tryin'," he says. I laugh and sit down to write this. Another porter sticks his head into my little roomette and says, " 'Scuse me, but didn't I see you on this train goin' to New Orleans about three years ago?" I remembered him, too! He had thought I was a dancer. He even remembered my name so we greeted each other like old friends. And now we're speeding through the night. I write it all down because that's what I do. If I don't write it down, I don't believe it. Heading home . . .

DECEMBER 5, 1982

It's morning on the Southern Crescent. The smell of coffee fills this sleeper car. I have slept and dreamed and smiled in my sleep. I have looked outside and looked inside and remembered everything. I have looked ahead and behind. So much coming up! The readings. The play. The L.A. trip.

The paper they have slipped beneath the door of my roomette has an article about a photographer who works with his wife of thirty years. They both look really happy. He says: "Living with a woman is either good or it's not. If not, it's better to live alone. One should never settle for mediocrity." Amen, brother, amen!

DECEMBER 10, 1982
Everything good is happening. Bruce calls from L.A. with an invitation to go see Lena Horne live since I'll be in L.A. for New Year's Eve. Sounds good to me. Out of all the people I met working on that awful Richard Pryor movie, Bruce is the only friend I made and kept!

DECEMBER 13, 1982
I feel a lot better. Don and I figured out a better ending for the play. It is really a trip, but I think it works.

I also figured out that I really don't care about this CNN radio gig and I don't want to write speeches for Julian Bond. Too late, Julian! I have reached another level now and I just don't want to do that stuff anymore.

And my friend says how come I never tell him about the other men who are close to me. I didn't know what to say. How to articulate it. Because of guilt? Because I'm fucking them, too, and don't want him to think about me fucking anybody else? Here is the crux of the matter:

 1. I am basically monogamous and I
    have guilt when I have more than

one lover, although I always reserve the right to do so.

2. He is basically polygamous and feels best when he has more than one lover; when at least the possibility exists.

Time to work/work/work.

DECEMBER 14, 1982

My goddamn "puppetplay" has sold out the whole downstairs of the Peachtree Playhouse for opening night! We are now selling balcony tickets!!

Oh yeah/oh yeah/oh yeah!

DECEMBER 24, 1982

Xmas Eve and all is well.

All is very well.

I feel good.

I don't feel hassled.

I have taken a little break though.

Have I?

Not really.

I've just been doing "puppetplay" work.

Gotta write a column tonight. About me, Oyamo and Sonia Sanchez. Not bad work if you can get it. So far, so good . . .

Good day. Getting ready to hit the road. Off to L.A. Don't wanna fly but will handle it. Will handle it! What to take:

1. 7 pairs of panties and 4 good bras
2. Toothbrush and toothpaste/ deodorant/etc.
3. Diaphragm and jelly
4. Eyeshadow/mascara
5. Black velvet knickers/black jacket/ white ruffled blouse/black tights/ black Chinese oxfords
6. Pearl earrings/gold bracelet
7. Brown boots/jazzy shoes with pointed toes
8. Leg warmers and tights with feet/ blue leotard
9. Green skirt/red boots/red sweater
10. Journal

Never a Christmas morning/Never the old
   year ends/
But someone thinks of someone/Old days,
   old times, old friends.

                        — Anonymous

DECEMBER 26, 1982
If I could just get rid of the interior eye. The constant eye. The eye that makes me

441

feel I could possibly be embarrassed when no one is here but me. Embarrassed in front of who? I actually think of myself as capable of embarrassing myself in front of myself! Is that vibe translated as: "I'd be so embarrassed if somebody could see me doing this . . ."? That must be it.

The thing about fucking is somebody is seeing you and if they like what they are seeing, it is almost impossible to feel embarrassed. Only if they make you feel odd or nasty or strange. I feel good. Michael Jackson singing Christmas songs on the radio. Deignan is with her father. I have a box full of old letters to read and save. Or burn. Good dope. Good food. And myself to myself. Yeah/yeah/yeah!

DECEMBER 29, 1982
I don't need a lover.
  I need a friend.

JANUARY 5, 1983
He hasn't called this morning because he hasn't gone out yet. Hasn't found a reason to head for the public phone. It's like Joan Baez in that song about diamonds and rust, asking Bob Dylan if he's calling from a booth in the Midwest.

And I wait, without wanting to. Listen for

442

the phone with an absorption that would guarantee me cracking fourteen hundred on the college boards. And I get angry at him. Angry at me. Just angry.

Q: What do you want to do? List things that are in your control only, pleez!

A: I want to unplug the phone and the machine and write all day and go see the play tonight.

Q: Why don't you?

A: Because I want him here.

Q: Why?

A: Because I want to be held and made love to and reassured that I'm not alone in the world.

Q: Do his visits reassure you?

A: While he's here they do. When he leaves, they just make it worse.

Q: Worse than being alone?

A: I think, yes, but I can't believe that.

Q: Why?

A: I don't know.

Q: What will you probably do?

A: Keep the phone plugged in. Wait for his call. Hope he comes over. Cry. Be angry. Let him confess. Make love. Cry. Watch him drive away. Feel mad. Feel bad. Go see the play. Go out with Bill and Jane. Cry. Get drunk at Gregory's.

Q: Sounds like the pits. Can't you not see him and skip the crying parts?

A: I don't know. One step at a time. The first step is to decide it.

Q: Can you?

A: I don't think so. Not yet. But I know I'm watching him. I know I'm losing trust; keeping score.

Q: Trust in what?

A: The fantasy of him appearing at my door with a suitcase. The fantasy of us living together. The fantasy of really being with him and not just being his mistress.

Q: What will happen then?

A: When?

Q: When you stop watching.

A: I don't know. I will stop fucking him, I guess. I don't know.

Q: Just try not to fuss at yourself. Try not to cry. Try not to sell yourself out. Try to be honest. Try to be calm. Try to write while you keep the radar out for his arrival. Try to relax. Try not to get mad.

A: I think it's gonna be okay.

Q: Do you really?

A: Yes. I think this is the last of this.

Q: Good. I think your financial plan will help you move toward greater independence. I think your New York work will help boost your confidence. Hang in there. You made it through 1982. Now it's 1983. The challenges are different, but you are stronger. And sweeter.

A: Sweeter?

Q: Yes. That's true. Relax.

A: I'm tryin'.

Q: I know you are. I love you.

A: I love you, too.

MAY 2, 1983

Just got fired from the paper. No more columns for the *Constitution.* My editor calls to say my writing is too esoteric and too intellectual! Makes me feel bad, but I'll deal with it. One way or another, I always deal with it.

I'm off the track a little. I gotta work more systematically. Gotta work more than mooning. Gotta write more. The time is now! You need product! Use tonight to get organized, and then hit it!

JULY 1983

Random thoughts on Judy Chicago's *Dinner Party,* Fox Theater, Atlanta, Ga.

The plates were all arranged on a big "V" shaped table. Nice soft lighting and all these ceramic plates shaped like vaginas and named in honor of famous women. I've been waiting and waiting to see it. Is Atlanta ready for a ballroom full of vaginas on a plate? I'm hoping for a blast of feminist wildness . . .

Alas! Turns out the plates are kind of boring. Too obvious, but a good idea. Well executed, but they didn't move me. The only literal plate is the black woman plate. Why we gotta be so realistic all the time? Why no flying of the spirit for us? No ambiguity. Just anguished big lip black faces. Why do we have to be the literal ones? I wanna be mysterious and magic. Mysterious and magic! Oh, yes!

SEPTEMBER 3, 1983
Sunday, 11:00 a.m.
Talkin' to myself:

The problem is — once again with feeling! — that it is so degrading.

Do you care about degrading?

Yes!

Why?

Because it erodes my self-confidence.

How?

Because I hate to watch myself twittering around, waiting for some attention. I never can win, so what's the point?

What is the fucking point?

SEPTEMBER 4, 1983

The moment of truth: We're riding up to the theater. He's gonna drop me off. We've been talkin'. We've been kissin'. We've been close. I look great. I know I look great. He tells me I look great. We laugh. When we get there, he says: "I'm gonna drive around the block." And he does without really asking me or anything. I laughed because I knew he didn't wana let me go. But he went around several blocks. He wasn't going to let me out! I got really mad. I felt like he was making me pretend something that isn't true. Making me not remind him I was going off somewhere looking good without him. It was that odd moment where I am supposed to be unaware of the reality of our situation or not acknowledge it so he won't feel bad about going home. I couldn't do it/wouldn't do it. "You don't want to let me go," I said, and he admitted it. And he was uncomfortable and I said, "Don't make me feel like it's my fault. I always want you to come with me. But don't give me mixed signals and make me ask you to come and then you deny me!" I was so mad. I said, "There's lots of things we can do. Pharoah Sanders is playing in the park right now!" I meant it, too, but I also knew he couldn't go there. Too many people we know. "Let

447

me out," I said, and he pulled over and stopped the car and I got out and walked away. "I love you," I said, and walked away. It was hard and scary but IT FEELS SO GOOD.

SEPTEMBER 18, 1983

I don't want to be
an anecdote
a truth serum
a refuge
a sanctuary.
I wanna be
a choice
a fact
a reality
a paradise.

OCTOBER 1, 1983

I begin book three of the Don Juan series today and get a letter from Kris in the mail quoting the following section of the same book after I have just underlined the same words in purple in the pages of my own book:

Fright never injures anyone. What injures the spirit is having someone always on your back, beating you, telling you what to do and what not to do.

Something in there touched both of us. She was clearing out her bookshelves, came across it and opened to that page. "I am hooked," she says. Me, too. We wonder what other truths Don Juan has for us.

There is a ring around the moon and the night is so soft and in the stillness a minute ago, I remember my lover's heart so close to mine and I feel so frantic. John Lennon said he knew when he met Yoko it was "magnificent love." Do people really change their lives for magnificent love?

Help me, Don Juan!

OCTOBER 6, 1983
Here 'tis:

I don't want to write novels. Or a novel. I want to write: articles, poems, screenplays. That's it. I don't want to have to sustain plot, characters, serious ideas, etc. Ain't no fun for the kid. Fuck 'em. I wanna play. I need an agent who can get me national freelance work and some screenplay stuff and then I'll be okay. Fuck a novel. Don't need the grief. If it ain't fun writin' the shit, I'd rather be a secretary.

So there, goddammit. So there!

OCTOBER 8, 1983

Last letter to you:

I'm not reading anymore of this Henry Miller.

Read it yourself/read it yourself/read it yourself!

And if you can, and if you do, can you still tell me NO?

NOVEMBER 13, 1983

Went in the backstage door to the Johnny Mathis show at Radio City last night with Phylicia [Rashad] and Seret [Scott]. Saw about fifteen minutes. Went to a party for Debbie Allen afterward at a beautiful, huge apartment on Park Avenue South. It was strangely subdued. I didn't feel awkward or anything, but just wished there had been more going on. It was fun, though. Walking back and forth to the theater between shows was fun, too. I love New York. I feel good. Strong. The play is getting better and better. Last night, Phylicia's mother told our director, Clinton Turner Davis, she heard me talking to the actresses, like I wasn't supposed to talk to them! Clinton was cool, though. He said: "She's working her magic." He's done so good. Everything is cool. I want to have a party. Not a Park Avenue party. Just a regular one.

NOVEMBER 25, 1983

Letter to a faraway friend:

How long you been gone? Six months or so? So far I've:

Cleaned my house.

Babysat a guinea pig.

Mothered my daughter.

Called Woodie and settled all that bad blood. He wants to do *Hospice* off Broadway in early March.

Talked to Don about the future of Just Us Theater.

Drafted a letter to Richard Pryor.

Figured out my creative output schedule for the next three months.

Heard from Woodie that Ray Stark Productions are nibbling at the thriller treatment we sent them.

Read a thing in *Essence* about Valerie Simpson where she says Nick Ashford is ". . . all in all, everything to me. Mother, father, lover . . . what can I say? I'm still mad about him."

Made a big change in *Essentials* based on the collision that occurred in my mind between Jesse Jackson and my father and Richard Pryor and Nick Ashford. Decided to let the brother live, okay?

Decided to buy groceries instead of paying my car note since it was Thanksgiving.

Wished you would call me a minimum of one hundred times or so and missed you/missed you/missed you.

My father has written down the dates of *Good News* because he wants to come and see it at Just Us. Mentioned it to me three times. Wrote the dates down. My father, who never saw me dance, never saw me do a reading! He came to see a play of mine at Howard once when I was nineteen. He was in town to meet with presidential candidate Eugene McCarthy. I went down to McCarthy's office with him and shook the man's hand. It was the weakest handshake ever. Maybe he was tired of shaking so many people's hands. Maybe his hand was sore, but it made me think: He can't beat any Republicans shaking hands like that.

Watched the Thanksgiving Day Parade with Deignan and Nick Ashford and Valerie Simpson come riding down the street and they stopped and sang a song from their new album. She was wild, hair blowing around everywhere, and he was cool, wrapped his arms around her waist from where he was sitting behind her and hugged her and she leaned back and shook her little padded shoulders and sang/sang/sang.

Went to rehearse for the Food Raiser event on Monday. I'm reading the piece about wanting to take tap-dancing lessons. Channel 5 will be coming to film the rehearsal and the director asked him to come at my time because he thought it would generate some audience. That made me feel good, but did I say miss you/miss you/miss you?

NOVEMBER 28, 1983

Whew.
This must be Joe Louis love.
If you not careful,
it will
knock
you
out.

DECEMBER 1, 1983

Have lost all track of days. Thanksgiving threw me off. Is it the weekend? Is there a deadline? Is there pressure? A rush? A stress ball headed my way? Can't remember. Sunshine coming in over my desk so strong I can see my shadow typing in unison with me on the rug.

Finished the new novel by Ernest J. Gaines, *A Gathering of Old Men.* It's a good book. There are some political things I didn't like, such as, how come the white girl is the catalyst to make the old black men come together, etc., but I figure the author has the right to decide what he wants to do and it could have happened that way. Just cuz I don't like that he wrote about it that way doesn't mean it shouldn't be there. And in the end, they, the old black men with guns, put the girl out, sent her back to her own people, and kicked ass.

DECEMBER 2, 1983
I ain't gonna fuss, I don't care how many times you tell me to.

Baby/baby/baby . . .

DECEMBER 3, 1983
Random Thoughts on Thirty-five or My Baby Loves the Western Movies:

It was the safest time to ask. I was lying with one ear against his chest at about the midway point in the six-minute grace period after you make love where you can ask the man whatever you want and he will stroke your back and nuzzle your ear and agree in the sweetest possible way to almost anything.

"Tell me," I heard myself say, "that I'm not old."

"What?" he said. I felt his arm shift so that he could lean back and look into my

454

face as if he figured the question warranted a quick visual check as well as a verbal response. "What?"

"Tell me I'm not old," I said.

"You're not old," he said calmly.

"Thank you," I said.

"Ask me again," he said.

"Tell me I'm not old," I said. After all, I was in the throes of the six-minute grace period, too, and there wasn't much he could have asked me, save the abandonment of my only child or the relinquishing of my writing, that I would have denied him.

"You're not old," he said. "Now!"

"Now what?" I said.

"I know you never believe me the first time I say anything," he said. "I'm not even sure two or three times works, but I'll give you the benefit of the doubt on this one because I think you want to believe me."

"I always want to believe you," I said.

He laughed and shifted his arm so my head was sort of cradled between his arm and his chest in a way that provided maximum closeness, excellent creative opportunities for random bursts of affection and a serious heartbeat. My favorite place. I sighed.

"I know it," he said.

"Know what?" I said.

455

"That you always want to believe me," he said. "You're not old."

"Thank you," I said.

"Three's the charm," he said.

I wish it was that easy, but this was a serious point we were discussing. This was no simple inquiry like, "Are you ever going to leave your wife?" Or: "You don't really want to have a baby, do you?" Or: "Can we make a living doing this stuff?" This was the big one.

The Big One. Mortality was definitely involved. Wrinkles around the edges of your eyes and a certain sag to the breasts. This was somebody saying, "You look really good to be thirty-five," and wondering what they thought you were going to look like. Somehow I never thought it would happen to me, turning thirty-five, that is, but it did. A turning point. Time to reassess. Take stock. All the books say so. So be it.

My writing has never been better. My daughter tells me I'm not THAT old, and my lover tells me I've never looked or felt or sounded better. But still . . . thirty-five? Is it middle-aged? Almost middle-aged? Whatever else it is, it forces you to admit that it's something other than young.

I have been considering my reactions to this terrible truth and have decided there are some good parts to being thirty-five. These include:

- I don't cry as much.
- I write better.
- My child is old enough to travel without Pampers.
- I'm desperately in love and haven't sold myself out yet.

Whew! Not bad. There were times when I thought I'd never get here. Like when I was thirty and left home looking for the way I used to feel in 1966. Or like when I was thirty-three and got so enchanted with feeling that kind of free again that I quit my job to concentrate on making love and writing, in that order. And now it is already December 1983, and in four days I am going to turn thirty-five. Thirty-five?

I remember my mother at thirty-five, one year before she married my stepfather and five years after she divorced my father. She was going out, something she almost never did, and she was wearing a blue crepe dress in the style they used to call a "sheath." On her feet were navy and white spectator pumps and on her head was a wide-brimmed picture hat, also in navy. She carried white gloves and a navy blue clutch purse. Her hair was coiled into a knot and pinned low on the back of her neck. She hardly ever wore her hair like that because it would invariably begin to slip out of its pins and she didn't like it wisping around her face. This night, though, she didn't seem to care.

She stopped to twirl for us on her way out the door and my sister and I were amazed and embarrassed by her beauty. We hugged her as if we had never touched her before.

"Can we drink some of that champagne," he says, as if it is suspect moonshine, "or will it make us go blind?"

"Not unless we drink vast quantities," I say. "I'll get it."

"It's your birthday," he says. "I'll get it."

There are three cases of champagne in my kitchen and twelve bottles of orange juice, freshly squeezed. Earlier this week, when the inevitability of thirty-five leaped upon me, I decided that if I couldn't be young, I could at least be thin. I devised a diet made up of equal parts orange juice and Andre's available-at-the-7-Eleven champagne. The state of my semi-hysteria can be measured by the fact that I went so far as to actually buy a two-week supply of the necessary elements before stopping to reconsider.

He hands me a glass.

"No OJ?" I say.

"You said you weren't starting your diet until tomorrow," he says. "We'll drink it neat."

"You sound like a refugee from *Gunsmoke,*" I say.

And he leans closer since he doesn't like to sing loud. "My baby loves the western movies," he sings and laughs into my ear. I laugh, too. I know that song.

So, thirty-five has certain compensations, I guess. But I will confess that I am not yet resigned to the fact that my seventeen-year-old body isn't coming back no matter how many laps I swim every day. I am still appalled at the new lines on my face and the veins in the backs of my hands and how hard it is to keep a flat stomach after you pass thirty-two.

But I think the other good stuff about thirty-five is realizing that life is shorter than you thought it was going to be, but sweeter. That people you love can deceive you, but it's usually nothing personal; it just is. Like love. And good reviews.

I don't have many resolutions for this thirty-fifth year. The ones I have are these:

- To keep an open hand;
- To be as loving as I choose to be;

- To tell the truth;
- To be gentle;
- And not to worry about nuthin'!

"So how does it feel to be playwright of the week?" he says, offering a toast.

"Great," I say. "It feels wonderful."

"Damn right," he says. "Congratulations."

"Thank you," I say. "You know, I think I might make it through this birthday after all."

"I'm counting on it," he says. "I'm counting on it."

JANUARY 1, 1984

I want utter devotion and complete unconventionality.

I want George Orwell to be wrong.

JANUARY 3, 1984

Yesterday I did an interview with cable TV about LeRoi Jones. Sitting at Spelman under a tree. It was fun. The interviewer kept talking about dialectics and I kept talking about art.

JANUARY 5, 1984

Letter to a far-off lover:

Dearest Darling,

Hey, baby, what's happenin'?

I love you so bad.

Why not pack a bag and come ride to New Orleans with me on the train and we'll make love and eat shrimp by the banks of the Mississippi?

And I love you more than Bessie loved the blues.

More than Simone loved Sartre.

More than Ossie loves Ruby.

More than Anaïs loved Henry.

More than Yoko dug John.

More than O'Keeffe loved Stieglitz.

More than Herschel wanted the Heisman.

I love you like Dr. J slamdunking against Boston.

And that ain't no joke.

FEBRUARY 4, 1984

Okay. Here's the thing about white literary critics:

They don't know about uncensored black stuff cuz they don't get to see it. No mystery there. We act different when there's white folks in the room. We talk different. We walk different. We laugh different. We can't be our unguarded, private selves. We didn't just survive all this race craziness because we

461

were strong and know how to fuss. We survived it because we are smart and know how to love. Because we are surrounded by and protected by the love, by the strength of us being us; together.

So here's the thing: Since they can't hear or understand it cuz they don't get to be around it, they can't judge it, all right? But what does that mean? It means that they reward the ones who speak in their language and talk to them. They are more comfortable with that. They are able to understand in the way they've been taught to understand things. And so we find that a writer like Toni Morrison gets better and better reviews as she writes more and more like a white writer. As she writes more and more about white folks. Then she makes the cover of *Newsweek* so that all of us who wanna make that cover, too, begin to write a little whiter. We begin to be conscious of the white people who will be in the room or in the theater or in the book biz. So we write into their ears and hope for the attention of Clive Barnes.

But here's my question: What if we didn't? What if we pretended for the sake of our work that there were no white people in the room? That it was us talking to each other? What would our characters say? They certainly wouldn't say the same things that they say to white ears. Those conversations usually are about: "You treated us so bad! Aren't you ashamed?" Or: "You treated us so bad! Look how sensitive and angry we are about it!" But in truth, in real life, we don't talk to each other about those two things only! Race isn't the only thing on our minds. We talk about love and the future and babies and sick mothers and dying fathers and pregnant sisters and how fine Herschel Walker is, in addition to being able to run so fast and hit so hard. But that's what makes the cover of *Newsweek,* so although we don't say it to ourselves, or to each other, we begin to write for white ears. The brother at the National Endowment meeting said, "We become white-speaking people."

So, what am I suggesting? Let's give it a shot and see what we would tell if we were talking to each other. I think we might surprise ourselves. And if you are good enough and true enough to your real self, to your real voice, and talk to the people who are as familiar with that real voice as they are with their own because it is their own, then it transcends what we have been told are our limitations and reveals not only our specific humanity, but our general connection to the company of other human beings. I think this is why we love Richard Pryor. He is us and he sounds like us!

MARCH 16, 1985
I haven't written here in so long. I'm out of practice! Relax. Talk about the music.

Some thoughts on "We Are the World."

I wanted to be cynical, okay? I mean, a star-studded song with video attached with proceeds earmarked for the starving Ethiopians. Don't get me wrong. I am glad to see help on its way to the people of Ethiopia. The problem is there are lots of starving children closer to home than that. But somehow they're not quite so glamorous. They're not quite so far away and exotic. There is a lot more glamour to worrying about Addis Ababa than there is to worrying about Vicksburg, Mississippi. So I was prepared to be politically correct and cynical. I also have a healthy suspicion of the artistic integrity of such a project. Does Diana Ross really care about the starving kids or is she just down after that Central Park rainstorm? Does Cyndi Lauper really need any more publicity? Is Michael Jackson ever going to take off those sunglasses? I had my reasons for not buying in right away.

I also had an amazingly disorganized

house staring me in the face demanding to be cleaned and no junk food in the cupboard. Oh, I had my reasons for thinking negatively about that song, but the truth of the matter is, I couldn't resist it! I played it once, then I played it again, then I played it again. Finally, I had to give it up. They kicked ass!! They sounded sincere and egoless and professional and passionate and communal and sweet and idealistic. They made me remember Simon when he was still with Garfunkel and Diana when she was still a Supreme and Ray when he was singing "Let's Go Get Stoned," and Bob Dylan when he was singing "Blowin' in the Wind" as if his life depended on it. It made me forgive Cyndi Lauper for being on the cover of *Ms.* and *Time* and *Rolling Stone* in one year. It also made me appreciate the producing genius of Quincy Jones, who understood that Stevie Wonder and Bruce Springsteen belong together.

I loved it. It is an anthem and a hymn. *Rolling Stone* says the sign on the door of the recording studio said "please leave your ego outside." That is the key!

MARCH 22, 1985
I think what hurts me the most is that I was there every step of the way. I was there,

465

agreeing, nodding, smiling, holding on, fluttering about. I was there!

I have never had analysis and the main reason is that I have always had great difficulty telling anyone what I know to be true. I lie. Almost constantly. The basis of the lying is fear tending toward terror about almost everything. Some of this, of course, is due to the fact that I am that most threatened of species: a black American woman between the ages of eighteen and forty. So I lie to protect myself; to hide myself.

The sad thing is that I have the temerity to think any of what I do makes a damn bit of difference.

What I write.

What I think. Does it? How can it?

APRIL 22, 1985

A young woman, age nineteen and working at a friend's clothing store, is raped at gunpoint by a white man who strips the other female employee naked, too, and makes her watch. This happens on Saturday. I get the call this morning. Another friend tells me what happened. It is horrifying. I begin to carry it with me. I begin to think about all the things you read and think and see and then it comes right to your front door. What can I tell these women to do? The store owner and the victims? How do they feel? How can we, their friends, help them go through this with as much clarity and compassion as possible?

I know that we cannot eliminate pain from people's lives. We can only try to help them achieve clarity, which make the pain less "personal," I think, if not more bearable. I cannot run the film backward and make the man decide to go to the next store and get cigarettes instead of terrorizing these women. I cannot take the gun out of his hand or make his victim a karate expert so that she can hit the police alarm and kick the gun from his hand while her co-worker gets him in a headlock and they hold him until the police come.

The most heinous crime in the universe, according to the John Varley books, is rape. There is a terrible rape in the book and because the victims are straight women, they let the rapist live. Gaby, the lesbian character, wants to kill him. But Cirrocco, the heterosexual woman, says let him live. Why? It is hard to think about all of this.

The clarity issue is paramount. I am reading/seeing/understanding so many feminist things. I am full of the visions I see. The horror. How to understand when it really happens?

The *Black Scholar* arrives in the mail today with an issue dedicated to black women and feminism. We shall see. But even as I flip through the pages, I am thinking and thinking about the rape. I go in and out of wanting to think about and not wanting to think about it. I just yanked myself back into considering it because I feel guilty for thinking or reading about anything else when someone in our circle has been raped. I feel guilty that I am not concerned enough. That I can forget for even a minute.

I am driven to try and help in some way. Maybe they should call the Feminist Women's Health Center, I think. I call Kay, but no answer. I call Karuna. No answer. I talk to the people at the Grady Rape Crisis Center. They are kind, concerned and gentle. They only put me on hold once and that's fair. They knew I wasn't a victim. I told the woman I spoke to that I was concerned about the victims' feeling guilty and responsible in some way for what happened. She asked me if I was a counselor, because I had a good understanding of what they were probably feeling. I said, "No. I'm a writer."

Clarity/clarity/clarity.

I write the numbers for the FWHC and

the Rape Crisis Center on a card and double-check to be sure I have written it correctly. I want to ease their pain. I want to help them get some feminist interpretation of events. I want them not to feel guilty and responsible and helpless and scared and I know they feel that way because I feel that way, too, and it didn't happen to me. I want them to feel like warriors that have been wronged. I want them to call all of us together and tell us what happened so that we can come together and help. So that we can come together and find the man and kill him with spears! I want us to feel that we should and must and can call upon each other for help!

There is a message on my answering machine when I get back from mailing the store owner the information I have gotten about places to go for help. I know she feels terrible. My letter gives her the phone numbers and says: "I love you and you are not guilty of the crime and please call the women you know for help. You are not alone. We love you." The message on my machine says: "Don't tell her I told you. I don't think she wants anybody to know." He's talking about the woman I just sent the letter to! He thinks she will be embarrassed if I know, but I am trying to round

up the posse! I am the damn federal marshall! And she doesn't want anybody to
know? This is all terrible. How are we gonna
form the posse if nobody is supposed to
know?

This shit is complex. Dangerous territory.
Don't want to hurt trying to help!

I want these women to know that it is a
political crime like lynching. Do we blame
Emmett Till for being lynched? Martin
Luther King for being shot? No! We know
those crimes happened because of oppression. White folks did some shit because they
felt like they could. No blaming the victims
when somebody gets lynched.

But in a rape, the victims are so freaked
out we can't even talk about it. Black people
don't try to hide when they get beat by the
Klan. They call *Jet*! They get on TV! They
get as many angry, indignant black folks as
they can find and go talk shit to some white
folks. Maybe not the ones who did it, but
any white folks who are supposed to be in
charge; who are supposed to prevent this
kind of shit from happening.

We should be out in groups when somebody gets raped, throwing shit in cars driven
by men. Would white people lynch a black
man on Tenth Street and then drive home
down Cascade Road? No! But men rape

women every day and drive home unmolested. And if we hold all white folks responsible for the ones of their group who act a fool, why don't women hold all men responsible in the same way? How come we don't say, "Hey, y'all are responsible for controlling the vicious ones among you!" That's what we tell white folks. "You Kennedys better stop these fucking George Wallaces and Bull Connors."

But what do women say? We say:

Don't tell anybody.

Don't tell any other women especially.

Don't tell the posse.

And I have a vested interest, too. Not just a friendly, sisterly interest. A rapist is running around my neighborhood, but the general attitude seems to be, well, there are lots of them, so why get excited? Men rape women all the time.

In *The Wizard,* Robin's mother warns her about parks because that's where men hide to rape women and since Robin is from an all-woman planet, she wouldn't necessarily know that. And I remember my mother telling me the same kind of thing. Not in such direct terms, but the same warning. Why did we have to be home on our bikes by the time the street lights came on? Might get raped! I was eight years old and I had to deal with being warned about rape without ever hearing the word; too young to understand it if I did. How do you tell an eight-year-old girl child what rape is?

And I look at my daughter and see her body, and I think, "Oh, shit! Men will be after her soon." We don't blame them because we are sleeping with them. We are in love with them. We laugh at the rape jokes (as if there could be such a thing as a rape joke!) and look the other way at all the sexual exploitation like we don't even see what it is doing to us and to our daughters. God!

I want to call her, but I don't know what to say without freaking her out about somebody knowing. I want her to understand. I want to understand.

I am walking up on some deeper understanding of the oppression of women. The oppression of women. Even the words sound terrible. Nobody will give rape the same credence they give lynching because the victim isn't usually killed in a rape and because men are usually the victims in a lynching. Men are lynched. Women are raped. Our lives are less respected so these crimes against us are perceived to be less serious. If somebody had been murdered, nobody would go on with business as usual.

Everybody would know and be talking about it and reacting to it and freaking out. But the rape is a secret current running through our circle. "Don't tell anybody! She doesn't want anybody to know."

But I have to tell somebody! We have to warn other women about the rapist in their neighborhood. We ought to be circulating wanted posters. We ought to be calling in his description to the paper so they can publish it on the front page. They gave big play to the woman who lied about a rape, which just feeds the idea that most charges of rape are trumped-up. Or: "She asked for it." By going to work. By moving around in the world. By thinking she was safe; protected.

And how do I fit liking Madonna into all this? And Prince, even when he slaps Appolonia in *Purple Rain,* we explain it as part of what he learned at his abusive father's knee, but damn, what makes her character continue to love somebody after he slaps her down and pushes her face in on the street and wants her to wear teddies and moan that song about being a "sex shooter/ shooting off in your direction." The women in the popular culture who seem so alive and seem to be having fun are like Madonna and Vanity and Tina and all of them are sex objects of one sort or another. They are women put forward by men in a manner that is supposed to make other men want to fuck them. Is that what sexy means?

Of course I wear big clothes. I don't want anybody to fuck me but men I care about and invite to fuck me. Random lust is dangerous. We are encouraged to generate it from everybody and then told we asked for it when somebody rapes us and it ain't even about sex, but just somebody who wants to hurt us/use us/humiliate us. He raped her with a gun to her head! It makes my chest hurt to think about it; to picture it.

"Don't obsess about this," my friend says, but I am crying on the phone, feeling like I am not obsessing enough about this. Our lives are not perceived to be worth as much as the lives of men and that affects the seriousness of everything. Childbirth. Cramps. Stuff men make silly or trivial cuz they don't do it. Getting hit in the balls? Worst pain in the world, they always say. And we believe it, too. Is it worse than the moment of transition in labor where you want to push so bad and you can't? Is it worse than when your bones separate to let the baby's head out? And who cares which is worse? Why do we keep score that way?

Because of oppression. Because if one is

going to be greater than, one has to be less than. Across the board. Straight through to the finish line. Same as white folks and black folks. It's always the same: oppressor and oppressed.

I am overwhelmed with sorrow; consumed with the need for clarity.

APRIL 23, 1985
I am determined to give myself the right to grieve for the woman who was raped. I am determined to make the men within this circle look at what happened as a political crime. As a lynching. As an attempted murder. As if a huge white woman with a big dildo had come into their offices, stripped them down and raped one of them up the ass while she made the others watch and then packed up her toy and faded off into the city. Would they think it was normal behavior? Would they say, well, it happens every day? What do you think the reaction would be if rape happened to them? They would be outraged. They would be enraged. I am determined to identify and claim the damn outrage!

APRIL 26, 1985
One of those moments when I don't know what I look like. When I don't know what I

feel like. When I want to look/feel/be a little different than I am. Don't know what it is, but truthfully? I think I know what it is:

Wanna be free/wanna be free/wanna be free.

I wonder what I look like. I feel great this way. New dress. Earrings. Bracelet. I know why Madonna dresses up in so much stuff. It makes you feel another kind of vibe. Another world. Another set of standards. Different aesthetics. Weirdness. Wild, but somehow comforting, too. Like dressing up in Mama's clothes. A costume.

I'm tired of being in here alone, day after day, typing away. I feel like I just had a baby.

Waiting to hear from Columbia Pictures. I don't know if I believe they will call or believe they won't.

I don't know if I even care. Don't ever say I didn't tell you I was crazy.

MAY 8, 1985
10 p.m. (or so . . .)
Somewhere between Lovely Atlanta and D.C.
Whew. The train has stopped to pick up or let out and it's dark outside. I'm so far to the back of the train that I never see where we are until we're in the process of moving on and only the hard core are still waving and grinning in the remains of this pretend-

it's-Paris mist. That's fine with me. I've got Deignan's Walkman and I'm listening to a tape of Philip Bailey singing about "Walking on the Chinese Wall." The song repeats over and over for about forty-five minutes, which is easier than running it back. I'm drinking AMTRAK wine, which claims to be a "product of France" and settling in for about another hour of wakefulness before I crash. I love to sleep on the train. You can sleep and cover great distances at the same time. You can also see the moon, the stars, houses where people are going about their lives, not knowing you are trying to catch a glimpse of them at dinner as you whiz on by in the darkness.

MAY 22, 1985
Adventures everywhere.

A call from Columbia Pictures to say, "Thanks, but no can use," to our screenplay treatments. I feel my throat clog up and my cheeks flush as I talk to the assistant to the Beeg Cheese who has been dispatched to call and give me the bad news. When I hang up, I am embarrassed, guilty, afraid of what my collaborator's reaction will be. I feel tears crowding out any sane thought behind my eyelids and I make what I now know to be a great move. I go to my bedroom; I lie down and nap for an hour and a half. I wake up with a slight headache, but no tears and a clearer vision of what it means.

I think what it means is this:

I have gotten a specific rejection of two specific ideas by a specific studio way off in Hollywood.

No more/no less.

I also realized in my half dream state that there is a part of me that is relieved. A part of me that wants to continue the slow . . . not so slow . . . pace of my real work. That is, projects that are coming from my heart and life, not made up according to the desires of faraway studio chiefs who don't know or love me. I'm not writing to sell, but writing to speak clearly about who and what and why. There is some relief at not having to throw myself into that movie world just now. There is also the realization that I don't have to worry about disappointing anybody but myself. It is up to me to decide where to put my writing energies. Me and only me.

The next phase includes the following (not necessarily in this order):

Revisions on *Hospice* and an attempt to tour it.

A good script for *Alias Johnny Valentine*.

A new play (possibly the athlete and the mom).

A teleplay (the little girl and the Vietnam vet) to send to Woodie for O'Neal consideration.

I think all this will keep me working in an arena where I am comfortable and where I trust the people around me. I would also like to approach *Essence* about doing some more writing for them. There are challenges and joys within the world where I already have a good reputation and some respect for what I do. There is more control of my work in theater and I want to control as much as I can. Movies are about stars and directors; not writers. I want to listen to my own voice and not throw myself at the movies where there is such a press to do commercial stuff.

JUNE 15, 1985

It is good to have this time alone. It is hard to figure everything out. Sitting in my window, surrounded by the work I should be doing. Smoking a joint, thinking about O. T. Hammonds dying; dreaming of my own demise. I am so afraid of all the ways it is possible to die. I am afraid of airplanes; rapists; murderers. The slow ravages of cancer. I close my eyes and allow myself to remember Ma's bald, flaking scalp at the end with just a few remaining strands of hair scattered here and there. I remember that last visit. The respirator making her breathe in a regular and artificial rhythm so that when Kris and I walk in her eyes widen, but she cannot catch her breath at the realization that she is, at last, dying. We are the proof. We all know it. We have come to see her one last time before she dies. Gathered at her deathbed. She breathes regularly and her eyes droop sadly. She wishes she were sitting outside in her garden listening to Puccini pouring from the windows. Her grandchildren running nearby. She wishes her husband was there, singing his unmistakable tenor accompaniment with Jussi Björling or Thomas L. Thomas or Caruso. She doesn't want to be dying.

We ache for her to rip out the respirator, rise and go with us, even at a hobble, even limping, dragging, with one of us holding each arm, pulling her out of here. We can help her die better than this. I will not die in a hospital like that. I will have morphine and I will die at home with people who love me and music. I am so afraid of it. Of the end of it. "Do you want to see the baby?" my stepfather says. She closes her eyes; pain and a flicker of something else. Irritation?

Exhaustion? "No," she shakes her head, pursing her lips like her mother. "No." And I know what it means for her to say no to looking at the newest baby's face. It's like the moment I wrote in *Hospice,* where the mother says to her pregnant daughter: "Can't think about that now. I'm dying. I've got to use all my energy to figure out what's happening inside me." In the play, Alice is weary; knows she doesn't have time to explain the unexplainable. Jenny is frightened; doesn't want to let her mother go. Both of them realize that the only hedge against death is sex. Love if you can get it; sex if you can't. When my mother told me about sex, she said, "Hold out until you find somebody you love if you can. It's always pleasurable, but if you love the person, it's so much more." When the doctors told her she probably couldn't have sex anymore, she was devastated. "I don't know if we will ever be able to make love again," my mother said to me. "He says it doesn't matter," and she lowered her voice so my stepfather would not overhear her sharing these intimate details of their life together. "But it matters to me," she said. "It matters to me."

My sister talks about her garden. What she has planted. What is coming up. My sister speaks calmly, but her eyes never leave our mother's face. Her swollen arms, bruised from so many needles. Dying in a room with a dying, anonymous white woman who looks at us as we come in and I look at her and away quickly. She is not my business here. My sister and I leave first, my stepfather stays to tell her good-bye and we are walking down the hospital hallway and I start to cry and I have never been so scared and sad and frantic and my sister puts her arm around my shoulders and hugs me as we keep on walking. I am amazed at my sister's strength and her ability to hold on to me like that. I think without her being there, I would fall to the ground. She is taller than me and I lean against her, grateful she is the big sister.

Before we leave the room, I lean down and speak into my mother's ear softly. "Are you scared?" and she looks at me and gives a tiny little nod. "Don't be scared," I say. "We love you so much." She closes her eyes but the machine keeps breathing.

"We love you so much."

JUNE 18, 1985
Statistics from a TV show on battered wives: Wife battering is the main cause of serious injury to women in the U.S. More than muggings, auto accidents and rape com-

bined! It is the main reason women ever show up at hospitals other than childbirth. How sad is that?

The choice is to stay and be hit or leave and live in poverty with your children. There were no battered women's shelters at all in 1970. The first shelter opened in 1974. Now there are over seven hundred shelters around the country and it's still not enough. We need safe spaces!

JUNE 19, 1985

I realize that my return trip to Indianapolis is my first extended out-of-town residency. I am pleased to realize it. Pleased that my friend arranged it. Pleased that I will be going alone. Pleased that everything is everything.

JUNE 21, 1985

If we don't believe in the existence of black men, we can't believe in the possibility of loving them.

JUNE 21, 1985
10:30 p.m.

It dawns on me that I will be alone for nine days. Both the men who I depend on for strength and companionship are away. I have to take care of myself. No protection.

So the tradeoffs become more obvious. It is only worthwhile to be what we are trained to be if the tradeoff occurs. It dawns on me that they are now getting everything. We have demanded equality, so they no longer have to protect us/defer to us. Did they ever? Was that a myth? Did anybody really act like my grandparents but my grandparents? How could my grandmother explain to my grandfather that she wanted to work? She was good with numbers. Had run her uncle Victor's store all those years ago in Montgomery, taking orders, waiting on customers, adding long columns of number in her head. But he didn't want his wife to work. Didn't want people to think he couldn't take care of her. So she kept their house and kept quiet about the headaches that sometimes got so bad she had to take to her bed. We would call them migraines now. She called them "sick headaches."

But now we are independent. Taking care of ourselves, thank you. So now what? We are still supposed to adore, adapt, admire. All that we are taught to do with men and they are taught to expect. It is difficult to talk about this to a man you're close to. It comes out sounding so accusatory. Does the man in question oppress me? Can he stop it if he wants to? Do I oppress myself?

Can I stop it? And if he does/and if I do, what in the world lies on the other side? How can we even begin to imagine what it would be like without all that bullshit?

Miles Davis stayed in his house for five years. Now I know why. He needed time to think.

JUNE 21, 1985

I am angry. Worse. I am put upon. I am neglected and emotionally abused. I entertain the thought of out-of-town trips to see old lovers. I invite men I do not care for to events that are meaningless. It is only June, but these are dog days as sure as shit.

JULY 3, 1985

I am awed by Doris Lessing. I am overwhelmed and exhilarated by my discovery of her work and angered and depressed that I am only finding her now. Where was Doris Lessing when I was twenty? Where was the teacher with enough guts to put her on the high school reading list? I am angry that her books lay hidden away while I was reading Steinbeck and Hemingway and Tennessee Williams and loving them and their work and, more dangerously, believing every word they said. Trying to be brave like Ma Joad in *The Grapes of Wrath*. Trying to be loving

and tragic like Kitty in *A Farewell to Arms.*
Seeking the sophisticated madness of
Blanche DuBois in *Streetcar Named Desire.*
Well, better late than never. I've got reading
to do!

JULY 5, 1985
Fragment of something I don't know yet:
    "I have found another perfect man. This
one shits rose petals and pisses champagne.
And I wanted this to be a love story."

JULY 6, 1985
The only thing I don't like about the beach
is sand in my diaphragm.

JULY 7, 1985
Part of an *Essence* query letter:

As a mother, I am less concerned with
mastery of multiplication tables and more
concerned with giving my daughter the
ability to observe and interpret current reality without also inculcating the hatred
and the violence and the sexism and the
racism that encourage her to think she's a
worthless piece of shit.

I'm too mad to write about this. You can't
say "shit" in a letter to *Essence*!

JULY 10, 1985

Have I forgotten how to be a mistress or grown out of it?

Did I always feel this way?

Is it rage or realization?

JULY 11, 1985

Don't know what vibe this is. Stood up for a date vibe, I think. All dressed up and no place to go vibe. Wronged-wife vibe and I ain't even married. Second choice vibe. She'll always be there so I don't need to rush vibe. I don't know. Yuck vibe. That much is clear.

Bill says: "You put your life on hold when he's in town. You rearrange everything when he's here."

Do I? Do I want to?

That sick feeling that always means insecurity about the beau. I set myself up. Again.

NOVEMBER 12, 1985

I watched myself getting ready: Change clothes twice; find the perfect outfit; check my bracelets; change my earrings ten times. Men never do this shit. I don't think they do, anyway. And if they do, they never write about it. They're too much in control. Yuck is right.

I don't think you can love a man and be

free. There is too much built-in bullshit. Ashford and Simpson on TV, touching and laughing and being in love. And: "Who's the boss?" Phyllis George asks them. They laugh. "We try to be equal partners," says Nick, "but I'm the boss." Valerie just smiles.

DECEMBER 18, 1985

I'm tired of being a mistress to married men who are bored with their wives. Bored with their houses filled with small children and home-cooked meals. Heads full of dreams, searching for the smell of incense and good sex.

I want someone who can go out and stay all night.

JANUARY 1, 1986

A thought from Ed Berrigan to start the year off right:

"Joy is what I like. That, and love."

JANUARY 12, 1986

I am so used to withholding.

I am so used to the silences.

I am so used to hearing my words thrown back at me; against me.

I am so used to not trusting.

I am so used to not opening my mouth, my hands, my heart.

I am so used to running and trembling.

I want to let the silence go. I want to let the tears go. I want to let the fear go.

It's time for a change!

MARCH 19, 1986

The most exhausting thing about men is their total self-absorption. I am seeing more and more my own complicity. I am more convinced than ever of the possibility of freedom.

Movies & office supplies = good things.

I believe if we can speak we can identify the root of the problem and then behavioral changes become minor. Or manageable anyway. Nothing is minor.

1. Discipline is remembering what I want.
2. Liberating myself is the initial act of revolution.

The good thing about this phase is that I am beginning to be able to see more clearly; to hear more sharply; to understand how sexism works.

All of us working and feeling motherhood guilt — CLICK!

A rape "joke" in *The Owl and the Pussycat* — CLICK!

Our male friends telling us how and what and why in the authoritative man voice (mantones) — CLICK!

I can hear it, feel it and know what to say about it when it happens. My brain is full of new feminist understandings. I think that it is critical for me to follow through; do the reading; go to Kay's "Feminar"; talk, think, protest, push myself to understanding!

Last night, talking to Kay on her veranda and she said: "It's that thing they do. Having to be the center of attention all the time. It is something they are taught to assume. Power, authority, privilege." — CLICK!

MARCH 20, 1986
Appointment at the Fulton County Court House. I'm early, so I go to the cafeteria for a cup of coffee. I'm carrying a briefcase full of the articles Kay gave me so I pull them out and read them. I can see the effect of sexism on women everywhere! I think study is a crucial part of action. Oppressed people are often so hostile and angry and threatened that they/we leap to the action phase without study. Action without a base of study drains energy very quickly.

So I am sipping coffee and observing the women around me. I become fixated on their clothing. I see the torture of their high-heeled shoes as they shift from one foot to the other when they stand in line, trying to take the pressure off of first one foot and then the other, toes gripping the shoe, butt thrown out of its natural line. All of the internal organs obviously tilted weird.

Part of the article I'm reading was about clothes. One style is obviously aimed at pleasing men, but runs you the risk of being dubbed a "slut" if you "go too far." The other, baggier style is not that way, but runs you the risk of being called a "slob," or accused of "letting yourself go." Whew! I know I worry about that stuff. I see that my almost forty-year-old stomach is not as flat as I might want it and I worry. About what? Not being attractive to men?

MARCH 21, 1986
I'm getting somewhere.

I am talking about my real feelings/reactions/conflicts/questions/fears/angers.

I am not humoring and pretending. I am learning to speak up and tell the truth to the men I love.

Life is so sweet and complex. Humans are so fucking weird. I love the clarity I am achieving. I love the love and energy and concern of the people around me. I love my daughter and I want her to be whole and happy.

I hope to live a long time. I can't control that.

I hope to continue to live a full, rich life that challenges me. I can control that and I am learning how to do it more.

MARCH 25, 1986
Good Feminar with Kay today. One of the personal things I am working on in the group is to listen and relax, rather than performing, joking, showing off either wit, humor or intelligence. I feel myself do it sometimes because I am feeling insecure. I know I interrupt everybody all the time! I don't want to be the one who messes up the vibe by hogging the conversation.

Had a really good conversation with Zaron today. I realize how much pressure I put on myself to hold up the pretense of monogamous devotion when everything I believe and say is against that.

It's a trap; offering proof of love in ways I have not promised.

MARCH 28, 1986
6:21 a.m.
Feel good. Early morning. Deignan is snoring lightly in the other room. I'm thinking

about writing.

I realize more and more that "a story is the theme of its location," means people are in circumstances that affect them. They don't "represent" those circumstances, and probably don't pontificate about them. That means that in *A Little Practice,* the people must have lives that go on inside and in spite of the racist/sexist culture. It is not a monolith, bearing down on them, but a backdrop. Present, but they're not always and only dealing with it. They're not representing it or opposition to it. They are just living their lives!

Remember *The White Hotel.* Thomas made me love that woman, care about her and then when the Nazis intruded, I was horrified. They are there during the whole book, building up, being Nazis, but they aren't the whole story until they knock on the door.

I have changed my house all around. Put the desk in my office; warmed up the living room in a very sweet way; hooked up my VCR. Zaron helped me move everything and we had fun. We were laughing and talking the whole time.

I feel like I'm doing well claiming myself, feeling out my space and loving my lovers and my friends. As of today, I got no complaints!

MARCH 29, 1986, SATURDAY BEFORE EASTER

I wake up to calls about the success of Sandra Deer's play *So Long on Lonely Street.* Start the day feeling competitive and negative.

I feel like I am not living up to my potential.

Thinking about Easter. People are shopping like mad to get those new clothes. A Pagan ritual if I ever saw one.

MARCH 31, 1986

I am working in my newly organized office. Zaron said in response to my saying I was stumped on what to write about for my "Southline" column: "Just write what you want to write and then decide later if you want to submit it to them or just keep it for yourself." Great idea! I'm saved! Maybe I should write about him!

APRIL 3, 1986

The question at the end of a love affair is: "How do you begin to tell the truth after lying for so long?" The only answer is: "Just do it!"

Wonderful call today from Tina Ansa. She's sending me a piece of her novel for *Catalyst.* We're going to pay her five hundred dollars. Already paid Zaron two hundred dollars for his piece. I love being able to pay writers for their work!

A rule for romance in long-term relationships: No house shoes!

APRIL 6, 1986

Alice just asked the Cheshire Cat which way to go and he said, "It depends on where you're going." And she said, "It doesn't matter." And he said, "If it doesn't matter then it doesn't matter which way you go." "That's the problem with me," said Alice. "I give myself very good advice. I just rarely take it."

APRIL 15, 1986

A long time between entries. There are many revelations to be recorded. The ones on my mind at this moment are involved in my writing. In how much my ability to see more truth and identify more bullshit in my personal life has allowed me to see the writing differently. Better.

I have just checked my calendar for May. I have no appointments. I have a beach trip scheduled. No business. I am planning to take May as a total writing month.

Why?

Because I have three plays in my head.

No. Because that is what I do.

Because I have goals for my writing that can only be achieved through my attention and diligence. I want to use my house as a one person artist colony. I am going to lay in supplies. I want to write as if I only had a week to live. As if the war was closing in. As if the germs were everywhere.

APRIL 17, 1986

Georgia O'Keeffe and Simone de Beauvoir died within a month of each other. I'll bet they are sitting at a café in heaven talking their asses off. I remember going through Ma's books and pulling out *The Second Sex* because the title sounded promising. I was too young to make sense of it, but it was still memorable for being the first place I saw the word "penis" in print.

JUNE 27, 1986

"Describe Pearl Cleage in one word," the interviewer says. A jazz station DJ with that cool voice. My nieces are peeking in the narrow glass of the studio door, big-eyed and giggly. "One word?" I say, thinking oh, god! What a question! And then I just say:

"Alive." "Alive?" he says, sounding surprised. "Okay. That's an interesting choice."

Shit, I want to say. Interesting my ass. That's the whole point! Live and in living color! All the way live! Life and death every time or not interested. I ain't angst-ridden over nothin'! What could be a better word than "alive"?

OCTOBER 5, 1986
(We are discussing the fact that racism and sexism restrict and confine movement.)

ZARON: Anything you wanna do, I'll do. Anywhere you wanna go, I'll take you.
ME: But that doesn't work, see? If I can't go alone when I want to, it's not the same.

Women exist in such small spaces. Bedrooms. Kitchens. Nurseries. Those little well-organized spaces right outside the president's office/the pastor's study/the mayor's private entrance.

OCTOBER 12, 1986
We're rehearsing *A Little Practice* and the process is making this impossible! I don't want to collaborate like this. I want my own way! I am self-righteous; abrupt; strangely

argumentative and vaguely unpleasant.

I don't care. I don't want to think about anything or anybody but myself until after I do the first performance on Thursday. That includes: family, friends, lovers, bill collectors and the IRS!

I can't believe this show isn't the most important thing on everybody's mind!

I feel so self-centered; scared; crazy; confident. ON POINT!

I want to say: Indulge me, okay??

I know this show is:
True/Timely/Good/Interesting/Well-written.

My only fear is not remembering my lines.

How can you address that problem most effectively? Study your lines every day! Go through the show twice a day, no stopping, every day until showtime.

I will!

OCTOBER 20, 1986
I can't believe it's over! The show went great! I feel free and wild and happy. I feel great! I feel strong! Strong and free! I've got a solo show in December. Can't wait!

DECEMBER 4, 1986
Opening night at Club Zebra, and it is what it promised to be! Zaron has made it exactly

like a Harlem speakeasy, down to the candles on the table and the band! It's going to be billed as "Live at Club Zebra, a solo cabaret performance by Pearl Cleage developed especially for the intimate setting of Club Zebra."

I like the show a lot. I like what it says and how. I like wearing Zaron's suit. I like how I look in the bodysuit at the end. I am ready!

Do it/do it/do it! I love my life!

January 12, 1987
Graffiti in the ladies room at Atkins Park Deli:
Statement: Don't wear high heels! They are victim shoes!
Response: I luv heels! Men & shoes!

JANUARY 14, 1987
Story idea:
"I used to live in a house where everybody had a pistol and everybody knew it."
Character idea:
"At thirty-five, he was a young woman's man. Long on experience and short on expectations."

JANUARY 20, 1987
Zaron sends a note after *Love & Trouble,*

our first full-length collaborative performance piece. We were a model of how to
collaborate the right way! Kenny Leon was
great, too. He let us do what we were doing
without being too "directorish." We had a
great time and the audience had a great
time, too. Here's the note:

> Pearline, *Love & Trouble* is everything I
> hoped/wished/thought/feared/expected
> and more. I want to spend the rest of my
> life with you. Sometimes in calm moments
> of reflection, I think of us in the abstract
> and ponder the odds. The way you make
> my stomach burn by driving onto the
> property suggests magic on your part.
> Don't let my madness throw you. I love
> you. I love being in love with you. I love
> everything with you in it. To life, love &
> trouble!

He wrote this on the back of a postcard
where he put our heads from the show flyer
on a *Miami Vice* photograph of Don Johnson
and Philip Michael Thomas as Sonny
Crockett and Rico Tubbs. It made me laugh
out loud. It must be love because he let me
be Sonny!

JANUARY 29, 1987
I'm thinking I'll add a group of pseudo

500

Amazons to my story: The Demonic Divas. They wear black leather skirts, high-heeled ankle-strap shoes, lots of makeup, extreme hair/wigs. What is their deal? What do they want??

It's a fairy tale: "Once upon a time, there was a race of black women warriors. Amazons. They were brave and strong and smart and loving and warm and spiritual and sensual and creative and free. And they could fly."

FEBRUARY 3, 1987

I think the story will be titled *The Return of the Amazon Queens.* They used to have powers, but the problem is that the women got distracted by men and so they lost it.

FEBRUARY 12, 1987

Exchange between two artists living in a town with no Sunday liquor sales:

ARTIST 1: You didn't get to the liquor store?
ARTIST 2: I forgot it was Sunday tomorrow. I fucked up, didn't I?
ARTIST 1: Yup. You fucked up big time.
ARTIST 2: Is there any vodka at home?
ARTIST 1: Not enough.

Artist 2 beats his head against the wall as

Artist 1 exits, in search of vodka.

Welcome to the Bible Belt!

MARCH 3, 1987
Places to be avoided at all costs:
   Receptions where all the men have on dark suits and tasteful ties and introduce the women hovering nearby as "my lovely bride," or "the little woman."

MARCH 5, 1987
He's not here. Left a briefcase behind to mark his territory. Am I crazy? Does he need space, whatever the fuck that means? I hate this kind of retro bullshit. If I wanted to feel sad and crazy I'd get married. Fuck it.

APRIL 24, 1987
I tell my father I rented a copy of the video of *Behind the Green Door.* I say it scared me. He says why. "Rape," I say. "They raped her." "Raped her?" he says, with the question mark. I describe what happened. They kidnapped her. They blindfolded her. Some women fondled her. Then a man comes out and rapes her. "I didn't think of that as rape," he said.
   There is a certain amount of craziness that

comes with being a black American feminist.

I decide that pornography is not something I want to talk about with my father.

APRIL 25, 1987
Note for *Amazon Queens:*
"In her dreams, she always saw herself flying."

A boy with a new bicycle and a puppy to sell asks Deignan how old she is. When she says she is twelve, he says: "You are so fine, I would do life for you."

"A poor exchange," I tell her. "Accept no pledges of love that are based on long-term incarceration."

APRIL 25, 1987
I am deep into my evidence-gathering phase. I am looking for the imperfections in order to make it easier to make a decision to let it go. We are hurtling toward weirdness. Was it something I said?

APRIL 27, 1987
Sitting in my car, somewhere in midtown. Tape player is playing Ben Webster doing "Willow Weep for Me," and I am adrift in the world on Monday morning. I wish I was writing notes for a book, but I'm *man-*

moaning; an unending keening at the moon about the unfairness of it all. He said: "I want you to keep telling me what's on your mind about this man/woman stuff." Like that was the answer! He wishes it could be like it used to be when I never questioned anything. He misses BABY GIRL. But I was a different woman then! I was a confused slave! I needed safety! But I'm stronger now. I'm freer. Is it fair for me to want something different because I'm different? What do I want NOW?

We are lost. No language. No passion. I think he misses having such an attentive audience, but I can't play that role anymore. Did we ever talk? I think we did. I know we did! About politics. About marriage. About love. About how we wanted to act toward each other.

Now? Nothing.

MAY 7, 1987
Man-moaning: It's not Monday anymore, but I'm still man-moaning. Sitting in a parking lot listening to Lou Reed on the radio singing about "closing in on death." It is destructive for me to be out like this; alone and sad. He's hurting me. No! I'm allowing him to hurt me. Why??

MAY 8, 1987

When Daddy and I went to see *The God-father,* I was struck by the similarities between him and Don Corleone. I asked him if he ever thought about himself as a gangster and he said, "Yes. The problem is trying to find a gang that's worth a damn."

MAY 12, 1987

It may be too early to call it a trend yet, but maybe not. It may be that it's still just a series of coincidences; a matter of timing, circumstances, the phases of the moon and flow of the tides, but I don't think so. I think it's more serious than that. Here's the situation:

In the last four months, three of the biggest white theaters in town have proudly presented three new works by three white playwrights. So far, so good. I'm a playwright myself and I love to see theaters willing to present new work rather than relying on Billy Shakespeare to rock the house because he's already been certified by the passage of time and the passion of generations of white scholarship. The problem is that all three of these new works — *An American Dollhouse* (an adaptation of Ibsen's *A Doll's House*), *Sweet, Sweet Auburn* (a musical set on Auburn Avenue), and *Cy-*

baris (a drama set in Martinique) — feature predominantly black casts and/or black protagonists.

Here's where it gets complicated, but in order for my reaction to make any sense, we've got to go back a ways. Haste makes waste. The thing is, we live in a nation that is undeniably racist. A place that continues to oppress its black citizens from the cradle to the grave as a matter of course. Even the most cursory perusal of any set of statistics will show that black folks are the poorest, the sickest, the angriest, the last hired and the first fired. Even the Supreme Court acknowledged it in their recent decision regarding capital punishment. They just didn't see fit to factor it in as a critical element in our criminal justice system, which makes no sense, but that's not this story.

So, let's say American racism is a fact. That means all of us — black and white — who are born and raised and live and die in this country are tainted by that racism. We are separated from each other by an intricate web of lies and laws, customs and traditions. And that separation is real. So how can they write about us? They don't know us! It is a fact that the oppressed is always better acquainted with the oppressor than the oppressor is with the oppressed. We have to be. Our lives depend on our ability to out-think that oppressor; to anticipate his desires; understand his whims; avoid his rages. There is no impetus for oppressors to carefully study and analyze their victims. They don't have to. They need only maintain sufficient firepower to keep control. The oppressed become not people, but one big dusky lump of problems. Angry teenagers. Unwed mothers. Hungry babies. Welfare cheaters.

So why are they so busy writing about us? Why don't they write from their own point of view; look through their own eyes? Because nobody wants to be the oppressor. It is easier to look at the victim, from a safe distance. Once at the end of a heated, all-day discussion about racism and the responsibility of southern-based artists to deal with it, a white artist jumped up in anger and said: "Can't we be done with this? We dealt with it all afternoon!" Which is the problem. It takes more than an afternoon. It takes a lifetime!

I'm not saying white writers shouldn't write about race, but why not write about your part in it? It's not as sympathetic, not as colorful and rarely as successful at the box office as the kind of exotica we're being subjected to.

The piece Zaron did with Celeste is what should be happening. *A War Story* incorporates two points of view — his as a black man and hers as a white woman — during the Civil War. He is finally free, searching for his family. She is trying to pick up the pieces after the South surrendered. What emerges is something brand new; a bi-racial piece that doesn't sell anybody out, that doesn't go for the cheap laugh; that digs deeper in order to find a way out. When I first saw the piece in Dalonega, it took my breath away. They were rehearsing outside and there was a mist in the mountains and when Zaron starts chopping wood, the sound of it put you right where they wanted you to be. It was like seeing Eiko and Koma at Nexus, except I know Zaron and Celeste. They're my friends and they did something that is one of the best pieces I've ever seen on the stage.

There are so many stories to tell and if we don't tell the story straight, then who will?

MAY 16, 1987
Zaron calls from a public phone with traffic noise in the background and says: "Come down! It's a beautiful night. The stars are out. Come down and see!" I am finishing a poem and I tell him so, but I tell him it's a

great idea and try me again another time. I can hear the sex in his voice. "But the stars are out," he says and laughs. "How do you know the stars will be out another time?" I laugh, too. How can I resist? Sometimes it's more fun to be a poem than to write one!

JANUARY 17, 1988

Collaboration is like slow dancing, except not as much fun because eventually you have to do it in front of people while you can slow dance in your living room forever and ever and never have to show nobody nuthin'!

Things Zaron and I know we have in common: race/politics/music. Things we struggle on that fuel our work: sexism & new definitions of love. How do you do it without replicating that old master/slave shit? It changes everything when you go on a trip with a man you love while you are working on an Amazon Oath to help women free themselves from sexist oppression. In order to make it work, you have to do a couple of things:

1. Teach him and work with him (tell him the truth!).
2. Work to talk always in the context of working together to identify the

outrage and survive/share the anger.

3. Reinforce progress without pandering.
4. Push the analysis so it isn't just personal but a total struggle we can engage in against the common enemy of sexism.
5. Make him understand that this is not a woman's struggle; this is a right and wrong struggle.

We already share a common struggle against racism. We are prepared to offer critical analysis and rigorous self-criticism. But there is still the question to be answered: Can you be a free woman and love and/or collaborate with a man? We trade information/ideas through the music. We both know that one of the reasons why "Try It Baby" is one of the most beautiful songs ever recorded is that Marvin Gaye was lucky enough to get the Temptations to sing backup. I actually believe that an incomplete knowledge of the discography of the Temptations from "Dream Come True" through the death of Paul Williams makes it almost impossible to understand black American men between the ages of thirty and fifty, so deeply has the music shaped their ideas about love and sex and life and death and what it means to be a black man in America. Shaped mine, too. I remember hearing "Dream Come True" and thinking *I want somebody to love me like that.*

FEBRUARY 8, 1988
The fact of the matter is I have more fun doing everything I like to do with Zaron. I feel like I've known him all my life and in several past lives, too. That first night we met in Princeton so many years ago (1971!!), I felt like we were picking up a conversation we'd been having in another time and place. We're still not through talking. How rare is that?

MARCH 3, 1988
And the question at the edge of the earth is, once you admit you want to know how it feels to fly, do you have the courage to jump?

MARCH 30, 1988
AN OATH AND PLEDGE TO THE GRAVE FROM ZARON WALTER BURNETT, JR., TO PEARL MICHELLE CLEAGE ON MARCH 30, 1988, ATLANTA, GEORGIA

Whereas I believe you to be the most special

511

wonderful intelligent kind inquisitive artistic creative correct concerned consistent fine woman in the history of the world as we now know it;

And whereas I am committed to the pursuit of your attentions and the sharing of your time on earth until death do us part for now;

And whereas you are the person to whom I write all the things I write so that you will know why I do all the things I do;

And whereas you are the only person in my life who has taken it upon herself to figure me out and then did it;

And whereas you are the person with whom I want to spend the rest of my waking and sleeping hours;

And whereas I believe you are the finest writer not named Zaron Burnett in the world;

I, Zaron Walter Burnett, Jr., do hereby pledge to always honor you and to always think of you 24/7/365 and to always be excited when I think-see-hear-touch-feel-smell-taste you and to always write to you and to always read and think about what you are reading and thinking about and to always share with you what I am reading and thinking about and to never tell you a lie either by omission or commission and to never, ever forget that you are uniquely unique and especially special and that you are with me because you want to be and that that always is your ultimate prerogative and one upon which I have no vote.

Now, therefore, I, Zaron Walter Burnett, Jr., do pledge my heart to you for eternity.

EPILOGUE

Okay. So I've read my way through the
seventies, plowed through the eighties, and
it's still hard to know what to say about my
journals. I am protective of the wild child
that I was, even when I wish she could have
spared me the details. I am protective of the
history these pages carry, even when I wish
that history wasn't quite so messy. Even the
most random sample of entries for these
years reveals continuing confusion about
the form and content of love, lots of moaning about the impossibility of deadlines and
the unfairness of self-imposed page quotas,
motherhood guilt and its twin sister, maternal pride. There are tasks and page quotas
and budgets and pep talks and job options.
There are character sketches and family
portraits and love letters and that list from
the move I made to the perfect apartment
back in March of 1981. There are plenty of
tears and a general, wistful mistrust of hap-

piness. There is a lot of fussing and not nearly enough soothing, but there is also real persistence. There is an almost maniacal commitment to writing it down and taking a look at it; at *me.*

I think the best thing about my journals has been that they gave me an easily accessible, non-judgmental place to try and figure out the things that were driving me crazy. For that, I am grateful. The worst thing about keeping them is the danger of becoming an observer of your own life. There were times when I found myself watching myself with the detached alertness that is required when I know I'm going to write about it later. That constant need to watch and write down everything is what led me away from these journals over the past few years. I realized I wanted to see what happy felt like, not just what the fantasy of it looked like on the page. I wanted to make a move, not craft a perfect paragraph to describe the projected motion. I wanted to wallow in the real thing with no thought of remembering the details to be carefully recorded later on secret pages meant for my eyes only.

I decided to try and write some pages for the outside world and see how it felt. And I liked it, and I still like it, but my journals are still stashed in closets and cabinets around the house, even as I type these lines, and if they could, they would probably be smirking a little, knowing that I always neglect them when I think I have things figured out. Knowing how long that usually lasts and certain that when it turns out that those things I thought I knew for sure are still in flux, as they always are, I'll be back, scribbling frantically, trying to see my way out by crawling far enough in to know that there is no way to go but up toward the light.

So I'm glad I didn't burn them. I'm glad that within these pages my personal history weaves its way through the history of my adopted hometown in a way that hopefully doesn't just tell the story of what happened to one small woman yearning to be free, but how it felt to be there, right up close, as Atlanta proclaimed itself "the world's next great city," and then, in typical Atlanta fashion, set out to make good on that promise.

I think my daughter was right about one thing. There are some things you probably don't need to know about your grandmother, but if I hadn't been so obsessive about writing down all that stuff, how would I ever remember that when I moved into that perfect apartment on March 27, 1981, the small ballerina in my music box was spinning to "The Viennese Life Waltz," and the moon was full outside my window? How could I remember that even when it was really hard, it was all worth it, even the messy parts, because I got smarter; I got stronger; I got *free*.

And that guy who sent me the pledge of true love as the eighties stumbled to a close? I waited six more years to be sure he really meant it, and then I married him. So far, so good . . .

ACKNOWLEDGMENTS

This book is dedicated to my daughter, Deignan Tucker, because I would never have survived all this without her, and to my husband, Zaron W. Burnett, Jr., who once read all the journals at my invitation and said: *Men don't know a damn thing about how women think. We're not just wrong. We're completely wrong.* Big love always to my son-in-law, Will Tucker; to my grandchildren, Michael, Chloe, Bailey, and Averie; and to my family. Thanks to my friends whose names appear here simply because their lives intersected with mine, and to those whose names do not. *You know who you are.*

ABOUT THE AUTHOR

Pearl Cleage is an award-winning play-wright whose play *Flyin' West* was the most-produced new play in the country in 1994 and a bestselling author whose novels include *What Looks Like Crazy on an Ordinary Day, I Wish I Had a Red Dress, Some Things I Never Thought I'd Do,* and *Baby Brother's Blues,* among others. She lives in Atlanta, Georgia.